Praise for *It's Not What You Sell,*

D0337892

"Roy Spence is a brilliant, sparkling gem. Dedicated to the idea that true greatness comes in direct proportion to passionate pursuit of a purpose beyond money, he has inspired and changed leaders in every sector. Spence has a peculiar genius for helping people articulate what they stand for, and any leader who cares to create a great enterprise would be fortunate to learn from this inspired guide."

—Jim Collins, author of *Good to Great;*
coauthor of *Built to Last*

"Roy Spence's instructive book reflects his charismatic genius, his evangelical zeal, and his synergistic understanding of what makes businesses lodge in the hearts, not just the minds, of employees and customers. Absent Roy's moving and idealistic articulation of the overriding and, indeed, noble, purpose of Southwest Airlines, I doubt that we would be as overtly meaningful to ourselves and others as we are. Roy has a great and visionary lesson of business success to teach; buying his book is a very inexpensive way to learn it."

—Herb Kelleher, founder,
Southwest Airlines

"Great leaders are leaders of great purpose, in the world of public service and the business world. If you're looking for a way to inspire people, mobilize the talent and energy of your organization, and make a real difference, the road map and case studies in this book will help you do it. I know because Roy and the principles in this book have helped guide our work at the Clinton Global Initiative. Having a clear and compelling purpose has enabled us to unite leaders and citizens from all over the world in order to convert pioneering ideas into solutions with tangible results." **—Bill Clinton**

"This book will help you navigate the challenging task of discovering and articulating a purpose that will inspire and motivate your entire workforce. Purpose makes employees feel like their job is important, that what they do matters, and is one of a handful of critical factors that we at Gallup have proven correlates with highly engaged, highly productive employees. If you can't articulate the purpose of your organization and you want and need to, you need this book."

—Jim Clifton, CEO,
The Gallup Organization

"Whenever I've seen a company or a brand that motivated me, inspired me, or gave me goose bumps, I've been able to link it to an incredible purpose at the heart of that company. Roy Spence has nailed the power of purpose in this visionary book, and it will motivate and inspire you to find and fulfill a purpose at the heart of your organization. It's a must read for twenty-first-century business leaders."

—Jim Stengel, former P&G global marketing officer
and president/CEO, The Jim Stengel Company

"Great companies have great purposes. This is a transformative idea and one that Roy Spence thoroughly understands and communicates brilliantly. His book is chock full of interesting stories and illuminating insights that will prove invaluable to entrepreneurs, the leaders of Fortune 500 companies, or anyone interested in business or leadership. I love this book!" **—John Mackey,** cofounder and co-CEO,
Whole Foods Market

"Roy's lovable, charismatic spirit stirs up every emotion to motivate us to look inside our businesses for our purpose. He beautifully shines the light on why finding what you stand for isn't something that can wait, it's a requirement these days to foster a thoughtful, thriving company. Readers will want to keep it close at hand—I do. It continues to be a go-to guide when I need an inspiring reminder of why doing business this way, absolutely, positively works."

—Kip Tindell, chairman and CEO,
The Container Store

"If there is only one book you read this year this is the one. Roy Spence lays out in detail why doing the work to discover and follow your PURPOSE will reap personal and professional rewards for the rest of your life. Looking back at my twenty years at Starbucks the one undeniable fact that led to our success was our commitment to a purpose that was bigger than any of us."

—Howard Behar, president, retired,
Starbucks Coffee International

"Thank goodness for Roy and Haley, the purpose trailblazers that have inspired so many. Their combination of passion and pragmatic guidance helped Dell unleash the hearts and spirit of 100,000 team members across the world. Soon I imagine most organizations won't wonder whether they should have a purpose, but instead they'll wonder what took them so long to realize how powerful purpose can be."

—Erin Mulligan Nelson, CMO of Bazaarvoice,
former CMO of Dell

"Purpose plays a pivotal role in the conscious business journey, and you will not find a better guide and companion than Roy Spence. Roy's inimitable wit, wisdom and warmth come shining through in this enjoyable, practical and deeply inspiring book, which should be required reading for business students, scholars and practitioners everywhere. Someday, every successful business will be run this way, thanks in no small measure to Roy Spence's pioneering work over the past several decades."
—**Raj Sisodia,** founder and chairman,
Conscious Capitalism Institute

"In the schoolyard as a kid, one of the worst things you could do was to do something 'on purpose' (usually something bad). As an adult and as a business leader, my life is completely focused on being 'on purpose.' Purpose is the fuel that has energized my work into a calling. Roy and Haley's book is my bible."
—**Chip Conley,** founder and executive chair,
Joie de Vivre Hospitality

"One of the most important things we did when we launched the new NBCUniversal under Comcast ownership was ask Roy and Haley to help us identify and articulate the new company's Purpose and Values. Those cornerstones of our culture enabled people from Day One to rally around a single vision and focus in unison on what matters most to us as we grow our business. This book serves as an invaluable springboard for anyone wishing to take their company to that higher plane of Purpose-based excellence."
—**Maryam Banikarim,** former SVP, Integrated Sales Marketing,
NBCUniversal and SVP and chief marketing officer,
Gannett Co, Inc.

"Haley Rushing stepped on our campus and shined a light on the difference that the University of Arkansas makes in the life of the students, the state and the world at large. Being clear about our fundamental Purpose here at home and in the world has ignited a pride and determination that you can feel when you step on campus. This book will serve as the only textbook you will ever need on the subject of how to discover and bring to life the Purpose of your organization. I give it an A+." —**G. David Gearhart,** chancellor, University of Arkansas

"Roy Spence's creative brilliance has been an enormous influence on helping people better understand what the PGA Tour stands for. The wisdom contained in this book is a great resource for those who want to lead their business with a purpose."

—**Tim Finchem,** commissioner, PGA Tour

"At BMW we live and breathe purpose. Roy's book and the powerful way he outlines how to bring purpose to life within your entire organization is the clearest game plan ever written on how to win on purpose." —**Jack Pitney,** vice president marketing, BMW of North America

"Roy Spence has a great gift for getting to the heart of the matter. Fearless in questioning the status quo and relentless in rejecting cynical shortcuts, he has his finger on the pulse of America like no one else." —**Margaret Heffernan,** author of *How She Does It*

"Roy Spence's book demonstrates the power of purpose in building successful organizations. He shows how to discover your purpose, cultivate it, and use it to make a difference as well as to make profits."

—**Bill Novelli,** CEO, AARP

"If there is a secret to success in business, Roy Spence has gotten to the heart of it: that the most winning organizations exude a genuine and truly distinctive sense of purpose—a powerful set of ideas that neutralize the competition, click with customers, inspire employees, and reshape the sense of what's possible in the marketplace. This book is nothing short of an instruction manual for the right way to win from the team that unleashed the power of purpose to help build some of the world's most legendary maverick brands—from Southwest Airlines to Wal-Mart. Like Spence himself, it will leave you inspired, energized, and well equipped on the path to purpose."

—**Polly LaBarre,** coauthor of *Mavericks at Work*

"Everyone knew Texas A&M was a great brand, but it suffered from a lack of real distinction, particularly for those with no A&M DNA. The Purpose Institute led us to better understand ourselves, and Rushing's insight in defining our purpose and values has created a solid foundation for our future. Let's hear it for 'leaders of character dedicated to serving the greater good'!"

—**Steve Moore,** CMO,
Texas A&M University

IT'S NOT WHAT YOU SELL, IT'S WHAT YOU STAND FOR

(Credit: Dave Mead)

Roy Spence is the cofounder, chairman, and CEO of GSD&M Idea City, a leading national advertising agency. A native of Brownwood, Texas, Spence moved to Austin to attend the University of Texas. Upon graduation in 1971, he and a handful of friends decided they wanted to stay in Austin, work for themselves, and make a difference. Since then the agency they built has helped grow some of the world's most respected and enduring brands and Spence has become a valued counselor to business, government, university, and nonprofit leaders who themselves want to make a difference.

Spence and his wife of thirty-one years, Mary Couri Spence, have three grown children. He was named Adman of the Century by *Texas Monthly,* is a distinguished alumnus of the University of Texas and a member of the Lyndon Baines Johnson Foundation board. His first book, *The Amazing Faith of Texas: Common Ground on Higher Ground* (Idea City Press), is a journey that proved that what unites us is greater than what divides us.

(Credit: Dave Mead)

HALEY RUSHING is the chief purposeologist and cofounder of The Purpose Institute in Austin, Texas. As chief purposeologist, Rushing leads a team of people who act as organizational therapists, anthropologists, and investigators dogged in their pursuit of uncovering the purpose at the heart of an organization. Every purpose project involves a thorough exploration of the passions, underlying motivations, and strengths of the organization as well as a thorough examination of the impact of the organization on the lives of the people with whom it comes into contact.

Over the past few years, the requests for Haley to help organizations discover their purpose have grown and the clients who have embraced doing business on purpose have prospered. As a result, she and Roy launched The Purpose Institute—an organization dedicated to helping clients discover and articulate their purpose and values in the world.

She lives in Austin with her twin girls, India Vida and Ziggy, and her twin Malteses, Lily and Champion of All.

IT'S NOT WHAT YOU SELL, IT'S WHAT YOU STAND FOR

Why Every Extraordinary Business Is Driven by Purpose

ROY M. SPENCE, JR.,

WITH HALEY RUSHING

PORTFOLIO / PENGUIN

PORTFOLIO / PENGUIN

Published by the Penguin Group

Penguin Group (USA) Inc., 375 Hudson Street, New York, New York 10014, U.S.A.

Penguin Group (Canada), 90 Eglinton Avenue East, Suite 700, Toronto, Ontario,
Canada M4P 2Y3 (a division of Pearson Penguin Canada Inc.)

Penguin Books Ltd, 80 Strand, London WC2R 0RL, England

Penguin Ireland, 25 St. Stephen's Green, Dublin 2, Ireland (a division of Penguin Books Ltd)

Penguin Books Australia Ltd, 250 Camberwell Road, Camberwell, Victoria 3124, Australia
(a division of Pearson Australia Group Pty Ltd)

Penguin Books India Pvt Ltd, 11 Community Centre, Panchsheel Park,
New Delhi – 110 017, India

Penguin Group (NZ), 67 Apollo Drive, Rosedale, Auckland 0632, New Zealand
(a division of Pearson New Zealand Ltd)

Penguin Books (South Africa) (Pty) Ltd, 24 Sturdee Avenue, Rosebank,
Johannesburg 2196, South Africa

Penguin Books Ltd, Registered Offices: 80 Strand, London WC2R 0RL, England

First published in the United States of America by Portfolio,
a member of Penguin Group (USA) Inc. 2009
This paperback edition with a new foreword published 2011

9   10

Copyright © GSD&M Idea City, LLC, 2009
All rights reserved

THE LIBRARY OF CONGRESS HAS CATALOGED THE HARDCOVER EDITION AS FOLLOWS:
Spence, Roy.
It's not what you sell, it's what you stand for / by Roy Spence, Jr., with Haley Rushing.
p.   cm.
Includes bibliographical references and index.
ISBN 978-1-59184-241-5 (hc.)
ISBN 978-1-59184-447-1 (pbk.)
1. Success in business. 2. Strategic planning. 3. Brand name products. I. Rushing, Haley.
II. Title. III. Title: It is not what you sell, it is what you stand for.
HF5386.S7515   2009
658.4'012—dc22   2008045305

Printed in the United States of America

To all my extraordinary
partners in purpose—
I love you all.

Contents

10. Southwest Airlines: How Purpose Can Take You Higher   167
11. Wal-Mart: How Purpose Can Make You Better   189
12. BMW: How Purpose Can Accelerate Your Momentum   201
13. Norwegian Cruise Line: How Purpose Can Set You Free
    from the Sea of Sameness   216

Membership Organizations

14. AARP: How Purpose Can Move You from Discounts to What Counts 233

Nonprofit Organizations

15. American Red Cross: How Purpose Can Create Common
    Ground on Higher Ground   243
16. American Legacy Foundation: How Purpose Is Activated
    Through Insight   255

Higher Education

17. American Council on Education: How Purpose Can Create
    a Grassroots Movement   267
18. Texas A&M: How Purpose Can Explain the Unexplainable   275

Sports Organizations

19. PGA Tour: How Purpose Can Tee You Up to Be Exceptional   283

Summary

20. Key Principles from the Book   293

    Acknowledgments   299
    Notes   303
    Bibliography   307
    Index   309

FOREWORD

When our book about Purpose-inspired organizations, leadership, and performance first came out, we were so blessed to have worked hands-on with legendary leaders and organizations that instinctively practiced the core principles of winning on Purpose. Herb Kelleher, founder and chairman emeritus of Southwest Airlines. Sam Walton of Wal-Mart. Former president Bill Clinton and the Clinton Global Initiative. Jim Stengel, former Procter & Gamble global marketing officer and now CEO of the Jim Stengel Company. And of course our dear friend and partner in purpose, Jim Collins, bestselling author of *Built to Last* and *Good to Great.*

We worked up-close and personal with these and other true visionaries who built Purpose-inspired organizations which, in that process, became organizations of great respect and sustained performance.

Then in 2009 the severe once-in-a-generation economic winter landed on the shores of America.

The game changed. And the practices, purpose, principles, and values of companies here and around the world were under immense pressure and scrutiny. Every leader and every organization was tested like never before. Those Purpose-centered leaders and companies continued to weather the economic winter and became even more respected while so many others either went dormant, out of business, or needed massive assistance to stabilize.

So what have we learned?

By continuing to stay very active in the Purpose arena, we learned that when a disaster, whether natural or man-made, decimates the very foundation of your world, your company, and your country, you have several options. You can play like you're doing something but actually do nothing. You can try to rebuild what was there before. Or you can begin building what you should have been building all along.

Before the economic winter, the public discussion of Purpose-inspired growth and leadership seemed to take a secondary role in most organizations.

But that world is changing. It's changing rapidly and for the better.

During the last two years, since the original publication of our book, we have once again been fortunate enough to work with some extraordinary leaders and organizations. Purpose-inspired leaders who are leading positive change and proving that there is a better way to do business. From best in the world organizations like Procter & Gamble, led by CEO Bob McDonald, to the intimate world of hotels like Joie De Vivre, led by Chip Conley. From the extraordinary world of John Mackey's Whole Foods Market to the global world of GE Aviation led by David Joyce. From the new world of Motorola Solutions driven by Greg Brown to the organized world of The Container Store led by Kip Tindell. From the world of content creation at NBC Universal, the academic world of The University of Arkansas and UT Arlington, the well-being world of Aurora Health Care and their leader Nick Turkal to the financial world in the heartland whose leaders like Greg Massey and his family bank, First United Bank, got it right from the start. And even from the economic meltdown world of the home building industry emerged Pulte's new, young, and Purpose driven leader Richard Dugas, Jr. who had the courage and brave heart to begin building again with a new foundational Purpose to create homes and communities that enhance the lives of everyone they serve.

Let it be known there is a new and authentic movement—a movement led by visionaries who are pioneering Purpose-based capitalism and Purpose-inspired growth. These enlightened leaders are building the kinds of companies that people want to work for, that customers flock to, that communities welcome, and that investors respect.

This movement is being fueled by a rise in the demand for Purpose in the workplace from two generations shaping the American business landscape: the millennials and the baby boomers.

The millennial generation rejects the idea that the only purpose of work is to make money. They want to break down the barriers between their business life and their personal life so that they don't have to leave their passion at home when they go to work in the morning. Almost every day we meet some young person with a passion and a determination to use his talent in the service of something he believes in.

There is possibly no greater evidence of this than to look at the work of a Harvard Business School student named Max Anderson. He crafted a "Hippocratic oath" for business grads in which these future business leaders pledge themselves to causes above and beyond the bottom line. When asked about his personal aspirations he said: "My hope is that at our twenty-fifth reunion our class will not be known for how much money we made . . . but for how the world was a better place as a result of our leadership." And that's from a Harvard MBA student!

We also have 78 million boomers in the United States—many of whom are now sitting in the proverbial driver's seat of American business. So many we have met have come to realize that they want to spend the rest of their lives not just being successful but being significant. These individuals are creating Purpose-inspired organizations that make money by making a difference in the lives of all of their stakeholders—employees, customers, vendor partners, investors, and the communities they serve.

For all of these reasons, we now have hard evidence that we are on the brink of a new model of capitalism that makes money by improving lives.

Bob McDonald, CEO at Procter & Gamble, calls it Purpose-inspired growth.

John Mackey, CEO at Whole Foods Market, calls it conscious capitalism.

Conscious capitalism advances the idea that the Purpose of business is to have a deeper Purpose beyond making money. As Aristotle said, "where your talents and the needs of the world cross, there lies your purpose." We now know that businesses with a deeper Purpose have employees who are motivated to go the distance, customers that remain loyal through the storms, and brands that stand apart from the competition. As the dust continues to settle and new life is beginning to emerge, it's increasingly clear that the only businesses that will be left standing—and standing tall—are those that stand for something. Conscious capitalism requires leaders to think about how they can conduct business in a way that creates value for every stakeholder they touch—not just the shareholder, not just the customer—but every stakeholder affected by their existence. More and more leaders are living proof that business is not a zero-sum game—a series of never-ending trade-offs where one stakeholder wins at the expense of another. The enlightened leaders of today's thriving, high-performing businesses understand that it's possible—not easy, but possible-to create value for everyone.

When we first published *It's Not What You Sell, It's What You Stand For,* our hope was that in some small way this book would inspire leaders of any size organization to go forth and win on Purpose. But what we are witnessing is a movement more deeply held than we thought. It seems we have tapped into a much deeper vein. For everywhere we go we find leaders who want to lead organizations of Great Purpose. Associates and employees who want to work in places of Great Purpose. Customers who want to do business and shop with companies of Great Purpose. And communities who take so much pride in companies of Great Purpose.

We hope that *It's Not What You Sell, It's What You Stand For* inspires you to build an organization for good that leads to extraordinary growth—Purpose-inspired growth. And we hope this work will accelerate the movement that is moving us all forward to the next frontier of capitalism.

Most of all, we wish you a Purpose-inspired life.

IT'S NOT WHAT YOU SELL, IT'S WHAT YOU STAND FOR

INTRODUCTION

On a cool November morning in 2002, I was sitting in my office at 6:00 A.M. preparing for an all-client Idea Summit at the GSD&M headquarters in Austin, Texas. I hear a tap on my door. I look up and there is Jim Collins, a good friend and best-selling author of *Built to Last* and *Good to Great*, leaning in and smiling like someone about to give you a gift that he knows you're going to love.

Jim was the keynote speaker we brought in for the summit. Before I could say good morning, Jim looked at me in that pensive way that he does, hand on chin and head cocked slightly, and said, "I've got it!"

I said, "Got what?"

He said, "What you guys can be the best in the world at!"

While this might seem an odd opener for a conversation, on many occasions GSD&M had been used as a test site for the principles Jim espoused in his first book. Recently, we'd been struggling with the answer to a very difficult question—*what can you be the best in the world at?*

"It's right in front of you. Look at the clients you've assembled here today. GSD&M has somehow managed to attract extraordinary companies with a purpose beyond making money. They're companies that want to make a difference. I think you can be the best in the world at delivering visionary ideas for companies that actually have a purpose."

After this declaration, Jim left just as abruptly as he had shown up. I was frozen—like when you catch a glimpse of your reflection and it takes a moment before you realize that what you're seeing is you. I realized he had put his finger on the unarticulated secret that has shaped the most successful client relationships we had developed in our thirty-five years of running the agency. While we often talk about the difference that our clients are making in the lives of their customers, we hadn't given ourselves enough credit for taking notice of that difference and using it as the cornerstone for building some of America's most successful brands.

We work with a vast array of clients and have always done whatever it takes to build their businesses. Some relationships have been a disaster from day one, while others have unfolded into lifelong friendships and true partnerships that have built both the esteem and the profits of everyone involved. Jim's comment made me realize that our most successful relationships are with clients who are genuinely passionate about making a difference in the marketplace. And our gift is being able to identify, simplify, and articulate that difference to the world.

This shouldn't have come as a surprise to me. From day one, my partners and I shared the same lifelong goals—to stay in Austin, to stay together, and to make a difference. Whether we did it consciously or not, over time we've gravitated toward industry mavericks, visionaries, and leaders committed to making a difference like Herb Kelleher, Sam Walton, Jim Collins, Norm Brinker, Colleen Barrett, Jeffrey Katzenberg, Paul Higham, former president (41) George H. W. Bush, former president (42) Bill Clinton, Tim Finchem, Red McCombs, Bernard Rapoport, retired Air Force general Rand, U.S. secretary of state Hillary Clinton, former U.S. secretary of defense Bob Gates, Bob Utley, Charles Schwab, Gary Kelly, Betty Sue Flowers, Jim Stengel, Bill Novelli, and Jim Clifton, just to name a few. These are all people with a great sense of purpose leading companies or organizations with a culture of purpose—cultures geared up to make a difference.

Just like we needed Jim Collins to point out our own obvious strengths, we help organizations identify and articulate the core purpose that's right under their nose. It started early, when we let Herb Kelleher, founder and chairman emeritus of Southwest Airlines, in on the fact that he wasn't just offering low fares and frequent flights, he was democratizing the skies. Later, we picked up on Sam Walton's real vision of saving people money so that they could live better lives. Today, we're attracting purpose-driven brands like BMW and John Deere and marquee philanthropic organizations like the American Red Cross and the Clinton Global Initiative. Great universities like The University of Texas at Austin and Texas A&M have called us in to help them articulate the difference they make in the lives of the students passing through their institutions. These are just some of the organizations that are winning in the marketplace because of their commitment to a higher purpose—a purpose that we have had the privilege of helping to discover and bring to life through the power of media and marketing.

The road we've taken comes from our values and our outlook on life in general—namely, that life is short, so live it out doing something that you care about. Try to make a difference the best way you can. We've had fun; we've cultivated the success of others and enjoyed a lot of it ourselves. At the end of the day, it's been much more rewarding to work with clients that are trying to make a difference than it is to work with clients that are just trying to sell more stuff. And there's always a sublime vindication in seeing our clients ultimately sell more stuff and make more money *while making more of a difference* than their competitors. There's also an enormous satisfaction in seeing the cultural transformation that happens when an organization is turned on to purpose.

We've all experienced corporate cultures in one form or another. While this language may be new to you, the experience is one you know instinctively. Think about all the organizations you've dealt with in your professional and personal life. You can probably readily identify organizations that have a strong sense of purpose, as well as those that don't.

In a company without a purpose, people have no idea what they're *really* there to do. There may be a flurry of activity and an abundance of "busy-ness," but it all seems frenetic, disorganized, and leading in no particular direction. They often look to the competition to decide what to do rather than navigate by their own sense of what's right. And your sense of who they are is probably quite muddled due to the fact that their ad campaigns change dramatically every year or so. This is what it feels like in an organization without a purpose. Unfortunately, it's an all-too-common feeling in corporate America.

Contrast this with a company that has a great purpose. You can usually feel it when you walk in the door. You can sense it in the confidence and clarity with which employees go about doing their work. You can see it in the remarkable ways they do business.

You witness leaders who have a knack for endearing themselves to the troops and harnessing the passion and talents of their employees to great ends. And you usually know what they're all about because their stories have been well told and consistent in the marketplace. This is what it feels like to step into an organization driven by purpose.

This book's primary goal is to get you to the same level as these purpose-driven companies. It will provide an actionable road map to discover your purpose, bring it to life, and then actively market and practice that purpose in all you do. The net result is that when a company is driven by purpose, everyone in the organization wins—both professionally and personally.

It's Not What You Sell, It's What You Stand For is driven by three interdependent components:

1. Building an organization that truly makes a difference in the marketplace;
2. Becoming a leader of great purpose; and
3. Bringing your purpose to life so that your constituents know exactly what you stand for.

You need to be firing on all three cylinders to truly experience the power of purpose in the marketplace.

The journey starts with an understanding of the difference that you want to make in the world. *What does this organization believe in? What does it believe it's here to do? What difference does it ultimately make in the lives of the people it is trying to serve?* At the intersection of the passions and strengths of the organization and the needs of the world stands a great purpose. Every company is capable of having one. No organization is too big or too small, too niche or too mundane, too high or low interest to have a purpose.

We've worked with every kind of enterprise imaginable: from soap to social causes (antilitter, smoking cessation, colon cancer), from airlines to AARP, retailers to restaurants, health care to hotels, country clubs to country music, and telecom to tortilla chips. It's not the category you work in, but the business model, the leadership, and the positioning that ultimately determine whether or not you will discover and live out your purpose.

My hope is that reading and practicing the principles of *It's Not What You Sell, It's What You Stand For* will inspire you to make a choice—a choice to go out there and either create or find work in an organization of great purpose. And in the process, you will make money, make a difference, and make history.

A pretty cool way to live your life at work.

PART I

PURPOSE
PRINCIPLES

WHAT IS A PURPOSE AND

WHY SHOULD YOU WANT ONE?

From the beginning, instinct told us that what a company stands for is as important as what it sells—I guess that's why we were naturally drawn to organizations that were known as much for their values as they were for the products and services they sold in the market.

I got my first official introduction to the idea of purpose when I picked up the book *Built to Last,* by Jim Collins and Jerry Porras, in an airport bookstore. I was interested in the book because two of the visionary companies that they covered were Southwest Airlines and Wal-Mart—two longstanding clients of ours (GSD&M's). I'm always curious to see how other people explain their success.

I was immediately struck by the description of core ideologies that separated the visionary companies from the mediocre companies. The visionary companies had a set of core values that were unchanging and a core purpose that fueled everything the organization did. As the authors put it:

CORE PURPOSE is the organization's fundamental reason for being. An effective purpose reflects the importance people attach to the company's work—it taps their idealistic motivations—and gets at the deeper reasons for an organization's existence beyond just making money.

The book listed the powerful purpose statements that had propelled some of the most visionary companies of our day to great success. For example:

> Merck: *To gain victory against disease and help mankind*
>
> Disney: *To use our imaginations to bring happiness to millions*
>
> Johnson & Johnson: *To alleviate pain and suffering*

These are big ideas—ideas that can make a meaningful difference in the world, ideas that separate the great from the ordinary. My heart was racing. I couldn't wait for the plane to land. The second the wheels hit the tarmac, I was on the phone. I called Jim Collins because, to be honest, I couldn't pronounce his coauthor's last name. We had a good conversation, and by the time we got off the phone we both agreed on the secret ingredient of extraordinary companies—purpose.

Purpose isn't everything, but it trumps everything else. Sure, every organization must also have strong leadership, management, succession planning, execution, strategy and tactics, innovation, and more, but in more than thirty-five years of working with a vast range of companies and organizations, my belief is that it all has to start with a purpose. That is the hinge that everything else hangs upon.

In my experience, the simplest way to explain purpose is:

> Purpose is a definitive statement about the difference you are trying to make in the world.

Having clarity about the ultimate purpose of the time and energy you spend doing what you do is the cornerstone of a culture of purpose. It's what drives everything you do. It's your reason for being that goes beyond making money, and it almost always results in making more money than you ever thought possible.

If you have a purpose and can articulate it with clarity and passion, then everything makes sense and everything flows. You feel good about what you're doing and clear about how to get there. You're excited to get up in the morning and you sleep easier at night.

If you don't have a clear and easy-to-articulate purpose, everything feels a bit chaotic, harried, and maybe even meaningless. Meetings may go on for hours with endless and arbitrary decision-making criteria being thrown out by anyone with an opinion. You may launch totally new business plans year after year. Without a core purpose in place, the way forward is often a real challenge.

The textbook definition of purpose is: n. The object toward which one strives or for which something exists. Without a purpose, what are you striving for? What are you resolved to accomplish? If you have no answer to these fundamental questions, your business (and your life) may be a real struggle.

> The power of purpose is not a marketing idea or a sales idea. It's a company idea. Purpose drives an entire organization and it answers why the brand exists.
> —Jim Stengel, former global marketing officer of Procter & Gamble (P&G)

SOUTHWEST AIRLINES: AN EXAMPLE OF GREAT PURPOSE

Before I go any further, let me give you one clear example of what I mean by purpose in the corporate world. For over twenty-seven years, I have worked side by side with the founder and other leaders of Southwest Airlines. Tons of stuff has been written about Herb Kelleher and the Southwest business model, and I will not rehash what's well known. I will, however, offer insight into the fundamental underpinning of purpose that fuels their famous culture and unrivaled success.

Herb conceived of the idea of Southwest Airlines with Rollin King one night in San Antonio. As the legend goes, it started as a simple triangle scribbled on a napkin: from Dallas to Houston to San Antonio and back to Dallas. At that time, it was a highly regulated industry, and Braniff and other airlines had a monopoly on routes and fare structures. Their incredibly high cost structures resulted in expensive fares that were only accessible to the elite, and as a result, only 15 percent of the American public had ever flown.

Herb and Rollin decided to single-handedly deregulate the industry and create a low-cost, efficient airline that would make flying affordable for people from all walks of life. Their clear purpose (although they hadn't yet articulated it as such) was to give people the freedom to fly—in essence, *to democratize the skies*. They may be in the airline business, but their true purpose is *to give people the freedom to fly*.

The result: Southwest Airlines has posted a profit every quarter for over thirty-six years now, a record unmatched by any other airline in the history of aviation. No one else even comes close.

And while that is a rewarding difference in the pocketbook, the most rewarding difference is the one that they've made in the lives of people across the country. As a direct result of Southwest Airlines, today over 85 percent of Americans have traveled by airplane. That's purpose in action. That's a real difference that the leaders and employees of Southwest Airlines can take pride in and that customers reward with their loyalty.

WHY SHOULD YOU WANT A PURPOSE?

So, you may be saying to yourself, that's great for Southwest Airlines, but I'm not really sure that I need a purpose.

Why does purpose matter? Why not just work on sound strategy and positioning year after year and have a good, viable business in the marketplace? You can certainly do that, and you may even have reasonable success doing it. But in our experience, purpose offers up a host of benefits, including easier decision making, deeper employee and customer engagement, and ultimately, more personal fulfillment and happiness. And in the end, a clear and compelling purpose is a huge tie breaker in the marketplace that will make not only your people and your customers happier but also your shareholders.

Here is a full list of the reasons we believe that having a purpose is so critical to succeeding in today's marketplace.

PURPOSE DRIVES EVERYTHING

With a purpose in place, decision making becomes easier. You can look at an opportunity or a challenge and ask yourself, *"Is this the right thing to do given our purpose? Does this further our cause?"*

> If it does, you do it. If it doesn't, you don't. If it's proof to your purpose, embrace it. If it violates your purpose, kick it out on its ass.

In Jim Collins's follow-up bestseller *Good to Great*, he describes how companies with average performance ascended to greatness after, among other things, they discovered their "hedgehog." Hedgehogs, as the economist Isaiah Berlin describes in his essay "The Hedgehog and the Fox," simplify complex environments into a simple view or principle that unifies and guides every move they make. All challenges, opportunities, and threats are examined through one unifying worldview. As Jim points out in *Good to Great*, "For a hedgehog, anything that does not somehow relate to the hedgehog idea holds no relevance."

So it is with companies with a purpose. They look at the world through the lens of their purpose. If a move is relevant to their purpose, they make it. If not, they don't.

For example, if a decision comes to the table and it violates the core purpose of Southwest Airlines' ability to keep costs down and fares low, it's thrown out. If a piece of automotive technology is presented to BMW that does not support the core purpose of enabling people to experience the joy of driving, they discard it. If some idea is put forward at John Deere that might compromise their quality, commitment, innovation, or integrity, it will be passed over. If any compromise on design is put on the table at Kohler, it is ignored. If a new policy at Norwegian Cruise Lines that would inhibit their passengers' right to go their own way is run up the flagpole, it is tossed out. If any new practice would cast doubt on the integrity of the game of golf, the PGA Tour would immediately nix it.

In short, leaders driven to fulfill a purpose will make decisions to ensure that the purpose is never violated.

Purpose should drive what's on your personal to-do list, what's on the R&D list, and what's on your mind as you assess the overall performance of the organization. Hiring and firing should be based on alliance with the purpose. Purpose should drive everything from the philosophical foundations of the company to that hot fourth-quarter promotion developed in the advertising department.

PURPOSE IS A PATH TO HIGH PERFORMANCE

A purpose is not developed in a vacuum. While the core of a purpose must be born out of the genuine strengths and passions of the organization, those strengths and passions must ultimately intersect with the needs of your audience.

As Aristotle said: "Where your talents and the needs of the world cross, there lies your calling." Your purpose, as it were.

In my experience, most purpose-based leaders and organizations understand the needs of the world instinctively. Answering those needs is the path to high performance.

Sam Walton knew that people in rural areas were sick of paying high prices for average goods. They needed a retailer they could trust to deliver low prices every day on quality goods that help make life a little better.

Herb Kelleher knew the 85 percent of the market that hadn't flown probably wanted to—they just needed someone to make it affordable for them.

Charles Schwab knew that individual investors were sick of getting ripped off by traditional Wall Street brokerage firms. People needed a brokerage firm that was on their side.

John Deere knew that the farmers who were having a hard time plowing through the tough prairie soil of the Midwest would appreciate a better performing plow that they could trust to get the job done.

Phil Knight and Bill Bowerman (Nike) believed that "if you have a body, you're an athlete." They knew that if they outfitted individuals with innovative gear and inspired them with a battle cry, a new generation of athletes would emerge around the world.

Howard Schultz (Starbucks) knew that people would probably appreciate a third place to spend time and enjoy a really good cup of coffee if they had it.

A purpose is informed by the needs of the world. Ergo, if you build your organization with a concrete purpose in mind—a purpose that fills a real need in the marketplace—it stands to reason that performance will follow.

Jim Stengel, former global marketing officer of Procter & Gamble, oversaw the world's largest ad budget of roughly $6.7 billion. Through his experience building and managing some of the world's most successful brands, he has come to believe in the power of purpose to drive incredible performance. Here's what he shared with us:

> *Over the course of my career, I've developed a deep sense that the companies—the brands—that really stood out above the rest in every way had something else going on that was much deeper than the functional benefit they provide to their customers or consumers. Whenever I saw something that motivated me, inspired me, or gave me goose bumps, it was something to do with purpose.*
>
> —Jim Stengel

Jim's observation led him to commission a proprietary study designed to identify brands from around the world that were growing disproportionately to their categories. This massive study began with over thirty thousand brands and focused on twenty-five top performers. When the group conducted an in-depth study on those top performers, they found that all the top performers were fulfilling a higher-order purpose. P&G believes so deeply in the idea of purpose and its ability to drive performance that it has recently codified everything the company has learned about purpose in an internal manual.

There have been many other studies that have proven the bottom-line power of purpose.

Jim Collins and Jerry Porras demonstrated in *Built to Last* that organizations driven by purpose and values outperformed the general market 15:1 and outperformed comparison companies 6:1.

Harvard Business School faculty members John Kotter and James Heskett studied blue-chip firms across twenty different industries and found that firms with strong adaptive cultures based on shared values significantly outperformed firms with weak, values-neutral cultures. Over the four-year period they observed these companies, revenue grew more than four times faster, rate of job creation was seven times higher, stock price grew twelve times faster, and profit performance was significantly higher than comparison companies in similar industries.[1]

In a book entitled *Firms of Endearment,* the authors identify thirty companies (three of whom include our past or current clients: BMW, Southwest Airlines, and Whole Foods Market) driven by a sense of purpose and humanistic principles. These companies put the needs of their stakeholders ahead of the needs of shareholders and are bringing about a profound change in the existing capitalist paradigm. The authors found that companies that choose to put their employees and their customers first are outperforming conventional competitors (who have an eye almost exclusively on profit and shareholders) in stock market performance on the order of 8-to-1. Not only is overall stock performance significantly better, employee turnover is lower, productivity is higher, and pricing strategy is not subject to the same low-pricing pressure experienced by pure profit-driven, shareholder-focused competitors.[2]

Far from being some touchy-feely concept, purpose and values have been identified by the best business gurus of our time as key ingredients of high-performing organizations.

Just to be clear, having a strong purpose in place does not make an organization immune to setbacks that may inhibit financial performance from time to time. We've all seen strategic decisions or marketplace forces derail even the most beloved purpose-driven organizations. But organizations with a strong purpose are much more likely to get back on track and create a legacy of high performance over time.

PURPOSE FOSTERS VISIONARY IDEAS AND MEANINGFUL INNOVATION

Let me share another story from Jim Stengel, which demonstrates how purpose can unleash innovative thinking in an organization. Jim believed that Pampers was more than just a diaper that prevents wetness. As he expresses it, "We're talking about babies and mothers and birth and life. Shouldn't we as a company have a higher aspiration other than to just keep the bottom dry?" He describes the powerful transformation that happened when Pampers began to earnestly explore how they could do more than "just keep the bottom dry":

> We asked ourselves: What's the one thing that every mother cares about? And what she cares about is her baby's development in every way. So we began to seize that idea. And we switched from being a brand about functional dryness to a brand that helps mothers around the world with their baby's physical, social, and emotional development. And in the beginning, that idea sounded crazy. But it started to get people inspired. It got the imagination going. The agenda for innovation started to change. The way we approached consumers began to change. We began having daily interactions with mothers and babies onsite. We began thinking about our product experience differently. We identified "sound sleep" as a key to healthy baby development. We began asking questions like what can Pampers' role be in helping babies have deep, healthy sleep so they can wake up with energy, with rejuvenation and better brain development? We did clinical studies in that area. We learned that mothers around the world care about one another. One thing led to another and now we have a partnership with UNICEF in over 40 countries; when a mom buys a bag of Pampers, we donate one vaccination delivered through UNICEF. And now, ten years later, the brand has doubled in size. It's one of the leading brands in the world and has become P&G's first $8 billion brand.

As they made the conscious decision to get out of the dryness business and into the baby-development business, new and innovative thinking spread like wildfire throughout the Pampers organization. The purpose provided the inspiration and direction necessary to develop innovations that have made Pampers a hugely successful brand.

Innovation is on everyone's mind. "Departments of Innovation" have sprung up in corporations across America. "Chief Innovation Officers" are being anointed. Innovation conferences in hotel ballrooms are regularly sold out. There is a restless urge to stay on the cutting edge of what's next. But in the absence of a purpose, innovative thinking can be difficult to ignite.

Without a purpose, there is no heartfelt motivation or inspiration to drive innovation in a constructive and meaningful way. Innovation for innovation's sake often results in a lot of wasted time and energy. Innovation designed to facilitate a core purpose in new and exciting ways is where meaningful progress is made.

BMW is an innovation machine. Every detail of a BMW is designed with the company's purpose in mind: enabling people to experience the joy of driving. BMW engineers know that anything that doesn't provide more exhilaration or more comfort or enhance driving safety simply doesn't belong in a BMW. For example, one of the greatest innovations BMW is known for among driving enthusiasts is the Near-Perfect 50/50 Balance. This creates the signature driving feel associated with a BMW that people love. By balancing the weight over the front and rear axles evenly, they deliver exceptional agility, enhanced safety, more control, and, ultimately, a better driving experience. What that means to you and me is that we can take corners really, really fast without missing a beat. That's the joy of driving and the kind of purposeful innovation that employees can wrap their head around.

Southwest Airlines is one of the most innovative companies in the country. But we've never been asked to help them develop something innovative in a vacuum. What we receive, instead, are assignments asking them how they can deliver "freedom" in new ways. What innovations can we create to deliver more freedom in the Rapid Rewards loyalty program? What innovative things might we do with the schedule to give people more and better flying options? What innovations can we create to deliver more spontaneous travel (i.e., freedom) to our customers while lowering our costs?

Having a purpose not only helps foster innovation inside your organization, it also helps all the stakeholders and partners that work with your organization to develop visionary innovations on your behalf. As a marketing firm that has worked with extraordinary purpose-based organizations and not-so-purpose-based organizations, we can testify to the fact that visionary ideas are much harder to come by for the latter.

When we are working on behalf of truly purpose-based organizations, the visionary ideas and innovations tend to flow much more easily. Ideas move beyond the realm of clever tactics that might be noted in an industry publication to meaningful messages, experiences, services, and interactions that will be loved by the customers who are being served.

I suppose our pursuit of purpose-based organizations may in some ways be self-serving. It's a hell of a lot easier to be in the business of "visionary ideas that make a difference" when we're working with organizations that are hell-bent on making a difference too.

PURPOSE MOVES MOUNTAINS

Purpose can make the seemingly impossible possible. It can rally the troops to overcome seemingly insurmountable odds. It can ignite a fire in the belly to fight the fights that seem impossible to win.

Don't Mess with Texas

It was 1982 and Mark White was elected governor of Texas. He had just appointed Bob Lanier to chair the very powerful Texas Highway Commission. Bob Lanier was on a mission to cut the fat out of this huge department. He started with in-depth briefings from every sector of the highway department. I mean *in-depth*. It finally came to the antilitter effort. The person in charge was going through the statistics: Each year litter on Texas highways grew at an average of 17 percent.

So, each year Texas taxpayers had to spend 17 percent more on clean-ing up that litter just to break even. This was the trend all over the na-tion, and no one seemed to have any solutions for reversing that trend. Bob was taking it all in, and finally the presentation stopped—with the annual request for a 17 percent increase in state funding of the antilitter program.

The room was quiet. Bob, in his typical way, pushed his glasses down, looked up, and said, "Excellent presentation. But what is the purpose of this program?"

No one spoke until the head of the division stood up and said, "The purpose of our effort is to make sure that our Texas highways are clean and beautiful and something Lady Bird Johnson and her whole *Keep Texas Beautiful* effort will be proud of."

Bob Lanier nodded and sat there peering off into space. Then he made the acute observation, "Has anybody ever thought about the notion of persuading Texans not to litter so that littering goes down each year, and therefore so does our budget?" Silence took hold of the room.

That mandate sent us down the highway to create a purpose that would change the face of Texas and cut Bob Lanier's budget. Other antilitter campaigns all had the same worthy goal of reducing litter: *"Give a hoot, don't pollute"* and *"the crying Indian,"* featuring a Na-tive American brought to tears after looking at the mess we had cre-ated. While these messages might have resonated with Lady Bird Johnson and Sierra Club members, to your average Texan in the early 1980s, the antilitter cause was not a cause that many took to heart. We needed a purpose that Texans could sink their teeth into—a pur-pose with the power to make a difference, a purpose that would move people.

Tim McClure, one of the founding partners of GSD&M, was walking down the highway one day and saw trash along the shoulder. He stopped and thought to himself, *"This isn't litter—this is trash. People are trashing Texas. We've got to stop people from trashing Texas."* Now, anyone who has spent any time in Texas knows how fiercely proud Texans are of their state. And that pride is exactly what we needed to tap into. We took the worthy goal of reducing litter and married it with Texas pride to create a purpose powerful enough to clean up our highways and cut our budgets. The purpose of this antilitter initiative was *to tap into the pride of Texas to keep our state clean.* That purpose was brought to life with one of the most well-known taglines in America: *Don't Mess with Texas.*

Sure enough, Texans rallied around the idea and changed the face of Texas in a way no one could have predicted. With purpose as our guiding light, litter took a nosedive and was reduced by 70 percent during the next five years.

Here's the point. If a problem seems impossible to overcome, then it's highly unlikely that well-intentioned tactics will see you through. Purpose is required to tap into the hearts of your constituents and make the impossible possible.

PURPOSE WILL HOLD YOU STEADY
IN A TURBULENT MARKETPLACE

When you know who you are; when your mission is clear and you burn with the inner fire of unbreakable will; no cold can touch your heart; no deluge can dampen your purpose.

—Chief Seattle

Markets are always changing. Competitors come and go. Trends rise and fall. Business strategies fluctuate in response to category dynamics. So what's going to be your anchor? What will you report back to on a day-to-day basis while you travel through the turmoil?

Without purpose to hold you steady, it's very easy to get distracted by marketplace fluctuations. You may find yourself reacting to every competitor that comes along. Wall Street pressure may send you desperately clamoring down unchartered paths. Trends may suggest you need to consider a new line of business.

Purpose provides a road map to hold your course along the journey. It ensures that everyone stays on track and you don't end up in a ditch, stalled out and confused as to how you got there.

I can't tell you the number of airlines that have come and gone, threatening to take out Southwest Airlines over the past thirty years.

They make their grand entrance with their so-called superior planes, enhanced first-class service, lavish airport lounges—you name it. But the culture of purpose at Southwest Airlines has bested them all. While there are certainly heated and fierce debates about how to strengthen its offering in the market, Southwest Airlines never questions its primary reason for being in the market—which is what frequently happens when clients without a purpose are besieged by the competition.

Instead Southwest takes stock of its beliefs and values and responds with product innovations that are uniquely and unapologetically Southwest. Some of the best innovations they ever created were the result of competitive pressures that forced them to figure out how to be a better Southwest Airlines.

Competitors said Southwest Airlines didn't have fancy flight attendants.

Southwest said, *"Hot pants are more fun."*

Competitors said Southwest Airlines didn't have a full range of jets.

Southwest said, *"Meet Shamu! He can fly you there just as fast."*

Competitors said Southwest Airlines' frequent flyer program didn't let you fly internationally.

Southwest said, *"With Rapid Rewards, every seat is a reward seat almost every day of the year."* Try actually using your frequent flier miles on another airline. The word "freedom" does not come to mind.

In each case, Southwest is true to who they are. They don't spend time trying to develop products or services to match the competition. They celebrate their own unique strengths and navigate by the core values and beliefs that set them apart from everyone else in the industry.

As human beings our minds easily wander off track. It's easy to lose focus. A strong sense of values, beliefs, and purpose will keep everyone on track.

PURPOSE INJECTS YOUR BRAND
WITH A HEALTHY DOSE OF REALITY

In Texas, when people talk a good game but have nothing to back it up, we say, "That cowboy is all hat and no cattle." In business, you want to have the cattle.

Historically, branding was pretty simple. Company X launched a product that offered a new and improved version of something, and the brand simply embodied what that product promised to do. Simple. But as the marketplace grew increasingly crowded—overpopulated with similar brands doing similar things for similar audiences—companies turned to advertising agencies to manufacture a meaningful difference on their behalf.

When companies don't have anything substantive to say and their product or service is relatively ordinary, they often rely on advertising to create an image they hope will add value to their brand. (Create the big ol' hat to create the illusion of being a cowboy.) And it may for a while. But Paul Higham, the retired marketing director at Wal-Mart who we worked with for almost a decade, always reminded us that the best advertising in the world will not save a mediocre company. The company has to have something of genuine value to offer to consumers.

This is not rocket science. It's common sense. If you tell consumers one thing in your marketing, and they experience something entirely different (or something entirely ordinary) when they go to use you, the relationship won't last long. Your behavior will catch up with you and people will notice.

When you have a purpose at the heart of the company, it will drive the business and ensure that something remarkable is happening with the product or service. The thing about purpose is that it starts with the leaders, works its way through the organization, and finds its way into the products, services, experiences, and, ultimately, into the marketing. If the company is not truly delivering it, the marketing shouldn't be talking about it.

FAKING PURPOSE

Let me give you an example of a company trying to fake a purpose. It happens. But fortunately it doesn't last. It was the late nineties and energy deregulation was just getting off the ground in Texas—spawning the infamous Enron and a slew of smaller players, one of whom came knocking on the door of our ad agency. At first we were excited about the prospect of helping a company that professed a desire to make a difference not only for the environment but also for the pocketbook of Texans. The harsh reality was that they only wanted us to profess it in the advertising. They didn't actually want to do business in any meaningful way to support it. They hoped that Texans—being largely uneducated about the intricacies of energy pricing and the challenges of offering truly green energy—wouldn't notice if the company didn't actually deliver on their promise. We knew the relationship was over when we were conducting research with people who were interested in switching, and one of the company's senior leaders said to the focus-group facilitator, "Hey, see if they'll buy it if we say it like this. It's actually going to cost them 20 percent more, but I don't think they'll figure that out."

It was not hard to make the decision to part ways. For one thing, our agency's purpose is delivering visionary ideas for clients with a real and genuine purpose. In short, our purpose is to help our clients fulfill their purpose. This company didn't have one. And second, imagine the futility of trying to build a great brand for a client that's not making any real difference except to add to the customer's cost.

The point is, if you profess a desire to have a purpose, what are you going to do to back it up? What are you going to do to make it real? Purpose is rooted in reality. The great purpose-driven organizations that have built great brands in the marketplace did so because they were actually creating products, services, and experiences that made a real difference in the lives of their customers.

PURPOSE RECRUITS PASSIONATE PEOPLE

"Don't ever take a job—join a crusade! Find a cause that you can believe in and give yourself to it completely."
—Colleen Barrett, retired president of Southwest Airlines

Human beings enjoy spending their time engaged in meaningful work. Unfortunately, work is often the last place they turn to engage in meaningful work. Jim Stengel wanted to change that.

> There is a woman that I work with at P&G in Paris who once said to me, *"Why is it that P&G people go home at night and on the weekends and do extraordinary things for their communities and other service organizations—but somehow when they come to work, they leave that at home. And what would happen if we invited them to bring that passion to life at work through our brands? What if we could fulfill their need to make an impact and change the world through our brands? What a powerful impact we could make!"* And it's true. Unleashing the people behind the brand in an inspired way—focused on a purpose they can believe in—has just been an unstoppable and positive force.
>
> —Jim Stengel

Human beings are a passionate species. We want to engage in meaningful work. So why does the world of work seem so devoid of meaning? Companies that are actively cultivating and communicating the purpose-driven nature of their work are quickly becoming some of the hottest employers in the country.

Healthways is one of the fastest-growing companies in the country today. The company works with health-plan sponsors to create proactive, custom health-care plans to slow disease progression, promote wellness, and, ultimately, cut healthcare costs.

Before you can enter its Nashville headquarters you have to literally walk across its core purpose etched in the floor in front of the main entrance: *Creating a healthier world one person at a time.* Healthways President and CEO Ben Leedle, Jr., told us that their purpose has helped them to attract "a certain kind of energetic person."

In fact, their purpose is one of the primary reasons why the company debuted on Fortune's 2008 list of "100 Best Companies to Work For."

> *At Healthways we focus every day on making a difference for more than 26 million individuals around the world by helping them be as healthy as they can be. We are able to impact the lives of the people we touch by attracting and retaining the best and brightest talent from around the world and then creating an environment where they can thrive. Healthways colleagues join our company because of our purpose and are collectively committed to what we believe is our obligation to succeed. Our colleagues' passion to achieve this higher purpose makes Healthways a great place to work.*

Working in the service of a higher purpose attracts highly energetic and highly motivated people to your organization.

Sometimes, you don't even have to pay them.

The game of golf stands for passion, integrity, charity, and sportsmanship. Those values attract more than seventy-five thousand volunteers to donate their time, talent and money to the PGA Tour. Tim Finchem, the commissioner of the PGA Tour explains it this way:

> *I am sure there are people who love other sports as much as some people love golf, but in my experience, the people who love golf are the most passionate, not just about the game or its players, but about the qualities the game represents. Integrity, charity, sportsmanship—these traits are important to golf—not just as a "lip service" checklist, but as a prescription for the proper way to play. . . . Volunteers are the backbone of our tournaments, and are a critical reason why PGA Tour tournaments are able to donate over $100 million to charity each year.*
>
> —Tim Finchem (Commissioner blog—PGATour.com)

Phyllis Wade is one of those passionate volunteers. She's almost eighty years old and she's spent sixty years volunteering for PGA Tour tournaments. At times she's worked three solid months, taken a brief break, and then worked another month straight. Passionate and committed volunteers like Phyllis save the PGA Tour $26 million a year (assuming minimum wage compensation for fifty-hour weeks).[3]

Are people drawn to your organization because of what you stand for?

Being clear about your values and purpose will attract people who share your values and feel passionate about the purpose of the organization. It will also create a common bond among employees.

Imagine what the culture of your organization would look like and feel like if everyone had knowingly and intentionally signed up for the purpose at hand. Realize that not everyone may choose to join your team. And ultimately, you wouldn't want those people in your organization anyway. Better to draw a line in the dirt and see who steps across up front than to find out later in the heat of battle. This "discriminating" factor was noted in a book written almost twenty years ago on purpose-driven organizations:

> When a company defines its purpose, it is with the understanding that anyone from a vice president to an hourly worker might choose to say, "I can't accept these values. It's not the game I want to play." The purpose tells people what they can be a part of. It declares, "Here's what we're all about, so you can decide if it's something you can commit yourself to. We're not saying you have to be this way. You decide whether or not you want to." When the organization's management defines what it will be, it also defines what the organization is not—what opportunities it will pass up. It establishes a screening process in which people either find something meaningful or elect to leave. . . . The power of a purpose-driven organization comes from everyone in the organization understanding what the organization is all about.[4]

Once the purpose is established, it's important to use it as a screening tool in your organization's recruiting process. Bringing someone on board who is not interested in your purpose or doesn't believe in it can, at best, demoralize the people around them and, at worst, can begin to derail the purpose altogether (if they're high enough in the organization).

On the flip side, when applicants have been drawn to your organization because of your purpose, you've just added a level of energy and passion necessary to create a high-performing company.

PURPOSE BRINGS ENERGY AND VITALITY
TO THE WORK AT HAND

What man actually needs is not a tensionless state, but rather the striving and struggling for some goal worthy of him. What he needs is not the discharge of tension at any cost, but the call of a potential meaning waiting to be fulfilled by him.

—Viktor Frankl, *Man's Search for Meaning*

We all know individuals who speak about their work with great joy and intensity—it's a major source of their fulfillment in life. These are the people who look forward to Monday mornings as much as most people look forward to Friday afternoons. For others, work is a necessary evil—something to be endured, a source of fatigue and complaints.

What makes the difference? Is the joyful experience a by-product of some happy gene that most of us were born without? Or do these people—the happy ones—lead or work for a company with a purpose that ignites their passion, their dedication, and their joy?

The Gallup Organization invested in a massive research study to determine the conditions that create loyal and productive employees which, in turn, create higher-performing companies. The study identified twelve core elements that need to be present to create, what Gallup calls, a highly *engaged* employee. About half the elements deal with the management style of supervisors. The rest have to do with the employee's sense of belonging. And one of the key criteria to determine belonging is captured by the statement, "The mission or purpose of my company makes me feel my job is important."

As the study describes it: "A uniquely human twist occurs after the basic needs are fulfilled. The employee searches for meaning in her vocation. For reasons that transcend the physical needs fulfilled by earning a living, she looks for her contribution to a higher purpose. Something within her looks for something in which to believe."[5]

If a company can provide its employees with meaningful work and something in which to believe, that company can benefit from highly engaged, passionate employees who are in it for more than just a paycheck. The employees who work in the service of something they feel true devotion to bring the most energy and vitality to what they do.

Mihaly Csikszentmihalyi, one of the world's leading researchers in the field of positive psychology, has researched what it takes for an individual to feel completely engaged, focused, and performing in a maximum state—a condition he calls "flow" in his book by the same title.[6] Having a purpose that provides context for all of one's effort is one of the chief criteria for flow. It allows a person's mind, body, and soul to commit to the task at hand. It turns work from a necessary evil into a completely absorbing experience, where talents are being pushed to their outer limits and energy is eagerly channeled to the purpose at hand.

Where you find this flow operating in the workplace, you'll also find happier and healthier employees—like the ones you might find at Whole Foods Market. The employees at Whole Foods Market are deeply passionate about what they do, and CEO John Mackey attributes that passion to purpose motivation (not profit motivation):

> It is difficult to impossible to truly inspire the creators of customer happiness—the employees—with the ethic of profit maximization. Maximizing profits may excite investors, but I assure you most employees don't get very excited about it even if they accept its validity as one of the legitimate goals of business. It is my experience that employees can get very excited and inspired by a business that has an important business purpose . . .

Whole Foods Market team members are driven by the fundamental purpose of that organization—*to provide choices for nurturing the body, the community, and the planet.* They want to change the way the world eats. They want to live by the *Declaration of Interdependence*— their paradigm-shifting business model that ensures that all stakeholders are served by the existence of Whole Foods Market. That's what creates the commitment day in and day out regardless of the company's stock price on any given day. And, paradoxically, that's what ultimately creates comp store sales growth, revenue per square foot, and gross margin and profit margin that are hands-down superior to anyone else in the industry.

Certainly, we've witnessed some companies that enjoy skyrocketing performance levels over a period of time and use that performance to energize and motivate their employees. But those same companies find themselves in a cultural crisis whenever the performance lapses or reaches a momentary plateau. Companies that try to motivate their employees purely through stock market performance are likely to find a corporate culture where the collective self-esteem rises and falls with the stock price. When the price is down, there's nothing to provide the energy, vitality, and motivation for employees. When employees are driven by a worthy purpose, it's much more likely to create a consistent level of commitment to the work at hand.

PURPOSE CONTRIBUTES TO A LIFE WELL LIVED

Many persons have a wrong idea of what constitutes true happiness. It is not attained through self-gratification but through fidelity to a worthy purpose.

—Helen Keller

Ranked by Forbes as one of the top five executive coaches in the world, Richard Leider[7] has dedicated his life to helping individuals lead purposeful lives. He's spent a lot of time talking with elderly people as they reflect back on their lives. He's asked them what would they do differently if they could live their lives over again. Answer: They would have discovered and been clear about their purpose earlier in life.

Fortunately, people are no longer waiting until the end of their life to start thinking about the difference they want to make in the world. Increasingly, people are exploring and seeking meaning and purpose in their personal lives. Bookstore shelves are now fully stocked with books about finding your personal purpose. But the reality is the vast majority of your time is consumed by your work life.

You wake up every morning and go to work. You leave your family, your dog, and your goldfish. Personal passions get put on hold. Whether you're a CEO or a secretary, the majority of your time, energy, and talent will be spent in the service of your work. So why not make it worthwhile? When you feel you're making a difference, you feel good about what you're doing. When you feel you're not making a difference, you want to go back to bed.

No longer do people—especially the next generation of young people—want to artificially divide their lives into their "real" life and their "work" life. A life of purpose is not something you can squeeze in on the weekends; it has to be something that infiltrates all aspects of your life. If work is devoid of any real meaning or purpose, it's going to be a real challenge to live a life of purpose.

And, on some level, everyone wants to live a life of purpose. Studs Terkel first wrote about the American worker's struggle to earn a living and also create a life and a legacy over thirty years ago in his classic book, *Working: "It is about a search, too, for daily meaning as well as daily bread, for recognition as well as for cash, for astonishment rather than torpor; in short for a sort of life rather than a Monday through Friday sort of dying . . ."*

A Southwest Airlines ramp agent shared a wonderful story about the meaning he was able to find in his work because of the larger purpose of Southwest Airlines. (Ramp agents are engaged in highly demanding work—among other things, they load heavy bags on planes in extreme weather conditions all year round, often on weekends and through the holidays.) This particular ramp agent had a wife, three children, and a Golden Retriever at home. He told me that when his kids start complaining that "Daddy has to work on Thanksgiving again," he gathers them around and tells them: *"If Daddy didn't go to work, many families wouldn't be able to fly around the country and be with their loved ones. Without Daddy doing his job, little kids all across the country wouldn't get to see their grandparents, their aunts and uncles, or any of their cousins. Daddy has to go to work to make sure everyone can be with their families."*

Now you tell me—would you rather go to work to deliver that

kind of freedom or go to work to load bags on a plane? That's how purpose infiltrates an organization and transforms lives of toil into lives of purpose.

George Bernard Shaw probably described this yearning for meaningful work best in this famous passage often invoked to describe a life well lived:

> *This is the true joy in life, the being used for a purpose recognized by yourself as a mighty one; being a force of nature instead of a feverish selfish clod of ailments and grievances complaining that the world will not devote itself to making you happy. I am of the opinion that my life belongs to the whole community and as long as I live, it is my privilege to do for it whatever I can.*

What if every organization lived by that passage? How much more joy might there be if people felt that their talents were being used "for a purpose recognized . . . as a mighty one"? By building your organization to serve a real need in the marketplace, organizations can help play a significant role in fulfilling the individual quest for a purposeful life.

Recent research into happiness demonstrates that the happiest people aren't those with the most money but those with a sense of purpose—a sense that they are contributing to something bigger than themselves. At least some of this has to derive from work. The purpose of a business, then, must be explicit and go beyond boosting the share price or fulfilling some bland mission statement. People want to believe that they're part of something meaningful. The sense of purpose doesn't have to be grandiose or revolutionary, merely credible and anchored in values.

—Margaret Heffernan, *Another Day, Another Mountain to Climb*, fastcompany.com (March 2005)

PURPOSE PRINCIPLES

Purpose drives everything. It will drive all major decision making and become the determining factor in how you allocate resources, hire employees, plan for the future, and judge your success.

Purpose is a path to high performance. It fulfills a deep-seated need that people have and will drive preference for your company.

Purpose fosters visionary ideas and meaningful innovation. It provides the motivation and direction necessary to create meaningful innovation.

Purpose moves mountains. It can rally the troops to overcome seemingly insurmountable odds.

Purpose will hold you steady in a turbulent marketplace. It will see you through when times get tough and the road seems unclear.

Purpose injects your brand with a healthy dose of reality. It is not something you can fake. It's genuine. It's real. And it's something that your customers honestly appreciate about you.

Purpose recruits passionate people. It will make your organization more attractive to value-based, passionate people.

Purpose brings energy and vitality to the work at hand. It provides meaningful and sustainable motivation for employees.

Purpose contributes to a life well lived. Work is no longer a 9-to-5 job to be endured but a meaningful source of fulfillment and satisfaction.

2

DISCOVERING YOUR PURPOSE

Your work is to discover your work and then with all your heart to give yourself to it.

—Gautama Buddha

You now know what a purpose is. You know the benefits. And, by now, hopefully as you consider your own organization, you're wondering: How do I get one? Often we find that a real and authentic purpose is right under your nose. With a little excavating, a little time travel, a little questioning, and a little inspiration, you can discover your authentic purpose.

YOUR PRESENT PURPOSE IS TO DISCOVER YOUR PURPOSE

If you don't have a clue as to what your organization's purpose is, don't be discouraged. You have one. It may have gotten lost along the way, distorted over time, or derailed by management turnover or marketing mumbo-jumbo. Or it may never have occurred to people to look for it—until now.

Start with the assumption that there is a purpose waiting for you— a purpose that will engage your heart and mind for years to come.

Make a commitment to finding it. That's your purpose until you find your purpose.

Discovering your purpose is more art than science. There are a variety of tools and techniques you can employ on your search for purpose—some of which may turn out to be dead ends but others may lead to the Holy Grail. We recommend experimenting with a variety of the following lines of questioning to figure out which one works best for you.

In Part IV of this book, we'll take you through examples of how a variety of our clients were able to find their purpose by exploring these questions. For now, we'll give you something to tide you over until we get to those stories.

REVISIT YOUR HERITAGE

You may have done this as a personal exercise at some point in your professional career. Often when you're in doubt about what you're doing or why you're doing it, it's helpful to ask yourself why you started doing it in the first place. The same goes for companies and organizations.

Many organizations that we work with, particularly government entities and nonprofits, were conceived with noble and grand goals in mind from day one. In some cases the purpose remains operative and well understood by every employee. In others it lies dormant in a storage facility, collecting dust as the years go by.

Well, it's time to call up the storage units and start dusting things off. Follow T. S. Eliot's advice and go back to where you started . . .

> *We shall never cease from exploration*
> *And the end of all our exploring*
> *Will be to arrive where we started*
> *And know the place for the first time.*
> —T. S. Eliot

Go back and dig up clues that reveal *why* the company began. Every company started somewhere with founders who had some kind of vision about what they wanted the company to accomplish. Johnson & Johnson has lived by a one-page credo that has existed for more than sixty years and begins with a clear indication of the overarching purpose:

> We believe our first responsibility is to the doctors, nurses and patients, to mothers and fathers and all others who use our products and services. In meeting their needs everything we do must be of high quality . . .

Use the founding charter of your organization. Find the original business plan. Keep in mind that what you're looking for is the fundamental motivation that set the organization in motion. You're looking for *why* it came into existence—not *how* it went about conducting business (which is bound to have changed dramatically over the years).

Jim Collins is an avid mountain climber, and he described the "why" of a company using this mountain-climbing metaphor:

> Why you climb mountains doesn't change. But the mountains you choose to climb and how you climb them will certainly change over a lifetime.

Talk to retired employees who were there in the beginning. They are the keepers of the stories that might hold the key to your future. This is especially true if you find yourself in a huge corporation that has radically changed since the earlier entrepreneurial days of the founders. The old-timers can tell you a thing or two about the original drive behind the organization, which may have been abandoned as times changed and new management began to try out short-term strategies to bring in more revenues, increase profit margins, etc.

Look for the common ground. Some companies have rather odd pasts populated with a variety or seemingly disconnected ventures and businesses. Sometimes the hodgepodge of initiatives reveals an underlying motivation that is part of the company's DNA. Look for the common-ground values behind seemingly disparate ventures that the company has embarked on over time.

Sometimes this exercise will prove to be a dead end. There may only be some people who saw an opportunity to make a buck. Don't let that take the wind out of your sails. Purpose doesn't have to emanate from day one. It can start whenever a heartfelt commitment to discovering a core purpose emerges. It's never too late to start.

A word to the wise: Beware of the all-knowing brand consultant and/or short-tenured CMO.

You would be amazed at how many "branding experts" or even some chief marketing officers (who now hold office an average of eighteen months) completely overlook or dismiss the origins and roots at the core of the organization. They are often so consumed with today's rapidly changing fads, trends, and technologies that they dismiss the company's heritage as yesterday's news. Driven to prove how smart they are about today's marketing environment and how out of touch the organization is, they often dismiss the true heart of the organization as irrelevant or antiquated. Follow their lead only if you wish to set the fundamental direction of your company at the mercy of marketplace fads or résumé-building individuals.

REVIEW FALSE STARTS

At one time in your organization's history there may have been an idea that everyone rallied around and everyone felt good about. However, for whatever reason, interest may have petered out or problems may have arisen that rendered the idea null and void. That happens. Sometimes perfectly viable purpose areas get left on the scrap heap because of a minor setback.

If you find an idea that you think may have been a viable purpose, ask yourself:

- Why did we walk away from it?
- What setback knocked us off course and how could it be avoided next time?
- Was the right leadership in place at the time?

- Did we get distracted by the competition?
- Did we compromise the business model that made the purpose possible?

Too often, great companies give up on a noble purpose too soon. Revisit ideas that resonated with your organization and see if there might not be a way to resuscitate or reincarnate the idea.

CONTRAST YOUR SUCCESSES AND FAILURES

Take the time to conduct an audit of all the times that your organization has achieved a successful outcome and, conversely, when it did not. What can you learn from contrasting the two situations? What's the difference between your successes and failures?

Take the time to really understand the ingredients that are present in successful endeavors, paying particular attention to intangibles that probably wouldn't register on a project-management worksheet.

I can use our own agency as an example of how this line of questioning really sent us down our own path to purpose. We looked at the types of accounts that we produced great work for, that we had no problem staffing, that we developed not only long-tenured business relationships with but also lifelong personal friendships through, and compared those with the types of accounts that were hard to staff, produced mediocre work, and usually lasted no more than two to three years.

At the end of much exploration, we found that the determining factors had nothing to do with the size of clients' budgets, the extent of their challenges, the category they were in, or where they were located, to name just a few of the likely variables. What set our successful relationships apart from our unsuccessful relationships came down to the very premise of this book: We are at our absolute best when we're working with leaders of organizations that have a great purpose. We get fired up about helping people who want to change the game and make a difference. Our people don't want to create ads that will effectively sell any old product or service. We want to *create visionary ideas that will make a difference*—for organizations and leaders trying to make a difference.

Whenever we encounter a prospective client who isn't interested in making some kind of meaningful difference, our hearts just aren't in it. And if your heart's not really in it, nothing great is likely to come from it. We've pursued those "opportunities" at our own peril, producing work that no one's particularly proud of and wasting time on partnerships that are not destined to last.

START ASKING WHY?

Why do you do what you do?

Why is that important to the people you serve?

Why does the existence of your organization matter?

If you ask these types of questions, eventually you'll peel away enough layers of the onion to get to the heart of your business. With each new "why," you may want to think about it from a variety of perspectives.

Why do you do what you do?

If you answered, "to make money," go back and reread everything up to this point. You missed the part about trying to make a difference first and letting the money follow. Ponder the question on a deeper level.

What is the functional benefit to your customers/constituents?

What is the emotional benefit to your customers/constituents?

What is the ultimate value to your customer/constituents?

In answering these questions, your purpose may very well jump out and start dancing around in front of you. Exploring the higher-order benefits and values of your work can reveal some rich purpose territory to play in.

NOTICE WHAT OCCUPIES YOUR MIND

You know those thoughts that fill your mind when you're trying to do your "real work"? Pay attention to those thoughts. There are positive, intoxicating ideas that keep you up at night or drive you out of bed early in the morning. When you wake up at 5:00 A.M., frantically searching for a pen and a pad to capture a brilliant insight into a problem, that's probably your purpose calling.

Notice when your heart rate speeds up just thinking about an issue. Notice when you look at your calendar and you're actually excited about going to a particular meeting or event. Notice where your mind wanders when it has a free moment.

The president of a local Austin engineering firm had built his business servicing a variety of sectors that ranged from semiconductors to nanotechnology, from medical equipment to clean energy products. After helping to design and build a piece of medical equipment that safely transfers patients from gurneys to hospital beds (apparently, hundreds of patients get dropped every year, and orderlies are often injured in the process), he noticed a discernable difference in the energy level and satisfaction he had with his work.

As he took up other projects in other sectors, his mind invariably drifted to problems with medical equipment that needed engineering solutions. Designing products that could potentially improve the quality of care to millions of people stirred a passion in him that he couldn't ignore. To keep his business viable, he could not get rid of all his existing clients in other sectors, but he could begin to aggressively pursue projects in the medical sector going forward. He rewrote his marketing materials to emphasize the medical solutions his firm had created, to begin to attract more of those types of clients and projects. He began hiring engineers who had more experience in this area. By noticing what really stirred his imagination and got his juices going, he began transforming his company into a more purpose-based organization.

Those thoughts that invade your head may be the world calling you to tackle something that needs to be tackled—giving you your concrete assignment that demands fulfillment.

LOOK AT WHAT YOU WON'T DO

Sometimes when you're having trouble identifying exactly what you want to do, it's helpful to flip that thinking on its head and take a look at what you're *not* willing to do. Values and priorities can start to become very evident when you write down the things that you want to avoid at all costs.

One of the founding documents of Southwest Airlines included a list of ten things the airline was going to be built upon, its foundation, if you will. Seven of those items were things they were *not* going to do. They were not going to fly anything but 737s. They were not going to issue conventional tickets or seat assignments. The affirmative items included things like cultivating a supportive and friendly culture and having the fastest turn times of anyone in the industry (which could have been stated as "not wasting time on the tarmac").

This list of the things that Southwest was not going to do was essentially a list of impediments to the fulfillment of their purpose: giving people the freedom to fly.

FIND YOUR HEDGEHOG

The hedgehog concept is an enormously helpful tool you can use to identify the strengths and passions of your organization. Jim Collins developed this tool after studying the best practices of companies that had transformed from good to great.[1] The hedgehog concept asks three basic but fundamental questions:

1. *What are you deeply passionate about?* Focus on the activities that ignite your passion. This is not about stimulating passion ("OK folks, let's get passionate about what we do!"), but looking for the areas where passion naturally resides. This may be the most important question to answer because without passion behind the purpose it will be difficult to achieve the momentum necessary to achieve success. This isn't something you feel you should do or might be nice to do. This should be something

that every fiber of your being tells you must be done. It's not something that might matter or might need doing. It's something you recognize as being critically important in your industry or in the world. It shouldn't be mildly interesting or somewhat intriguing. It should keep you up at night because you can't stop thinking about it. Take a good hard look within your organization and see where this level of passion occurs. It won't be found in every initiative or in every employee. But if you look hard enough you'll find it somewhere, residing in the hearts of your best people.

2. *What can you be the best in the world at?* Equally important, what can you *not* be the best in the world at? If you're no better or worse than other competitors in your category, why bother? Take a good hard look at yourself and identify the areas where you have a real and genuine strength above and beyond your competition (whether it's in your core business area or not). This is not about identifying what you would *like* to be the best in the world at, but understanding what you're truly capable of.

3. *What drives your economic engine?* Discover the single economic denominator—profit for x—with the greatest impact on your economics. In highly competitive and ever-changing markets, companies need to attain profound insights into the real source of their economic engine. (By the way, it's important to share this information with your advertising agency so that they can understand the ultimate objective of the work they create.)

The ultimate objective is to identify the intersection of these three circles, simplify it into a crystal-clear concept, and then let it drive everything you do.

TALK TO YOUR EMPLOYEES/INTERNAL CONSTITUENTS

Without your employees, your organization wouldn't exist. They're living, breathing, developing, creating, servicing, interacting with customers, and making things possible. So it's critically important to explore the aforementioned questions with them directly. They know what works and what doesn't. They know when the organization is at its best and when it is likely to flounder. They know what really drives the heart of the organization and what doesn't.

Trying to develop a purpose without considering their perspective will likely result in a purpose that never takes root in an organization. It's like trying to plant a seed in an alien climate—it's unlikely to flourish and will most likely die. By enlisting your people in the process, you not only gain valuable insights that shed light on your true purpose but you also create a built-in constituency that will be far more likely to nurture the purpose once it has been firmly planted in the organization.

So start asking people: When they're at their best, what are they doing? What are they most passionate about? What do they think the organization does better than anyone else out there? Ultimately, what difference do they think the organization makes in the world?

START AT THE TOP

We tend to begin this line of questioning with the leaders of an organization. Sometimes there is great consistency. Everyone is on the same page. Then there are times when we've had a hard time believing that the leaders are talking about the same organization. At the very beginning of the process, it's helpful to do this type of questioning on a one-on-one basis to give people the opportunity to be completely honest in their responses. This can be done through in-depth interviews or homework assignments. The responses can then be analyzed and common ground can be identified. This will facilitate a far more productive session when the leaders of the organization are called together for a group discussion.

The alignment that exists at the top is often a good indication of the unification (or fragmentation) that will be found as you go deeper into the ranks of the organization. If consistency isn't found at the top, don't despair. Just know that you will need to address it there to fully maximize the power of purpose throughout the organization. Often, just getting the leaders of an organization into the same room and exploring these types of questions proves to be quite an enlightening and aligning experience. More often than not, common ground can be found.

ENGAGE YOUR BEST AND BRIGHTEST
THROUGH ANY MEANS POSSIBLE

It's equally important to gain input from the best and brightest, the top performers throughout all areas and all levels of your organization.

We purposely exclude the average and bottom-performing employees in the purpose discovery process. Great insights and brilliant observations about the true purpose of an organization rarely come from the mildly or underengaged. The star performers who "get it" hold the secret to what makes your organization a dynamic entity designed to make a difference in the world.

The methodology you choose to question employees is not important. We've used the most high-tech Web applications that enable us to engage hundreds of employees throughout the world in a dynamic, interactive online brainstorming session. And we've also sat down with frontline employees during their lunch break and engaged them in the most informal fifteen-minute conversation imaginable. Both methods can yield equally valuable insights.

How you will execute the discovery process will depend on the number of employees you need to include in the process and the resources you have available to you. Don't wring your hands about it. The point is to use any means available to gather insights from your internal constituents. This might mean one-on-one interviews, focus groups, online sessions, day-long intensive workshops, self-administered surveys, or journals. Just use whatever combination of methodologies you need to gather input from the evangelists within your organization.

LISTEN TO YOUR CUSTOMERS

Talk to your fans. Talk to the people who love and rely on you. Talk to the people who are committed to your brand and forsake all others. You want the evangelists. They will be able to talk to you about the difference you have made in their lives. If you talk to someone who isn't that excited about what you have to offer, you're unlikely to hear any keen insight about a difference you've made in their life. You'll probably just hear that you haven't made any difference and end up discouraged and believing you have no purpose. Your fans will let you in on your value to the world. With that knowledge in hand, you can begin building your business to reinforce it or deliver it at ever-greater levels.

Here are some good questions to ask your fans:

- What difference has your product/service made in their life?
- What would they lose if you ceased to exist?
- When would and wouldn't they use your brand versus the competition?
- What do they think you do better than anyone else in the world?
- How do you make them feel?

AND FOLLOW YOUR HEART

"Your vision will become clear only when you look into your heart."

—Carl Jung

This process truly is more art than science. No quantitative survey or scientific formula is going to be able to reveal your purpose. Organizations that turn to such methods for direction are organizations that ultimately sacrifice their heart and soul to a set of survey results.

The great leaders that we've been privileged to work with side by side ultimately set their course by sheer gut instinct and a heartfelt drive toward some purpose that demands fulfillment (regardless of what any survey or analyst might say). Hearts tend to be in the right place. Listen to what your heart is telling you to do. Listen to what your heart feels needs to be done in this world, and then use your head to make it happen.

A WORD TO THE ENTREPRENEUR
AND BUSINESS OWNER OF TOMORROW

In Victor Frankl's classic work, *Man's Search for Meaning,* he believes that the ultimate meaning of life is "to carry out a concrete assignment which demands fulfillment." Life is full of challenges and problems that need to be solved. Before you go out and spend your blood, sweat, and tears to build a business, find a concrete assignment that demands fulfillment that your new entity could address.

Fortunately, you don't have to look very far to see work that needs to be done. In every industry there are fundamental problems that need solving. There are ways of doing business that would be more helpful to the planet, more helpful to the communities served by the organization, and more helpful to customers and, ultimately, to shareholders.

Take a good hard look at the world and listen for what it's calling you to do. Look for something you are deeply passionate about—something you think is vitally necessary and worthy of the time, talent, and energy of the people who will be working with you, and something you have the wherewithal to address.

What is the concrete assignment that demands fulfillment that your organization could address?

DISCOVERING YOUR PURPOSE

Revisit Your Heritage. Explore the genesis of the organization. Talk to the founding fathers, review the founding documents, and find the motivation that's been present since the inception.

Review False Starts. Review the "inspirational" initiatives that have been undertaken only to peter out for any number of reasons. The seeds of a great purpose might reside within the rubble of a historical initiative that was given up on too quickly.

Contrast Your Successes and Failures. Take the time to deconstruct your successes from your failures. Move beyond obvious variables to find both the tangible and the intangible factors that are present when you are at your best.

Start Asking Why? Look at all the major initiatives under way at your organization and start asking why—to what end, for what purpose, to make what difference.

Notice What Occupies Your Mind. Take notice of where your natural energy and attention tend to gravitate. If enough of your best and brightest people share this natural passion, the universe may be trying to tell you something.

Find Your Hedgehog. What are you genuinely passionate about? What can you be the best in the world at? What drives your economic engine? Collins discovered that truly great companies can answer these questions. Can you?

Talk to Your Employees/Internal Constituents. Talk to the people who make your organization a success, and gather their insights on any and all of the aforementioned exercises. They know the real deal and are ultimately responsible for the fulfillment of the purpose. Bypassing them is not an option.

Listen to Your Customers. Customers can tell you how you make a difference in their lives. Focus on your die-hard fans and find out exactly what you mean to them.

Follow Your Heart. When all the insights have been gathered and exploration has been done, listen to what your heart is telling you to do. Then use your head to make it happen.

3

ARTICULATING YOUR PURPOSE

TRANSCEND THE GENERIC MISSION STATEMENT

Before we start working on what your purpose statement is, let's talk about what a purpose statement is *not*. Purpose is *not* a mission statement—at least not the mission statement of the modern era.

Organizations often tell us that they don't think they need a purpose because they already have a mission statement. *"Great,"* we say. *"What is it?"* To which they often respond by rolling their eyes and saying with a hefty dose of cynicism, *"Oh, I don't know, something about being the best in the world at what we do."* And that's the problem. Frequently mission statements do not provide a mission, let alone a purpose.

Historically, mission statements were intended to be a powerful declaration of a company's purpose. Peter Drucker once described a mission statement as a "statement of purpose." He went further to explain: "Words should be chosen for their meaning rather than beauty, for clarity over cleverness. The best mission statements are plain speech with no technical jargon and no adornments."[1]

When a mission statement is done well, it *is* a statement of purpose. Today's corporate mission statement, however, has become little more than a descriptive statement about what the company produces and some aspiration to be the best in the world at it. Bestselling author Seth Godin laments the dilution of the mission statement on his blog where, using the following mission statement—To satisfy our customers' desires for personal entertainment and information through total customer satisfaction—he observed:

> "Mission statements used to have a purpose. The purpose was to force management to make hard decisions about what the company stood for. A hard decision means giving up one thing to get another. Along the way, when faced with something difficult, many managers just punted. Like the one above."

And management consultant Nikos Mourkogiannis has also noted the modern-day meaninglessness of most mission statements:

> "[A]s everyone knows, a corporate mission . . . are often utterly trivial: a description of the current product attached to some not quite sincere aspiration."[2]

By this point you should understand that a purpose is not a trivial description of the category the organization is working in alongside some explicit performance goal. It is a definitive statement about the difference you are trying to make in the world.

Once you have discovered and articulated your purpose, we recommend plastering it everywhere and getting on with it. Purpose trumps mission and vision. Purpose is all you need to get everyone marching in the same direction.

However, if you find that your organization still has an addiction to mission and vision statements, you should craft them in the context of your purpose. The mission can explain how you are going to go about fulfilling your purpose—the marching orders given to the internal troops—while the vision might paint a picture of what it means to fulfill the purpose of the organization. If you're going to write them, make them meaningful. Purpose provides that meaning.

Purpose: The definitive statement about the difference you are trying to make in the world.
>   Example: Wal-Mart's Purpose
>   *Wal-Mart's purpose is to save people money so they can live better.*
>
> Mission: The mission (core strategy) that must be undertaken to fulfill the purpose.
>   Example: Wal-Mart's Mission
>   *We're on a mission to drive down the cost of products and services, making them more accessible and affordable for everyone's benefit.*
>
> Vision: A vivid, imaginative conception or view of the world once your purpose has been fulfilled.
>   Example: Wal-Mart Vision
>   *We have a vision of a world where all people can afford to live better.*

One other thing: Purpose is NOT a tagline.

A purpose statement is designed for internal guidance. It is not your tagline, and, consequently, should not be written with that end in mind. If you develop a purpose statement that can easily be translated into a tagline, that's great. But the criteria that one utilizes to develop a tagline (clever, catchy, breakthrough) are not the same criteria you will use to articulate the fundamental purpose of your organization.

Invariably this issue will come up. Just when you think you've developed the perfect statement that clearly articulates the difference you're trying to make in the world in a way that everyone can understand and be inspired by, someone will say, *"I don't think it's catchy enough,"* or *"I don't know if our customers will get it."*

Your customers should feel it. They should instinctively and intuitively relate to your purpose (should they happen across it on your Web site or company brochure) because they are the beneficiaries of it. But it's not written for them. It is written for all the stakeholders who wake up every morning to help fulfill that purpose in some way, shape, or form.

Often the purpose will be translated into consumer language when it comes time to create a tagline. Southwest Airlines' purpose of *giving people the freedom to fly* ultimately expresses itself to customers in the highly memorable tagline: DING! *You are now free to move about the country.*

When you try to get too clever or creative with your purpose statement, you risk minimizing the clarity that's necessary for it to be truly meaningful and effective.

THE ART OF CRAFTING A GREAT PURPOSE

Once you have a good idea of your purpose, it's time to put pen to paper. The key is to articulate your purpose in such a way that will secure top-management buy-in while inspiring key constituents. It's also critical that the purpose be simple and clear enough for everyone to understand. This is no small task. Here's what we've learned from a decade of working through this process with our clients: Stay focused. Keep it simple. Aim high . . . but don't end up in the ether. Focus on what you do rather than how you do it.

LESSONS LEARNED FROM GREAT STATEMENTS OF PURPOSE

Stay Focused

As you go through the purpose discovery process, what often happens is that you unearth a wealth of potential purpose possibilities. You may start falling in love with all the great things your organization may be doing in the world. You can't decide where the real focus resides. No one wants to sacrifice any one piece of it. And then what happens—a verbose, kitchen-sink purpose statement is born. A statement no one will be able to remember, much less articulate; a statement incapable of providing the kind of single-minded focus necessary to accomplish something truly great. Or you end up with multiple purpose statements, and you bounce from one to another without gaining traction in any one area.

While getting a number of people together is critical for formulating ideas, that same large body of people can generate an ever-expanding hodgepodge of unworkable ideas if left without a master gardener to prune away the extra bits and pieces. What begins as an inspiring bounty of ideas can quickly drift toward complication and mess, an overgrown purpose in need of pruning.

I spend a lot of time in the backyard of the agency where I plant

PURPOSE STATEMENTS

Southwest Airlines
To give people the freedom to fly.

Wal-Mart
To save people money so they can live better.

Charles Schwab
A relentless ally for the individual investor.

Norwegian Cruise Lines
Defying cruise convention to deliver a liberating experience for all.

BMW
To enable people to experience the joy of driving.

Air Force
To defend America by dominating air, space, and cyberspace.

AARP
To champion positive social change that will enhance the quality of life for all as we age.

American Legacy Foundation
To build a world where young people reject tobacco and anyone can quit.

American Red Cross
Enabling Americans to perform extraordinary acts in the face of emergencies.

The University of Texas at Austin
To transform lives for the betterment of society.

Texas A&M
To develop leaders of character dedicated to serving the greater good.

and tend a considerable rose garden. Crafting your purpose can be like tending a rose garden. You have to constantly prune—even when there are lovely roses that everyone admires—in order to end up with a bush that produces perfect roses. If you don't, it will turn into a sprawling, complicated, tangled mess. You have to keep pruning away—pulling out the weeds, keeping it manageable, and revisiting it often to see where distracting complexity has crept in and where you need to prune again.

Let me share one example of a corporation that had a bit of trouble with the pruning. This is actually an admirable corporation that believes in a variety of really good things—all of which ended up in a statement describing their corporation as follows:

> We succeed only when we meet and **exceed the expectations** of our customers, owners, and shareholders. We have a **passion for excellence** and will deliver the highest standards of **integrity** and **fairness.** We celebrate the **diversity** of people, ideas, and cultures. We honor the **dignity** and **value of individuals** working as a team. We improve the **communities** in which we work. We encourage **innovation,** accept **accountability,** and embrace **change.** We seek knowledge and growth through **learning.** We share a **sense of urgency, nimbleness,** and endeavor to have **fun,** too.

All these ideas are wonderful things to believe in. But what is the ultimate purpose of this organization? How much more powerful would it be if it could articulate a focused purpose?

Contrast that example with the purpose of another corporation in the same industry—The Hilton Family. It articulates its purpose through one simple philosophy:

> *Be Hospitable.*

Be ruthless about scrutinizing the number of ideas in your purpose statement. Put your heart into it and sacrifice what needs to be sacrificed to cultivate a rich, fertile purpose. The most powerful purpose statements are crystal clear and single-minded in their focus.

Keep It Simple

Keep your purpose statements as clear and simple as possible.

Simplicity is the antidote for organizations that might, in fact, have multiple divisions that need to be reconciled under one purpose. The Hilton Family has nine different hotel chains and over fifty self-contained resorts, and its corporate philosophy, *Be Hospitable,* works for all of them.

The American Legacy Foundation was created to help reduce tobacco use in the United States. One side of the organization creates powerful messages designed to help teenagers reject tobacco and avoid the cycle of addiction altogether. The famously effective "truth" campaign has done a brilliant job exposing the tobacco industry as the ultimate manipulative authority figure—inspiring teens to rebel against the tobacco industry in the process. The other side of the organization is dedicated to smoking cessation—helping smokers kick the habit. They've created a suite of support mechanisms that give adults the know-how to break their addiction successfully.

We were very impressed with the wonderfully simple purpose statement that the American Legacy Foundation crafted. It did a great job of representing both sides of the organization:

> *To build a world where young people reject tobacco and anyone can quit.*

It's simple, understandable, and clearly focused on the ultimate goal of reducing tobacco use in the United States.

When crafting your own purpose statement, make sure that it is so simple that even a child could understand it (as the old adage goes). Initially, we had crafted Wal-Mart's purpose to read:

> *Improving the quality of life by lowering the cost of living.*

We quite liked the turn of phrase and found it a very eloquent articulation of what the company did best. But Greg Chandler, the director of reputation marketing at Wal-Mart, pushed us to go back and write it in a way that any one of his six young children could understand. That's how *"to save people money so they can live bet-ter"* was born.

> *"Being simple is vitally important for the Purpose of every com-pany. A powerful, simple Purpose statement is important because it allows a company as big as Wal-Mart to act like a small, entrepre-neurial company. Every person is empowered to make decisions and lead without spending loads of time seeking alignment that may be impossible to ever get without a memorably simple yet pro-found Purpose."*
>
> —Greg Chandler

The simpler the statement is, the greater the understanding, adop-tion, and ultimately, alignment throughout the organization.

Aim High

As you start to formulate some ideas about your purpose, it's impor-tant to aim high. You want a purpose that inspires people. If the pur-pose is something that you and several of your competitors have already achieved or deliver without any real effort, you haven't aimed high enough. If it reads like an ordinary, run-of-the-mill, dime-a-dozen mission statement, you're not there yet.

A purpose should feel like a lofty and noble goal that's worthy of your life's work. The higher you aim (while still being authentic), the more motivated and energized your employees will be. And the more personal fulfillment they will find in their work.

Once you have identified the nugget of the idea, take some liberty and elevate it to its ideal. Don't hold back because you're not all the way there yet. You may not achieve perfect alignment right away, but that doesn't mean you need to handcuff your purpose to your current reality. Don't get me wrong. There must be some evidence that you can deliver on it, but don't beat yourself up if you're not *yet* living it in every way all the time.

We were hired by the American Council on Education (ACE) to clarify the purpose of higher education in America—a noble cause rich with purpose. We conducted a six-month purpose-based brand-ing audit that included interviews with opinion leaders, academics, college and university presidents from across the country, students, parents, you name it. After a tremendous amount of soul-searching, it was time to present the purpose to a board of directors that consisted of academics and college and university presidents from community colleges to the Ivies. Smart crowd. Tough crowd.

We articulated their purpose as:

> *Transforming lives for the betterment of society.*
> *One discovery, one student at a time.*

Initially, there was a sense that we had nailed it. They were inspired. They said, "That's it!" Everyone could see how their institution could fulfill this purpose in some way, shape, or form. Then reality and second-guessing set in. They didn't really transform *all* lives. They only transformed some lives. Did they really need to transform lives or did they just need to provide students with basic skills to get by in the world? If we were bettering society, that might make higher education too utilitarian. Would it undermine learning for learning's sake? And what about that word "discovery"? Discovery sounds like a research word and that omits all the colleges and universities that aren't research institutions. And on and on it went. If all these considerations had been accounted for, we probably would have ended up with a purpose statement that read something like this:

> *Sometimes we transform lives in a way that might or might not be beneficial to the world—and sometimes we do breakthrough research but sometimes we don't but we make a genuine effort to give students useful skills for operating in the world.*

Just when we were starting to get a bit discouraged a Jesuit priest from Fordham spoke up: *"If you want accuracy about the state of higher education, write a white paper! A purpose is meant to embody the ideal. It should be evocative by nature. It should inspire us and remind us what we're really here to do. If we don't think that's what we should be doing, we need to rethink higher education altogether."*

He went on to give a powerful marketing lesson, pointing out how GE doesn't always *bring good things to life* in everything it does but that's its goal, its aim. How Coke may not really be *the real thing* but it sure believes it is and preaches that message around the world. By the time his speech was finished, everyone in the room understood the powerful simplicity of the purpose statement (and I wanted to become a Jesuit!).

Your purpose should give you a sense of meaning, not be a confessional for your shortcomings. Aim high. You may not always deliver, but if that's why the organization ultimately exists, then put it on a pedestal and preach it.

Another reason to aim high is that if you aim too low, it will be dismissed as a purpose unworthy of rallying the troops. Many people think they don't have a purpose because they have remained too close to the ground. They haven't found the moments where the organization swelled with pride and excitement and isolated those moments as potential purpose territories. They haven't raised the stakes.

As George Bernard Shaw said, *"The true joy in life is being used by a purpose recognized by yourself to be a mighty one."* Make sure that when the searching is done, and the crafting has taken place, you can look at your purpose and recognize it as a mighty endeavor worthy of your talent and energy.

Aim High, but Don't End Up in the Ether

Clearly, we believe in aiming high. But aiming too high can result in a purpose statement that doesn't provide enough clarity about what your organization actually does. For example:

To make the world a better place.

To change the world.

To revolutionize the industry.

To save the next generation.

Can you guess what organization might be associated with each purpose? Do you have any idea what they might be doing to fulfill these lofty visions?

A simple way to gauge whether or not you've floated into outer space with your purpose statement is to imagine that someone turned to you on an airplane and asked you what your organization does. If you communicate your purpose to them, will they have any idea what you are talking about? If not, you've probably gone too far.

Set the "How" Aside

While a purpose does need to be clear about the unique difference you are trying to make in the world, it does not need to be burdened with a description of how you are going to go about achieving it. When crafting your purpose statement, leave the *how* out of it. Focus on *what* you are trying to accomplish because *how* you will accomplish it will probably change and evolve over time.

Southwest Airlines didn't need to explain how it gives people the freedom to fly in its purpose statement. There are dozens of ways Southwest operates differently from other airlines, all of which enable the airlines to keep its costs low, its schedules robust, and its people engaged. And those tactics continue to evolve and change over time in response to shifting market conditions.

BMW didn't explain how it delivers *the joy of driving*. Every year BMW ups the ante on the innovation that creates the *ultimate driving machine*.

Charles Schwab didn't explain how exactly his firm acts as *an ally for the individual investor. How* Schwab serves as "an ally" changes dramatically in response to the needs of individual investors. Let me explain.

In the 1970s, Chuck was among the first to realize that millions of Americans had money to invest in the stock market, but the market was set up to cater exclusively to the very rich. So he created the first discount brokerage in America, enabling a huge new segment of the marketplace to invest and grow their wealth.

In the 1980s, he noticed that individual investors were having trouble managing their scattered mutual funds. Schwab invented a Mutual Fund Marketplace enabling individual investors to manage their funds all in one place.

In the 1990s, he recognized that the Internet would enable individual investors to have a level of control over their investments never before possible. In contrast with traditional brokerage firms that kept research and information in the hands of the stockbroker, Chuck developed the most robust online brokerage firm available and put the information in the hands of individual investors.

In the 2000s, after the market crashed, individual investors were paralyzed. They couldn't trust traditional full-service brokerage firms, many of which were being indicted for conflicts of interest. So Chuck, once again, found a way to become an ally for the individual investor by developing advice that was completely unbiased, not driven by commissions, and not compromised by any conflicts of interest.

Schwab's purpose, *"To be a relentless ally for the individual investor,"* never varied. But the specifics of how he did that evolved in constant response to the needs of the market.

Your purpose should embody your unchanging motivation behind your existence. Innovations in your field, progress in solving your most vexing problems, evolutions in your business model—all will conspire to influence *how* you fulfill your ultimate purpose.

ARTICULATING YOUR PURPOSE

Transcend the Generic Mission Statement. A great purpose statement goes far beyond the modern-day mission statement that is often no more than a basic category description wrapped in corporate performance goals. Be clear and definitive about the difference you are trying to make in the world and leave the category descriptions and sales goals for the annual report.

Remember, This Is Not a Tagline. A great purpose statement errs on the side of clarity over creativity. It is intended to inspire your internal constituents by giving them a clear sense of purpose for all they do. Leave clever taglines for the branding process.

Stay Focused. A great purpose is single-minded and focused. Prune away multiple ideas that can end up cluttering and sucking the life out of a great purpose.

Keep It Simple. A great purpose statement should be immediately understandable and easy for anyone to repeat in an elevator without the aid of Cliffs Notes.

Aim High. A great purpose statement should feel like a lofty and noble goal worthy of putting your life's work into. Understand that this is the ultimate reason for your existence and not a wholly accurate assessment of all your current operations.

Aim High, But Don't End Up in the Ether. A great purpose statement should have enough definition that people understand what you're talking about.

Set the "How" Aside. A great purpose statement is very clear about the difference that you are trying to make in the world but is not encumbered with the details of how you are going to go about doing it (which will most likely change over time).

PART I

Are Purpose Principles Alive and Well in Your Organization?

The following survey is intended to gauge whether or not your organization has a purpose in place. To begin assessing the work that needs to be done to lay the foundation for building a culture of purpose, answer a simple yes or no to each question.

Question	Yes	No
1. Do I feel like the work of my organization matters?	____	____
2. Would our customers notice or mind if our organization ceased to exist?	____	____
3. Does everyone know why we all show up for work in the morning, that is, what we're ultimately here to do?	____	____
4. Do we have a North Star that guides all the new investments we make and innovations we develop?	____	____
5. Is our organization fulfilling a deep-seated need in the marketplace?	____	____
6. Does our organization have a sense of a *concrete assignment that demands fulfillment*?	____	____
7. Is there an energy and vitality that is palpable among the employees of the organization?	____	____

If you answered yes to the majority of the questions, congratulations! It appears you have a strong purpose at work in your organization. You know what your organization is here to do, and you use that to guide your decision making and your workforce.

If you answered yes to roughly half of the questions, you may have some sense of your purpose but it may not be as well defined or as well understood as it needs to be. It may reside in a handful of people, but it hasn't made it throughout your workforce or into a sufficient number of operating practices. Or it may be just an ideal that, when push comes to shove, doesn't really affect decision making within your organization. Study where you answered no and let that be your guide as you proceed through this book. Focus on the areas where your organization needs help to ensure that your purpose seedlings really take root and flourish.

If you answered yes to only a handful of questions, don't be discouraged. By picking up this book you've proven your desire for purpose, and desire for purpose is often the first meaningful step on the journey. With discipline and dedication, every organization can find and fulfill a meaningful purpose in the world.

BUILDING AN ORGANIZATION THAT MAKES A DIFFERENCE

4

FIND THE THRILL!

WHAT DIFFERENCE DO YOU WANT TO MAKE?

Purpose-based companies are passionate about making a difference. Whether they were "born" that way, stumbled into it, or had an awakening along the way, the drive to make a difference is what fuels the company. It's the thrill of being in business.

Companies with a purpose have a way of seeing a need in the marketplace and conceiving of a never-before-thought-of solution to meet that need. Sam Walton looked at people in rural America and envisioned a day when they could afford to buy the same merchandise that was readily available to more affluent people living in metropolitan areas. Herb Kelleher looked at the highways and envisioned a low-cost airline that would get people out of their cars and in the air. John Mackey of Whole Foods Market looked at the grocery industry and envisioned a way to provide choices for nourishing not only the body but also the community and the planet.

This chapter will provide examples of inspiring visions that birthed companies and organizations designed to serve previously unfilled needs in the market. It will also offer methods to get you thinking about where the thrill may reside in your own life or organization. There's no better place to start than in Bentonville, Arkansas . . .

THE THRILL FOR WAL-MART: FANATIC ABOUT SAVING MONEY FOR THE CUSTOMER

Sam Walton began with a single dime store in Bentonville, Arkansas, and transformed it into the largest retailer in the world. A product of the Great Depression and the son of a fierce negotiator of all things (from farms to hogs to wristwatches), Mr. Sam understood how important it was to get the most out of every dollar. And he was driven to help everyday people in rural America get the most out of every dollar they worked so hard to earn. He did this by being absolutely relentless—almost maniacal—in his pursuit of saving money for the customer.

Mr. Sam still drove his red pickup truck, got his hair cut at the local barber shop, picked up nickels that he would find on the street, and shared rooms at a Holiday Inn when traveling for business, all well after he had been named *Fortune's* "Richest Man in America" in 1985. For Mr. Sam, his drive for success was never about the money. The money came as a result of his relentless passion to compete, his love of retailing, his belief in the value of a dollar, and his heartfelt desire to help make merchandise affordable for people living in small towns on modest incomes.

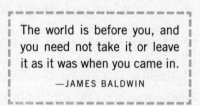

> The world is before you, and you need not take it or leave it as it was when you came in.
>
> —JAMES BALDWIN

Don Soderquist described the simple vision of Sam Walton beautifully in his recent book, *The Wal-Mart Way:*

> When he looked into the future, Sam [Walton] didn't see Wal-Mart as the largest retailer in the world. He simply wanted to provide a better shopping experience for people living in small towns. He wanted to improve their standard of living by providing quality goods at low prices in a pleasant shopping environment . . .

Sam never articulated a vision of being the biggest and richest. He did have a simple business plan that would make money and that he believed would likewise make the world a better place. And his team embraced the vision.[1]

Deep in Mr. Sam's DNA was a passion to do right by the customer. He said that the customer was the only one who can fire the CEO, by spending his or her money someplace else. That empathetic heart coupled with his entrepreneurial spirit, hard work, and vision got him where no one could have imagined. Success never changed Mr. Sam; he never lost his passion or the ultimate thrill of being in business:

> **We exist to provide value to our customers,** which means that in addition to quality and service, **we have to save them money.** Every time Wal-Mart spends one dollar foolishly, it comes right out of our customers' pockets. Every time we save them a dollar, that puts us one more step ahead of the competition—which is where we always plan to be.

From day one, Mr. Sam ran his business with a relentless focus: Do anything you have to do to save money for the customer. He found the thrill in saving people money and, in the process, made Wal-Mart the success it is today.

THE THRILL FOR SOUTHWEST AIRLINES: SEEING A MARKET NO ONE ELSE SEES

In 1971, Rollin King and Herb Kelleher got together and decided to start a different kind of airline. They began with one simple notion: if you get your passengers to their destinations when they want to get there, on time, at the lowest possible fares, and make darn sure they have a good time doing it, people will fly your airline.[2]

So the story begins.

A simple vision for a different kind of airline. When Rollin and Herb initially hatched their plan over thirty years ago, air travel was reserved for the elite. Either you were flying on the company's nickel or you were a part of America's upper class. Herb and Rollin weren't interested in serving that audience. There were dozens of other airlines fiercely competing for that very small market. They wanted to go after a much bigger market that was largely abandoned by the high and mighty legacy carriers of the day. They wanted to serve the 85 percent of the market that couldn't afford to fly or saw flying as impractical. They wanted to serve the people in the buses and in the cars on highways across Texas. They saw an opportunity to make a difference in the lives of people across the state, across the country, and, through emulation, around the world.

It's always wise to look for a niche that you can own. It's even better when that niche happens to be the majority of the market. And it's even better when no one else has been able to see the value in that market.

Southwest was created and sustains itself by being the defenders of the ideal that everyone should be able to fly.

THE THRILL FOR CHARLES SCHWAB:
DEMYSTIFYING AN INDUSTRY

Not too long ago, investing in the stock market was seen as the exclusive domain of the wealthy. You had to have money, financial advisers, and high-paid stockbrokers to play the game. The idea of investing caused, and still causes, many average Americans to feel overwhelmed and out of their league. The Merrill Lynches and the Smith Barneys perpetuate the belief that you *"Shouldn't try this at home! Leave it to the professionals."* Unfortunately, this belief can drive people away from investing and result in devastating consequences for their financial freedom toward the end of their lives.

Charles Schwab wanted to turn fear and intimidation into confidence and empowerment. He set out to design a discount brokerage firm that would empower average Americans with the know-how, the tools, and the low-cost access to the market that people need to get started. He set out to explain investing in plain English and help people get on the path to financial independence. As Chuck describes it:

What intimidates people about investing is largely a myth, a web of misconceptions that has been around so long and has become so pervasive as to seem unquestionable. People think the stock market is too risky, they don't speak the language, they don't know enough about economics. All common ideas, and all untrue, because the good news—the really good news—is that investing is easily demystified. Although a lot of brokers wish it were otherwise (and work very hard and make a lot of money by convincing you that investing is magic that only they know), investing wisely just isn't that hard. . . . If I sound passionate about this, I am. I remind my employees that we are the custodians of our customers' financial dreams, and it's not something I take lightly."[3]

The thrill for Schwab is demystifying investing and empowering investors. He is passionate about helping average Americans realize that they can essentially learn as much as they need to know about investing in a few hours and have affordable tools in their hands to secure their own financial freedom. He has shared his wisdom and set up his business to deliver on this passion. And he's made a huge difference in the financial security of millions of Americans as a result.

THE THRILL FOR AARP:
ANSWERING A BURNING QUESTION

When most people think of AARP, they think of discounts. While AARP certainly does offer discounts to people over the age of fifty, that is not the driving force behind this powerful organization. When we first set foot inside AARP, we were awestruck by the public policy and advocacy work being pioneered by AARP—from lowering prescription drug costs, to strengthening Social Security, to eradicating predatory lending practices, and to demanding affordable long-term care.

AARP's CEO, Bill Novelli, did not found the organization. He didn't lay out the vision. But Bill Novelli is definitely a man on a mission. A man who is kept up at night by the question, *Can our country afford to grow older?* This question fuels his commitment to the work that AARP does every day. It rallies the troops, guides the public policy and research, and determines how they allocate their resources. As he puts it:

> Many are asking whether our nation can afford to grow older. Given an aging population, huge budget deficits and other challenges, there is a call for changes in Social Security, Medicare, Medicaid and other programs in order to ease the financial burden.
>
> So, can America afford to grow older? We believe that—with the right policies and a strong partnership among government, corporate America, not-for-profits and individual citizens—the answer is yes. We can afford it, and benefit from it as well.
>
> We can create a society where people 50+ will have independence, choice and control in ways that are beneficial and affordable for them and for society as a whole. . . . This is our goal . . . to make progress and to create a society where all Americans can age with dignity and purpose."[4]

That is a much more thrilling endeavor than securing a 10 percent discount on your next rental car or hotel room. The people of AARP are truly motivated to create a world where people can age with dignity and purpose *and* do so without pitting the needs of the old against the needs of the young. They are driven to find new solutions that will make a difference in the lives of the aging and not leave future generations holding the tab. That's a formidable task and a mighty purpose worthy of expending one's life energy toward solving. As Bill put it in a recent speech, this seemingly insoluble problem is a challenge the organization looks to with great anticipation:

> And now, the time is here. As a nation, it's time to cut the doom and gloom and attack the issues, following John Gardner's approach. He said that, *"We are all faced with a series of great opportunities, brilliantly disguised as insoluble problems."* Today's America can afford to grow older, we will benefit from it as a society, and AARP will play a constructive and important role in making it happen.[5]

The desire to create a world where all Americans can age with grace and dignity while also leaving a legacy that helps future generations is a powerful motivation and a great way to make a difference in the world.

THE THRILL FOR WHOLE FOODS MARKET: PIONEERING A NEW PARADIGM

John Mackey looked at the existing paradigm of business and said, "Something's wrong here." He set out to prove that you could be mission driven and stakeholder focused (rather than shareholder focused) and still build a thriving business that creates value for everyone.

> *Think about how people think about business in our society. Business is greedy, business is selfish, all business cares about is profit. At Whole Foods, we've not made profit the primary goal of the business. We've put the mission of the business, selling the highest quality natural and organic foods, first. We've put the customer as the most important stakeholder. We've organized our business around satisfying the customers, and then we've put team member happiness as our second-highest value. I mean, you can't be a successful business unless you make a profit, but if you set that as your primary goal, that doesn't inspire anyone. That doesn't tap into anybody's idealism about how to make the world a better place, so I think it's been our idealism and our mission that's been kind of our secret formula to success."[6]*

While conventional wisdom says that the only responsibility of a corporation is to maximize profit for shareholders, John Mackey says that there has to be a better way. The thrill for Whole Foods Market lies in creating a new model that generates value for all stakeholders.

The primary stakeholder is the customer, followed closely by team members (employees), then vendors, communities, the environment, and shareholders. By creating value for all stakeholders, more value is ultimately created for shareholders—as the unrivaled performance of Whole Foods Market has proven. Whole Foods Market has shown that there is an alternative to the current business paradigm. Mackey calls it "conscious capitalism" and it's catching on in American business—consumer expectations are changing and nothing short of a movement has been ignited throughout the country. *"We wanted the philosophy of our stores to spread throughout the culture. We wanted to change the world."*[7] That's a thrilling proposition.

THE THRILL FOR THE CLINTON GLOBAL INITIATIVE: CHANNELING YOUR POWER WHERE YOU CAN REALLY MAKE A DIFFERENCE

I have known former President Bill Clinton and Senator Clinton since 1972. After Bill Clinton left the White House, like all former presidents, he began to focus on what he was going to do next. His thought process went something like this:

> *When I got out of office I had to figure out what I was going to do—I wanted to do something at home and around the world. There's no real job description of a former President so I started with what I couldn't do. I couldn't play my horn well enough to be a full-time musician. I couldn't play golf well enough to go on the Senior Tour. I'm too much of a Calvinist to just lay around and pontificate the rest of my life. So I decided to go to work . . . there are a lot of things that I cared about when I was President that I still care about but I can't have an impact on them. I could go down to my library and talk about them till I was blue in the face but it wouldn't make a difference. So I decided to work on things I care about that I believe I can still make an impact on . . . economic development here and abroad, racial and religious reconciliation, education and community service and AIDS work.*

Bill Clinton launched the Clinton Global Initiative (CGI) in 2005. It was set up as a nonpartisan catalyst for action, bringing together a community of global leaders from every walk of life to devise and implement innovative solutions to some of the world's most pressing challenges. Its purpose was clear and unequivocal: to help turn good intentions into real action and results.

In just over four years CGI has generated over 1200 "Commitments to Action" towards initiatives in poverty, education, climate, and health that will ultimately improve over two hundred million lives. These commitments have involved more than one thousand organizations working in one hundred and fifty countries and over $46 billion in commitments.

Using your power and influence to positively influence the lives of more than two hundred million people around the globe is quite a thrill.

THE THRILL FOR CANCER TREATMENT CENTERS OF AMERICA: *THERE'S GOT TO BE A BETTER WAY*

In the early 1980s, Mary Brown Stephenson was stricken with an advanced form of cancer. Her son, Richard (Dick) J. Stephenson embarked on a mission to find the most advanced and effective treatment available, hoping his efforts would enable his mother to recover and remain an integral part of his life and the lives of his children. What he found was deeply disappointing. What were regarded as world-renowned cancer facilities were focused more on the clinical and technical aspects of cancer treatment, ignoring the multidisciplinary nature of the disease. Even worse, he and his mother's input to her treatment was rebuffed and pleas to try alternative approaches were rejected. After Mary lost her fight with cancer, Dick vowed to change the face of cancer treatment. And that's exactly what he has done.

Dick founded Cancer Treatment Centers of America—the only institution of its kind in the nation. It practices a unique and revolutionary approach to treating advanced-stage cancer called Patient Empowerment Medicine (PEM). PEM is a philosophy of care that puts patients first and in the center of their care. The centers work with each patient to develop a personalized cancer treatment plan that includes nutrition, mind-body medicine, physical therapy, naturopathy, and spiritual wellness—as well as the best oncology treatments that science has to offer.

For Dick, the thrill resides in bringing warmth, humanity, and an integrated solution to an individual that desperately needs it and probably wouldn't find it anywhere else.

THE THRILL IN SERVING THE CUSTOMER

As the examples hopefully demonstrate, there are a lot of places you can look to find the "thrill": You can look for signs of fanaticism among your employees, for new market opportunities unnoticed by others, for noble causes no one is willing to take on, for underserved audiences left behind, or for new business paradigms people believe can't be done. But at the heart of each exploration, you'll find the customer.

All the companies showcased above put the customer first. They started with the customer and observed a deep-seated, unmet need they were passionate about fulfilling in some unique way. Take a good hard look at the people you are trying to serve and find something thrilling to do for them.

The pursuit of the thrill begins with a question:

> *What do people need or want that we have that no one else is offering them?*

Finding the answer to that question is a lot of work. But if you can identify that need, you can begin to align your existing resources around it and build an organization in the service of it.

It's much easier to get an organization to rally around serving the needs of a particular group of people than it is to motivate people around increasing profit or shareholder value. I'll give you a quick example. Imagine you're at a dinner party. A typical first exchange between two people meeting for the first time includes the great American question, *"What do you do?"* Now whether they would actually use this language or not, you tell me which response you think someone would prefer to give in answer to this question.

Option 1: I negotiate with vendors until they give me the lowest price possible.

Option 2: *I improve the quality of life for millions of Americans by helping them save money.*

Option 1: I work for a grocer that has the highest profits as a percentage of sales, the highest sales per square foot, and the highest same-store-sales growth rate.

Option 2: *I help provide food choices for people that nourish their bodies, their communities, and the planet.*

Option 1: I treat cancer with aggressive cancer treatments.

Option 2: *I treat people who have cancer and provide them with the physical, mental, spiritual, and emotional support they need to fight their battle.*

All the responses are true, by the way. But the orientation toward the customer is where the real thrill resides. That is where you will find the motivation for great purpose.

WHAT DO PEOPLE NEED THAT MY ORGANIZATION COULD FULFILL?

Great purpose-based organizations put the customer first. Start with the customer in mind and find a deep-seated, unmet need that your organization is passionate about fulfilling. Take a good hard look at the people you are trying to serve and find something thrilling to do for them. Ask yourself: *What do people need or want that we have (or could create) that the competition isn't giving them?*

What Turns My Organization On?

What is your organization genuinely fanatical about? Where do you naturally go above and beyond the status quo? Look at behaviors, attitudes, and beliefs that exist within your organization to discover signs of fanaticism that may hold the key to your true passion. Some of the organizations we covered found the thrill by:

- Serving underserved populations
- Creating new paradigms
- Fighting for noble causes
- Enlightening and empowering people
- Seeing what others can't see

What Difference Does My Organization Want to Make?

Ultimately, the answer to this question will be the source of the passion that fuels the culture of your organization. Next up—do you have the will to make it happen?

HAVE THE WILL!

Go put your creed into your deed.
—*Emerson*

Once you have identified the thrill of doing business for your organization, you must look at how you are going to behave as a company to fulfill the thrill in a meaningful way. In essence, once you've found the thrill, you must be able to answer the question—how are we going to do it? *How are we going to put our creed into our deeds?*

This chapter will showcase *the will* that brought about remarkable and sometimes revolutionary ways of doing business that enabled purpose-based companies to walk the talk. Entire books have been written about the business models highlighted in the following examples. But what most of those books fail to acknowledge is the motivation behind those business models.

This chapter is very important because operations have to be in alignment with the purpose for the purpose to have any chance of being fulfilled in the place that Peter Drucker called "the only place that mattered"—the marketplace. We've witnessed the derailing (and sometimes demise) of many great purpose-based organizations when operational decisions disregarded the real purpose of the organization.

HOW WAL-MART *SAVES PEOPLE MONEY*
SO THEY CAN LIVE BETTER

More for less.

Mr. Sam found the thrill in saving people money. He was driven to provide rural America with affordable access to better-quality merchandise that could improve their standard of living. So how did he do it? What decisions did he make that enabled him to fulfill the thrill and build a successful business while doing it?

The secret to keeping costs low, when Mr. Sam explained it, is really not that complicated. Mr. Sam made the decision to pass the savings along to the customer. That decreased the percentage that would go to his bottom line. However, by cutting prices, he sold more than everyone else, which helped him to make more than everyone else. Here's Mr. Sam's simple explanation of the economic model that Wal-Mart is built upon—an economic model that set it apart from every other retailer in the market:

> *If you're interested in "how Wal-Mart did it," this is one story you've got to sit up and pay close attention to. Harry (a NY Buying Service) was selling ladies' panties—two-barred, tricot satin panties with an elastic waist—for $2.00 a dozen. We'd been buying similar panties from Ben Franklin for $2.50 a dozen and selling them at three pair for $1.00. Well, at Harry's price of $2.00, we could put them out at four for $1.00 and make a great promotion for our store.*
>
> *Here's the simple lesson we learned: Say I bought an item for 80 cents. I found that by pricing it at $1.00 I could sell three times more of it than by pricing it at $1.20. I might make only half the profit per item, but because I was selling three times as many, the overall profit was much greater. Simple enough."*[1]

This explanation shows that when you do right by the customer—whether it's saving 20 cents or getting an extra pair of panties—the purpose and the performance of the company can be fulfilled at the same time. This desire to do right by the customer and right by your business is captured in two of Mr. Sam's "Top 10 Rules of Business,"[2] including:

Rule #8: Exceed *your customers' expectations. If you do, they'll come back over and over. Give them what they want—and a little more. Let them know you appreciate them. Stand behind everything you do.*

Low prices used to mean low quality. To live up to the thrill of helping people live better, that association with low quality had to be disrupted. That's why you'll find in Wal-Mart a wealth of America's trusted brand names like KitchenAid, Hallmark, Sony, Canon, and Black & Decker, to name a few. Today Wal-Mart is committed to exceeding customer expectations in delivering organic food and clothing and energy-efficient products that have been too expensive for middle-class Americans to consume before now.

Wal-Mart enables its customers to participate in the same "good life"—the Saturday afternoon BBQs, Friday-night movie nights, dinner parties with friends—that wealthier Americans often take for granted. Moms can send their kids to school dressed as stylishly and as well supplied as any other kid. People can trust Wal-Mart not only to have the lowest prices, but to have the lowest prices on the brands (and the quality) they trust. That's what Mr. Sam meant by exceeding expectations. If Wal-Mart wasn't bringing higher-quality goods and services to all Americans, it wasn't fulfilling its purpose of helping people live better.

Rule #10: Swim upstream. *Go the other way. Ignore the conventional wisdom. If everybody else is doing it one way, there's a good chance you can find your niche by going in exactly the opposite direction.*

This rule is CRITICAL. If you are trying to make a difference, you will need to look at the status quo and figure out how you can bust it up in order to bring something fresh and new to the marketplace. Mr. Sam recognized that the conventional way to make money in the retail category was to increase prices to make a higher profit margin. He decided to go the other way: to decrease the margin but increase the volume of products sold. He made the decision to behave in a way that would save his customers money, believing that success would come from putting the customers' interests first.

With Wal-Mart, we found a company with a real and genuine passion for its customer. It competes fiercely to keep every last dollar it can in the customers' pockets. And it is a company run more efficiently and cohesively than any retailer in history. This is the DNA of Wal-Mart, and it establishes an authentic foundation for its purpose.

HOW SOUTHWEST *GIVES PEOPLE THE FREEDOM TO FLY*

The Lean, Mean, Efficient Machine

To look at the marketplace and say, "let's create an airline that allows 85 percent of the market that has never flown to fly and fly often," is one thing. To pull it off is another.

Always Low Fares

To get people out of their cars and in the air, Southwest cofounder Herb Kelleher knew that he would have to bring down dramatically the price of flying. This required radically rethinking the economic model of the airline industry. Similar to Sam Walton, Kelleher wanted to bring everyday low pricing to an industry that fluctuated wildly from extremely high fares to basic high fares based on demand. He mustered the will to create an entirely new pricing model that, like Sam's, relied upon the belief that if the customer wins, he'll thank you with his business and your business will prosper (despite all conventional thinking that would suggest otherwise).

> Southwest applied the concept of price elasticity to the economics of passenger flight, further cutting fares on off-peak flights to fill more seats and thus achieving higher revenue than with fewer seats sold at higher prices. . . . The company's pricing strategy is to keep fares consistently low regardless of what the market will bear. The conventional wisdom of supply and demand would suggest that, when flights are full, prices should go up. However, throughout its history, Southwest has flown in the face of convention. Instead of raising fares when load factors are up, Southwest increases the number of flights and expands the market. On routes

*like Dallas–Houston its discipline in keeping fares low has given
the company 69 percent of the market.*[3]

Without reinventing the fundamental economics of the industry,
the idea of giving people the freedom to fly would never have gotten
off the ground. But it didn't stop there. To make the new low fare
structure work, Herb had to rethink how to maximize the productivity (and profitability) of his planes.

Keep 'Em Flying

This is no big news flash, but airplanes only generate revenue when
they are in the air. So the more time the plane is in the air, the more
money Southwest Airlines can make. This rather obvious insight led
to some other breaks with industry convention: the point-to-point
system and the open-seating process. The decision to go point-to-
point can be best explained as follows:

> *Simply put, the more flights you can make with each airplane in a
> day, the more revenue you will produce and the lower your unit
> costs per flight. The hub-and-spoke system augments costs because
> airplanes spend more time on the ground waiting for passengers to
> connect from "feeder" cities. [Southwest] flies point-to-point be-
> tween cities, thereby maximizing its use of aircraft. A typical Boe-
> ing 737 in the Southwest fleet is used 11.5 hours a day, compared
> with the average 8.6 hours a day of other carriers.*[4]

More time in the air means more flights for passengers (i.e., more
freedom to fly) and more money for Southwest. It's clearly a win-win
situation.

Now what does the simple process of assigned seating have to do
with keeping costs low and giving people the freedom to fly? It can't
possibly have that much of an impact, can it? This is an ongoing debate both inside and outside Southwest. It is a raging debate that has
sparked heated arguments. If the purpose of the company is to keep
costs low and make it more affordable for more people to fly, what's
the big deal with giving people an assigned seat?

The big deal is *not* the financial cost of providing assigned seating.

The big deal is the cost of *time*. Assigned seating is a time killer. It slows down the boarding and deboarding process and therefore decreases productivity and plane utilization. Southwest used to be famous for their ten-minute turnaround time (the ability to deplane, clean, board, and pull back within ten minutes). Cutting ground time to ten minutes reduced operating expenses by 25 percent. Because of using larger 737s, carrying more passengers, and adding freight service, Southwest now turns its planes in twenty minutes—which still stands as the industry record.

Southwest has no particular prejudice against assigned seating. However, since management knows that assigned seating would raise costs and cause them to raise prices, they won't do it. And the majority of the flying public seems to agree to this minor inconvenience in exchange for a low-priced ticket. An assigned seat on an airline someone can't afford to fly doesn't do them a whole lot of good.

Southwest has a radically different economic model, flight system, and turn-time advantage. One would think that ought to do it. But Southwest doesn't stop there. They look at everything they can possibly do to keep costs low so that they can pass along those savings to the customer.

We'll Take the 737

Another way that Southwest Airlines has saved billions of dollars in operating expenses has been with the strategic decision to use only 737s.

> *Flying this type of aircraft has a strong impact on the bottom line. First of all, training requirements are simplified. Pilots, flight attendants, mechanics, and provisioning agents concentrate their time and energy on knowing the 737—inside and out. Thus all Southwest pilots are qualified to fly, all flight attendants are qualified to serve in, all maintenance people are qualified to work on, and all provisioning crews are qualified to stock every plane in the fleet. This makes it easy for Southwest to substitute aircraft, reschedule flight crews, or transfer mechanics quickly and efficiently. With only one type of aircraft, the company can reduce its parts inven-*

tory and simplify its record keeping, which also results in savings.
Sticking with the 737 series also helps the company negotiate better
deals when acquiring new planes."[5]

This decision has been tested again and again as new competitors
have come on the scene with a wide variety of aircraft. Southwest's
decision to stay the course, however, is not that difficult when viewed
in the context of the purpose. They're not in the pretty airplane
business—although they do make improvements whenever possible,
such as upgrading to all-leather seats and adding more leg room.
They are in the business of giving people the freedom to fly, and maintaining a standardized fleet of 737s is the most cost-effective way to
fulfill their purpose.

From fare structure to equipment, point-to-point system to open
seating, Southwest took a fresh look at everything and had *the will* to
make the decisions that needed to be made to make the thrill a reality.

HOW CHARLES SCHWAB BECAME *AN ALLY* OF THE INDIVIDUAL INVESTOR

A Higher Interest in the Customer

We first began working with Charles Schwab in 2002. The market
was in the toilet. Investors had lost 30 percent of their stock wealth.
Enron had erupted and celebrity analysts were going to jail. Individual investors were feeling betrayed by Wall Street analysts, corporate
America, accountants, and the government. There was a growing
sense that the game was rigged against the little guy. No one had any
confidence in the market, and every individual investor we spoke with
distrusted the system. They were paralyzed. Any brokerage firm trying to advertise in this environment faced a tough challenge, to say
the least. But Charles Schwab had an antidote for the malady that had
overwhelmed investors. He had made tough decisions about how his
firm would operate to truly serve the interests of the individual investor in the most ethical way possible.

The stated mission of Charles Schwab couldn't have been any
more appropriate for the times:

To provide investors with the most useful and ethical financial ser-
vices in America. Be fair, empathetic and responsive. Always earn
and be worthy of customers' trust. . . . Staying focused on their in-
terests will ensure we have no limits in pursuit of our vision.
—Charles Schwab

A thrilling proposition but one that requires proof—particularly in an investing climate plagued by corruption. To be the most useful and ethical financial services firm requires you walk the talk. And Schwab had built a model to do just that.

Schwab's way of doing business was born out of frustration with the way business was done on Wall Street. Stockbrokers were getting incentives to push stocks that were being underwritten by investment banking divisions an elevator ride away. They were also getting paid on commission, which often translates to bogus recommendations to "buy" stocks that benefit the pocketbook of the broker—not the investor. Traditional brokerage firms also charge a host of hidden fees, front-end loads, and other markups that erode the capital of the investor—usually without their knowledge. They get away with this because of the myth of incompetence that most high-end broker-age firms impress upon their own customers: *This is very compli-cated. Don't ask questions. Leave it in our hands. We earn every penny.*"

Charles Schwab wanted to change all that. He had the courage and willpower to behave very differently from the traditional Wall Street brokerage firm. Here are some examples of the changes he made.

Pioneering the West Coast

Geography can be a powerful symbol. His choice to headquarter his new firm in San Francisco was about as far from Wall Street as one could get. And culturally, the radical bohemian, countercultural, crea-tive environment of San Francisco was the opposite of the traditional, elitist boys club, suit-wearing environs of lower Manhattan. It was an important symbolic gesture that this firm was going to be different.

First Discount Brokerage

Prior to Charles Schwab, a trade could cost the individual investor hundreds of dollars in fees. Schwab revolutionized the ability to get in the stock market game by allowing people to trade at a vast discount (reducing an average commission from $250 a trade to $29.95 a trade).

First Online Brokerage Firm

While all the other brokerage firms were hoarding their research and analysis to justify their prices, Charles Schwab put research, analysis, and investing tools in the hands of individual investors—trusting in their ability to make wise decisions for themselves.

No Conflicts of Interest

Schwab decided that he was going to do away with the old system of paying brokers commissions for their livelihood. His employees would be on salary and would have no interests other than serving the real needs of the individual investor.

No Hot Stock Tips

Schwab decided not to build an investment banking division—the bread and butter of most Wall Street firms. When you have an investment banking division, your analysts and brokers become cheerleaders for your own "hot" investments. Again, the investor gets stuck with advice that is serving the interests of the firm more than the interests of the individual investor.

He launched a host of other products and services that were designed to help individual investors fulfill their financial dreams— Schwab Quotes, the Mutual Fund Marketplace, Mutual Fund One Source, and Schwab Equity Ratings. Charles Schwab built his company with the individual investors' interests in mind.

When Pressure Derails Purpose

Charles Schwab is a company that I deeply admire and respect. It has a mighty purpose and one that clearly makes a difference in the lives of the people it serves. But it also operates in a fiercely competitive industry that is often at the mercy of investor confidence. This type of pressure can often cause *the will* to break down.

When we parted ways, the company was being forced to make some very tough decisions. Fees were creeping in where they hadn't been before. We could no longer say things like "no conflicts of interest" or "no hot stock tips"—principles that were central to being the most ethical and useful firm in the world. Traditional full-service brokerage practices were being deployed, causing one to wonder if it was now putting shareholder interests ahead of the interests of the individual investor. We could see *the will* slipping away.

And when the will begins to erode, the purpose begins to unravel. And so too does the thrill of working for the organization. We witnessed a malaise come over the culture as employees began to question the direction of the company. You simply can't state that you're on the side of the individual investor while creating a way of doing business that could undermine that same investor. It's demoralizing to everyone involved. The thrill was gone and the will was out the window.

The good news is that Charles Schwab appears to be experiencing a renaissance—acting as an ally for the investor again. It's not uncommon for companies—even great visionary companies with a purpose— to get off track from time to time. The important thing is to recognize it as quickly as possible when it happens and start making decisions in alignment with the *purpose* again.

HOW AARP *CHAMPIONS POSITIVE SOCIAL CHANGE THAT ENHANCES THE QUALITY OF LIFE FOR ALL*

360-Degree Thinking

Creating a world where people can age with dignity and purpose requires a lot more than offering discounts. It requires taking a 360-degree look at the factors impacting the quality of life as we age. That's a big job. But to truly enhance the quality of life for all, AARP mustered *the will* to identify the issues and made a commitment to tackle them. The all-volunteer board of AARP identified three critical priority areas that must be tackled to truly make things better for everyone, particularly those over the age of fifty.[6]

Economic Security

Economic security entails ensuring the solvency of Social Security, building up pension systems, and increasing options for private savings accounts. It means eradicating age discrimination so that older citizens have the option to continue working, and protecting older people from financial fraud, scams, and predatory lending practices. Finally, security comes from access to affordable, reliable utilities.

Health Care and Supportive Services

Access to health-care coverage, the quality of Medicare, and affordable prescription drug coverage can make or break the quality of life as we age. Long-term support and services are also critical as people strive to maintain personal independence as they age.

Livable Communities

Communities should be "livable" for those who are aging—with realistic housing options, ways of getting around, and access to services and public spaces that promote independence.[7]

AARP fights for solutions in all three of these areas and supports a vast network of state-run divisions to organize local efforts and volunteers to do the same. If it didn't take a 360-degree view and commit to making a difference in all areas, it wouldn't be able to truly help people age with dignity and grace.

As you set out to fulfill your purpose, make sure you have your eyes wide open as to what it will truly take to make a difference at the level you have in mind. Walk a mile in your constituent's shoes. Leave no stone unturned. And be honest about *everything* you will need to do to get the job done.

HOW WHOLE FOODS MARKET *PROVIDES CHOICES* FOR NOURISHING THE BODY, THE COMMUNITY, AND THE PLANET

Practice What You Preach

When Whole Foods Market went public in 1992, founder John Mackey announced, *"We're creating an organization based on love instead of fear."*[8] He's built a company where everybody wins—an organization in which value is created for everyone. Animals, farmers, customers, employees, suppliers, communities, and the planet are all served by his company.

The success of Whole Foods Market is attributable in large part to the philosophy it represents—a philosophy that turns customers into fans and employees into evangelists. When your brand is built on a philosophical foundation, it's absolutely essential that you practice what you preach. Whole Foods Market has *the will* to live by its beliefs in almost everything it does, as one can see in the following small sampling of practices.

Commitment to Whole Foods

Whole Foods Market is committed to offering the highest-quality, least-processed, most naturally preserved foods possible—unadulterated by artificial additives, sweeteners, colorings, and preservatives.

Creation of the Animal Compassion Foundation

The Animal Compassion Foundation was built to provide funding for research toward more humane methods of raising farm animals for human consumption. Many attribute Whole Foods Market for applying the pressure that is changing the face of industrial farming in America.

Commitment to Employees

Team members are encouraged and paid to contribute twenty hours of community service each year.

No Secrets Management

Whole Foods Market lives by the rule of transparency. It communicates more information about its financials than just about any other company in America. It does this so that employees will understand how the company is performing and how the money is being spent. This disclosure includes a pay book outlining how much every employee made the previous year.

Commitment to the Planet

Whole Foods Market takes its responsibility as a custodian of the planet seriously. The company supports organic farming, sustainable agriculture, and environmental protection. Locally, it supports nonprofit community organizations like food banks, shelters, and animal compassion leagues.

5 Percent of Profits to Charity

In 1985, Whole Foods Market publicly announced its commitment to donate 5 percent of company net profits to nonprofit organizations. This initiative was unanimously approved by the board of directors and today accounts for about $8.5 million in philanthropic donations each year.

5 Percent Days

Five times a year, Whole Foods Market stores across the country donate 5 percent of their sales on "5% Day" to a nonprofit organization selected by the local store management. This effort directly supports the individual communities served by Whole Foods Market.

With all the philanthropic efforts that Whole Foods Market participates in, one might wonder if there is any profit left over for the firm's investors (certainly that's what many analysts criticize them for). The numbers tell the tale. The stock has increased over 3,000 percent in the past fourteen years, proving that taking care of all your stakeholders is, in fact, a great way to do business.

PURPOSE IS EVERYONE'S RESPONSIBILITY

What these examples show is that for a purpose to be meaningful, everyone throughout the organization must be involved and committed to building an organization that is consistent with the purpose of the company. Your purpose cannot just reside in a few places, such as in the marketing department or in the imagination of top management. It has to pervade every part of the company. It has to influence how you operate, innovate, and grow your business. Without the involvement of operations, you don't stand a chance of making the difference you want to make.

THE WILL TO MAKE A DIFFERENCE

Every organization will need to look at the inner workings of its firm and find the opportunities to conduct business in a way that fulfills its unique purpose.

What's Up? Conduct a Purpose Audit
Begin by auditing your current operations: Which practices are enhancing versus detracting from your purpose? This will provide you with a frank assessment of how much work must be done to align the organization around a purpose.

What Now? Putting Purpose to Work
Once you have an idea of what you're trying to accomplish with your organization, roll up your sleeves and determine what must be done to accomplish it. What products/services/experiences need to be created? What pricing models could be developed? What procurement strategies could help? What R&D investments need to be made? What employee programs would reinforce the direction?

What's Next? Use Purpose as a Springboard for Growth
Don't just ask, *How can we grow?* Ask, *how can we fulfill our purpose in more ways?* What other products or services might you offer that are in alignment with your purpose?

IGNITE THE PASSION!

Nothing great in the world has been accomplished without passion.

—Hegel

You found the thrill and identified the difference that you want to make in the market that you serve. You have the will to create a business model that is actually capable of making a difference. The last element you will need to build an organization that makes a difference is passion. Passion is the fuel behind every organization that has soared to great success. Passion is born when your heart gets carried away with a purpose greater than yourself.

Passion is difficult if not impossible to manufacture. You can't fake passion or turn it on and off like a light switch. It has to emanate from an authentic source and once it's on, *it tends to stay on.* With the will intact and the right support in place, it only grows stronger, building momentum and spreading throughout the organization like wildfire. Eventually outside constituents will feel it, too.

This chapter highlights how passion plays out inside purpose-based organizations: what it looks like when your employees have it, how it affects expectations of what's possible, and why your job is never done.

When you walk into an organization with this kind of passion, it's palpable. You can sense it. You will probably also notice a unique culture born out of this passion: descriptive titles, rituals, symbols, ways of interacting, credos, even secret handshakes are not out of the question in organizations that share this rare quality.

As a customer, you definitely notice a difference. You can feel the power of purpose through the passion of the workforce. You're greeted by employees eager to tell you about what they can do for you and you're struck by the sense of personal satisfaction and *pleased-to-be-there-ness,* which is sadly absent from much of the American workforce.

TURNING EMPLOYEES INTO EVANGELISTS

Do your employees have a clear understanding of what you stand for and what the organization is ultimately fighting for? If not, it's unlikely that you'll find evangelists in your organization.

Organizations that are well known for their purpose, like Whole Foods Market, magnetically attract individuals who share their beliefs. Healthways, the health-care company introduced in the first chapter, attracts people who are passionate about helping people get healthier. The Air Force attracts young men and women who are passionate about defending America's freedom. The people who make up these organizations are much more than employees. They are evangelists.

When you are known for what you stand for (rather than what you sell), you attract people who want to stand (and fight) for that, too. Those people will be more passionate about making your organization successful than any corporate training or motivational workshop could ever instill in the typical employee.

If your purpose is not so apparent, then *step one* in igniting the passion is preaching the message so that it ignites a fire in everyone who comes in contact with the organization. Don't leave it solely to the advertising (although we will share examples of employee communications that were created to ensure the purpose was understood by everyone in the organization in Part IV on bringing your purpose to life). Your purpose should be easy to find on your Web site. It should be incorporated into corporate materials like annual reports, company newsletters, and employee intranets. Your PR should be tailored to tell stories through the lens of your purpose. It should be woven into your new-hire orientation process and in the interviewing and candidate-selection process. You should celebrate and reward people who help fulfill it in highly visible ways.

If you do, you will soon find that you have a workforce of evangelists who will be more engaged in their work, more loyal to the company, and more invaluable to your customers.

Whole Foods Market Evangelists

I'd like for you to meet some of the team members from Whole Foods Market. We went around the country visiting stores and interviewing frontline team members about working for Whole Foods. We didn't cherry-pick "Team Members of the Month" to stack the deck. We randomly intercepted people throughout the stores from the registers to the produce aisles and everywhere in between. Some had been there twenty years, some a few months. Regardless of position or tenure, a passion and a pride emanated from every single person we interviewed.

It was clear that these were not your average supermarket employees. These were full-blown evangelists ready to give testimony. When we asked them the simple question, *what's it like to work at Whole Foods Market?* here's what they had to say:

I got hired here and I am so thankful that I did because it has changed my family's life. Now, we eat all organic and natural, I'm 48 years old and I'm not on any prescriptions, I am super healthy, my kids love the food, and we're getting more into supplements. The longer I'm here the more I learn about things. And I share what I've learned with the customer since I know it works for me . . . I think the world would be more unhealthy if there was no Whole Foods. —Celina, Tempe, AZ

Working here is satisfying and gratifying because I am able to do something I believe in . . . I think that you have to be excited by the product that you sell in order to enjoy the work that you do.
—Nancy, Santa Fe, NM

I've never dreaded a day coming into work. That's hard to say. It's hard work, but I love it . . . I think we don't just talk the talk. We're

*not really going for trendy, we're just trying to make a difference . . .
To better the world—better people and their health and better the
environment.* —Marissa, Scottsdale, AZ

*I think our goal is to leave this planet better than when we found it.
That trickles down to everything: the food supplies, supporting local farmers, being out in the communities. I absolutely love it. I
want to heal the world. And that's why I'm here. Hell yeah, that is
why I'm here. I want to promote Whole Foods, whole people and
whole planet.* —Cal, Austin, Texas

*It's what I believe in—composting, recycling, it's more than just a
job. It's a way of life. It gives my life purpose to make a difference—
it absolutely gives my life purpose.*

—Myra, Scottsdale, Arizona, store

You can't fake this kind of passion or just turn it on for the cam-
eras. It's genuine, it's real, and it's incredibly persuasive. By the end of
the fieldwork, my daughter Courtney, who worked on this project,
was ready to go work for Whole Foods Market.

*Purpose turns employees into evangelists, which turns strangers
into customers, and customers into fans. It's absolutely contagious.*

If you were to interview the employees of your organization about
what it's like to work there, what kind of responses would you get?
Would anyone say that they be-
lieve in what the company believes
in? That their work is personally
meaningful? Would they say that
working there changed their life?
Would they talk about the difference they are making every day—a
difference they feel is important?

> Passion persuades.
>
> —ANITA RODDICK,
> THE BODY SHOP

Sadly, for too many companies in America, the answer to those
questions is a resounding no. But it's never too late. And you don't
have to be explicitly out to "save the planet" to generate this kind
of evangelism among the troops. *Any* act that makes a difference in
the lives of your customers can fuel this kind of passion among your
employees.

BMW Driving Evangelists

BMW wants to enable people to experience the joy of driving. At the BMW Performance Driving School the instructors show up every day to undo the bad habits of drivers and impart the skills necessary to have the ultimate driving experience. Many of the instructors are former race car drivers. They have a profound and genuine love of driving, and their work enables them to pass that passion on to brave and willing students. At the end of the day, they help people become better drivers and that, in turn, helps more people experience the true joy of driving. That's the source of their passion.

> We all enjoy it—we're passionate about driving, about the car. It's the kind of job you want to get up and do in the morning.
> —Jim Clark, lead driving instructor, BMW Performance Driving School

John Deere Land Evangelists

John Deere is a company that was built for people who love and work the land. Whether the customer is a developer, a farmer, or a suburban homeowner, John Deere has pioneered products and services that help their customers move, shape, and enrich the earth they rely on.

When you walk into a John Deere dealer, not surprisingly, you'll find employees who have a profound appreciation for customers who build, live, play, and rely on the land. The hundreds of employees throughout the John Deere dealer network do everything possible to ensure that customers are always up and running. They believe in and embody the John Deere values—*integrity, innovation, quality,* and *commitment*—and build multigenerational relationships with customers that are almost impenetrable to competitive advances. They feel honored to don the green and yellow colors of John Deere and inspired to behave in ways consistent with the brand values. As one John Deere dealer told me:

> I knew I wanted to work for John Deere ever since I was a child. My family always worked the land so I know what it meant to have a tractor break down and your livelihood threatened. My dad had a lot of different tractors but I always remember that the John Deere never broke down. The brand means something to America. It's

about integrity and taking care of the land and being there through thick and thin. Not a bad set of principles to dedicate your life to. I wake up every day thinking about how to carry on the tradition and push it further.

Wal-Mart Savings Evangelists

"Wal-Martians," the affectionate name used among Wal-Mart Associates to describe one another, are just as evangelistic as the John Deere dealer about saving money for their customers. In fact, Rule #1 of Mr. Sam's top ten rules of business is focused on the idea of believing in and being passionate about the business you're in.

Rule #1: Commit *to your business. Believe in it more than anybody else. Love your work. Be passionate about it.*

Everyone who ever had the pleasure of working with Mr. Sam could attest to his unquestionable commitment to the purpose of the company. He was always looking for ways to save money to pass the savings on to the customers. He was passionate about it. Totally relentless.

To this day, when you go to Bentonville to meet with the leaders of the company, you won't find them sitting in marble towers or eating in private dining rooms. Wal-Mart's world headquarters is a modest cinder-block building that more closely resembles a warehouse than it does the command center for the largest retailer in the world. And if you're traveling for business, forget the Four Seasons. Holiday Inn will be your home away from home.

Years ago, one of our marketplace planners was doing some research for the Wal-Mart film-developing department and two senior vice presidents from the corporate headquarters in Bentonville decided to attend. At the end of the night, as the groups were breaking up, the planner asked where they were staying and here is how one proudly responded: *"Well, we're at the Red Roof Inn which is $59 dollars a night. That's a little pricey. But since the two of us are going to share a room, that works out to just about $30 per person. That's a pretty good deal."* All of a sudden, staying at an Embassy Suites for $99 felt a little extravagant. She decided not to mention it.

The point is, they are just as passionate about keeping expenses low and passing those savings on to the customer. They're proud of saving money. It's in their blood. If they didn't behave in this way, their low-price promise wouldn't be possible. Employees wouldn't be evangelists and customers wouldn't have lined up to make Wal-Mart the number one retailer in the world.

Right now, do your employees have anything to be evangelistic about? Have you given them something to be passionate about? Have you articulated your values, philosophies, and ultimate purpose so that they have a clear

> **Role Modeling:** For over a decade, Wal-Mart created advertising that featured real Associates telling simple stories about the relationships that they had with customers. We always believed that our Associates were Wal-Mart's best ambassadors because they are real people who see firsthand how Wal-Mart saves people money and helps them live better. This approach not only helped communicate customer service to shoppers, it also built pride and passion among Associates.

understanding of why they should get out of bed in the morning and be excited about working for you?

If you are trying to motivate them through revenue goals and market share gains, good luck! Every organization should have something to get excited about. It may be rusty, hidden, or in a coma, but if you take the time to find the thrill, it's likely your troops will share your exuberance and a genuine passion will begin to take root.

PASSION BEGETS PASSION:
USING CUSTOMER FEEDBACK TO FUEL THE FIRE

You may be wondering how you generate passion over the long haul. Sure, when a purpose is launched there may be a wave of enthusiasm that takes over the organization as they rally around a common cause for the first time. But you may be skeptical as to how long that passion can be sustained.

When you begin to make a difference in the lives of your customers, the quality of the relationship you and your employees have with the customer changes. The relationship evolves from a transaction to a partnership characterized by gratitude, respect, and sometimes even joy. This new dynamic will fuel a level of passion and engagement in employees that gets reinforced by every positive interaction with a customer. Consider how each of the following employees might feel in response to making a difference in the life of their customer.

When a Wal-Mart Associate gets thanked by a little girl who saved up her allowance for six months to buy her mother a necklace, that Associate will look for ways to help allowances everywhere go further.

When a student at a BMW Performance Driving School yells "Holy S#@!" as she takes a corner at top speed, squeals with delight, and then emerges from the vehicle exclaiming, *"Oh my goodness, that was wonderful!"* the instructor has a pretty good idea that he has just delivered an unforgettable experience and will be highly motivated to deliver that experience again with the next student.

When a Charles Schwab adviser has an individual investor tell him that this is the first time in her investing life that she's been treated with respect and dignity by her brokerage firm, that "Schwabie" will no longer need a mission statement reminding him to behave ethically. He will take heart in acting with integrity and doing right by each client. He'll check up on each portfolio to see what adjustments need to be made and swear never to call unless the advice is truly in the client's best interest.

When a new AARP employee reads a letter from an elderly widow who was able to find a livable community and public transportation through her local AARP office—thereby, maintaining her independence and reducing the financial burden on her children—that employee begins to see a larger vision of AARP's purpose take shape, and is energized to do more.

When a Southwest Airlines flight attendant seats a grandmother and grandfather on their very first flight ever to see a grandchild across the country, that flight attendant will know firsthand that she has done her part in delivering freedom in helping to make that reunion possible. And that knowledge will keep her energy up when it's time to hit the ground running, turn the planes quickly, and keep smiling through it all.

When a Whole Foods Market team member hears a customer ask the question *"How were these ducks treated when they were alive— were they allowed to swim free?"* she can smile and know that she is changing the way Americans think about the food they eat. Next time she sees a customer, she'll be happy to take an extra five minutes to explain about organic versus conventional produce, or tell someone about the company's Animal Compassion Foundation, or share a story about where a product came from. An enlightened customer motivates team members to learn more and share more with other customers they meet.

When an American Red Cross volunteer looks in the eyes of someone who has just lost his home to a fire at 3:00 A.M. and hears *"Thank you, I don't know what I would do without you here to help me through this,"* she'll be more than willing to pick up the phone the next time it rings in the middle of the night asking her to report for duty.

When a Texan looks out the window of his pickup truck as he travels along I-10 and sees a pristine highway free of litter and quilted with bluebonnets and Black-Eyed Susans, he can take pride in his state and say to himself, *Yeah, that's right, Don't Mess with Texas.*

Passion begets passion. The organization that's making a difference will generate customers who tell powerful stories about how the organization is impacting their lives. This will encourage employees to want to make even more of a difference, which will create more customers who tell more stories, and on and on. Real-world feedback is a powerful motivator that will ensure that passion takes on a life of its own within your organization.

CREATING FEEDBACK LOOPS

Customer feedback has two powerful benefits. First and foremost, it instills your workforce with pride and keeps your employees motivated to carry on the cause. And second, it's a great way to spread ideas throughout your organization about ways to make a difference. Even the very best employees need a flow of fresh ideas to help them serve their customers better.

Do you think that all those songs sung and jokes told by Southwest Airlines flight attendants came about naturally from each individual employee? They're good, but even the best jokesters need new material on a regular basis. So flight attendants try out material, get feedback from passengers in the form of laughter or silence, and spread the word about what's worked and what hasn't.

The point is to guarantee that there is some kind of feedback loop to ensure that ideas and encouragement from the front lines are circulating freely throughout your organization.

Do your customers have any channels for telling their stories? Are customer stories circulated throughout your organization? Do your employees have any real sense of the impact they have on the lives of the people they serve? Do your employees have any way of sharing what's working and what's not? If not, why not?

A FINAL THOUGHT ON CREATING HIGHLY ENGAGED, EVANGELISTIC EMPLOYEES

The hit sitcom *The Office* provides countless examples of the ineffectual (sometimes pathetic) approaches often taken in uninspired workplaces to create employee morale. From "constructive compliment" suggestion boxes to pretzel days to impromptu pep talks, we've all experienced these types of approaches aimed at engaging the unengaged. If only suggestion boxes, pep talks, and pretzel days did it for people.

The thing that has always struck me about the countless books on strategies and tactics for creating a more productive and engaged workforce is the absence of any discussion about the fundamental purpose of the organization. All the team-building and motivational speeches you can muster won't make up for working for an organization that doesn't make any perceptible difference to anyone.

If you have a genuine purpose, you won't need to manufacture silly tactics to try to inspire people to come to work. Not that purpose is a panacea for employee engagement. You can quickly turn off even the most evangelical employees if your company is plagued with bad management practices and ineffectual leadership. But ultimately, it's purpose that will create the kind of evangelism and passion that well-run organizations thrive on.

SHOOT FOR THE MOON

> Believe it! High expectations are the key to everything.
> —*Sam Walton*

When you've found the thrill and have the will, and employees share that passion, don't be afraid to set audacious goals that would seem inconceivable to your competitors.

I remember when a representative from Sears was asked about the threat posed by Wal-Mart spreading around the country—right into Sears' backyard. It went something like this:

REPORTER: What do you think about Wal-Mart coming to Chicago?

SEARS: We're going to send that squirrel hunter right back to Arkansas. That discount concept won't fly in the big city.

To be fair, if you didn't know Mr. Sam and his commitment to shooting for the moon, you too may have been guilty of thinking the same thing. Don Soderquist, retired chief operating officer and senior vice chairman of Wal-Mart, tells a great story of the ambition of Sam Walton that propelled him further than anyone would have expected. At the time, Wal-Mart was just a small regional discount store, and Mr. Sam, along with several other small regional discount stores, would meet regularly to strategize about how to compete against KMart.

> [In the early 1970s] [t]here was a group of eight small regional discount store chains whose executives met several times a year to share ideas on how to improve operations. None of their stores were in competition with each other, as they were in different geographical locations.
>
> At the end of one of these meetings in 1971, one of the CEOs thought it would be interesting to hear what each thought his

company sales would be in ten years. The first CEO said that his sales were at $40 million in the past year, and he believed that they could move them up to $80 million in a decade. The next said that his company's sales were $60 million, and he expected to be at $100 million in ten years. Another said that sales were already at $100 million, and he believed his stores could reach $160 million in that period. Finally, Sam said that Wal-Mart sales were at $44 million, and he expected that in ten years they would reach $2 billion. Everyone laughed. What they didn't understand at the time was that Sam was serious. Ten years later, Wal-Mart sales exceeded $2 billion. Sam modeled the power of high expectations.[1]

When you have a difference you're trying to make in the world, and you've established a business model to make it possible, you suddenly have the passion and the permission to think big. And since most of your competition won't have this level of passion, they'll never see you coming . . . until it's too late.

Sam Walton's goal was to reach $2 billion in sales—that meant increasing sales by more than twenty times in less than ten years. Had he not established the reason why he wanted to succeed (i.e., to save people money so they could live better), and if he had not established a business model to make it feasible (i.e., an economic model based on more for less), that colossal goal may never have seen the light of day.

NEVER REST

A purpose never changes and it's never "finished." Purpose is always on the lookout. People who lead purpose-driven organizations know what work is left to be done, and are constantly searching for ways to do things better, faster, and more efficiently.

The American Red Cross is in the business of *empowering Americans to perform extraordinary acts in the face of emergency situations*. Over the years, it has continually asked how it can create systems that enable ordinary people to respond effectively in a crisis. The exploration of the question has led to the development of everything from training people in life-saving techniques (e.g., CPR and first aid), to collecting blood from thousands of Americans every year that saves lives, to helping people prepare for natural disasters that are increasingly facing the planet. Its purpose will never change, and it will never stop searching for ways to harness the best of humanity to effectively address emergency situations.

The purpose of higher education is to transform lives for the betterment of society—and in so doing create solutions that will benefit everyone in the future. This is a purpose that demands an ongoing search for problems that need solutions. Higher education must continue to step up every day and figure out how it is going to be a part of the solution machine for serving society at large.

The purpose of the Air Force is *to defend America by dominating air, space, and cyberspace.* Every year there are new threats, new enemies, new approaches to warfare that threaten the security we often take for granted. The Air Force's purpose will never change but it can never rest.

Schwab has never stopped pioneering new investing products and services that served the needs of the individual investor. Driven to be the most useful and ethical financial-services provider in the country means always finding new ways to be useful to investors.

Wal-Mart has to wake up every day and ask *what can it do today that will save people money and help them live better?*

BMW has to continually search for ways to perfect the ultimate driving machine to deliver the joy of driving in new and fresh ways.

AARP has to roll up its sleeves and tackle new issues that affect the quality of life as America ages *as it never has before.*

With every ship that Norwegian Cruise Line builds, it takes a fresh look at what it can improve upon and tries to develop new and better ways to deliver the type of liberating experiences people want when they take a vacation.

Purpose-based organizations are never satisfied with the status quo. They don't stop to rest on their laurels. They're always looking for new ways to fulfill the promise of their purpose.

Whole Foods Market epitomizes this drive to go further and do better at the end of its *Declaration of Interdependence* (a grand manifesto of all that it believes in), which concludes with the following:

> Our Vision Statement reflects the hopes and intentions of many people. We do not believe it always accurately portrays the way things currently are at Whole Foods Market so much as the way we would like things to be. **It is our dissatisfaction with the current reality, when compared with what is possible, that spurs us toward excellence and toward creating a better person, company and world.** When Whole Foods Market fails to measure up to its stated Vision, as it inevitably will at times, we should not despair. Rather let us take up the challenge together to bring our reality closer to the vision. The future we will experience tomorrow is created one step at a time today.[2]

What an incredibly forward-looking vision statement. The road to the future is paved with dissatisfaction of the present. Don't wait for your customers to tell you what they need. Take a long hard look at what needs to change and get started on it before your customers even have to ask.

Use the passion of your convictions to muster the energy to continue taking steps in the direction you want to go. When you stumble, regroup and take another run at it. The point is to channel your energy into creating better ways of delivering on your purpose. One step at a time.

> Every great accomplishment is the story of a flaming heart.
>
> —ARNOLD GLASOW

IGNITE THE PASSION

Turn Employees into Evangelists

Purpose turns employees into evangelists, which turns strangers into customers, and customers into fans. It's absolutely contagious once it catches on. Giving your employees the language of purpose and examples of purpose in action will give them something to take pride in, to behave in alignment with, and to preach about to your customers and prospects.

Let Passion Beget Passion

When purpose takes root within your organization and is operative in the marketplace, your employees will begin to feel it from your customers. Stories will come forth about the difference your organization has made. And employee motivation will begin to kick in naturally and consistently from the power of those "testimonials." Create channels to ensure that those stories circulate throughout your organization.

Shoot for the Moon

When you have a purpose you truly believe in, anything is possible. Aim high and dream big because your employees will rise to the occasion and just might take you there. In the meantime, your competitors won't take you seriously and won't know what hit them when you fly right by them.

Never Rest

Building a culture of purpose in order to make a difference in the world is an ongoing process. It's never over. You never rest. Maintain brutal honesty about where you are delivering the goods and where you're not. Take it step by step and keep on walking.

PART II

Are You Building an Organization That Makes a Difference?

The following survey is intended to gauge whether or not your organization is capable of making a difference in the marketplace. Even the best purpose-based companies will answer this survey differently at different times in their history. So think of it as a point-in-time assessment that will help you determine the level of work that needs to be done to create an organization that's capable of making a real difference in the life of the customer.

Question	Yes	No
1. Have you identified "the thrill" for your organization?	___	___
2. Does my organization have the will to change practices, processes, or products in order to deliver on our purpose?	___	___
3. Does my organization behave any differently than other organizations in our industry? (Be honest.)	___	___
4. Does my organization behave in ways to ensure that we can fulfill our purpose?	___	___
5. Would our customers say that we are doing business in a way that is uniquely suited to serve their needs?	___	___
6. Do our employees understand their role and take pride in fulfilling the purpose of the company?	___	___
7. Do the majority of people within my organization feel deeply passionate about the business at hand?	___	___
8. Is my organization made up of more evangelists than employees?	___	___
9. Do our customers tell stories about the difference that we've made in their lives?	___	___

Question	Yes	No

10. Are our employees constantly on the lookout for ways
to improve the way that we make a difference in the
lives of our customers?   ____   ____

If you answered yes to the majority of the questions, congratulations, you
are well on your way to building an organization that's equipped to make
a difference. You have a strong sense of purpose, you're willing to do
what needs to be done to get there, and you have a passionate workforce.
Let's hope you have purpose-based leaders and a marketing arm that is
telling your story to the world.

If you answered yes to roughly half of the questions, you can see the
light at the end of the tunnel but you've got some work to do. You may
have found the thrill but not been able to muster the will. Or maybe you
have the will—you're behaving in remarkable ways—but you're just not
sure what it's in the service of. You'll need to spend time thinking about
the examples from each chapter in this section and assess where the
work needs to be done.

If you answered yes to only a handful of questions, don't despair.
Everyone can have a purpose if they set their minds to it. You may in fact
already have one that has not been articulated in a focused or disciplined
way. In any case, you will need to spend time reviewing each chapter in
this section until you:

* *Find the thrill*—figure out what difference you want to make in the
world.
* *Have the will*—determine what you are going to do to make that
difference come true.
* *Ignite the passion*—develop ways of channeling the energy and
enthusiasm throughout your organization.

BECOMING
A LEADER OF
GREAT PURPOSE

STEWARDS OF PURPOSE

It takes great leaders to bring a purpose to life. And if there is one thing there is a shortage of, it's leaders who have a sense of purpose. [Leaders] must inspire employees and other stakeholders to bring to life that purpose day in and day out. And, at the end of the day, that is what distinguishes ordinary companies from extraordinary companies.

—*Jim Stengel, former P&G global marketing officer*

The primary responsibility of a leader in a purpose-based organization is to build, nurture, and sustain the core purpose of the organization. By anchoring leadership in purpose, you can drive progress, innovation, and change in a cohesive way that creates high-performing organizations.

By far, the number one driver shared by the masters of purpose is the desire to make a difference. Making a difference is the fuel that drives their energy and commitment to their companies. Making a difference is not some soft, feely, touchy New Age theory. It is the exact opposite. Having a definitive conception of the difference you are trying to make in the lives of all your stakeholders will drive all the tough decisions that need to be made and ensure maximum alignment between all the constituents required to pull it off.

Most books written about the great leaders in corporate America tend to showcase the brilliant strategy and execution associated with their reign of leadership. And for sure, all great leaders are great strategists and executors. Ultimately, a purpose cannot be fulfilled without great strategy in place to pull it off. We've seen a lot of well-intentioned, change-the-world entrepreneurs who floundered miserably because they didn't have the know-how to get the job done. So please don't read this book and think that all you need is a mighty purpose and everything else will take care of itself. Strategy is essential. Read Michael Porter. Study Jack Welch. Practice the principles of great companies identified by Jim Collins. Hone your strategic skills from the gurus who know what it takes to run an effective, high-performing organization.

But understand that great strategy is not the whole story. Having had the good fortune to work side by side with some of America's most notable and successful leaders, I know that there's more to their success than is often reported.

What these stories often leave out is the fire-in-the-belly sense of purpose that fueled the will to develop and execute such brilliant strategies. Purpose and strategy go hand in hand and both are required for any organization to fulfill a mighty purpose and win in the marketplace.

Great leaders use purpose to fuel their own personal energy, which is taxed beyond what most people will ever have to experience. We've seen firsthand how purpose influenced their decision making in spite of what the analysts and consultants were recommending. And we've seen how purpose has helped those leaders generate a level of alignment that most organizations only dream of.

What follows is a list of Stewardship Principles born out of our own observations and experiences working with leaders who make decisions *on purpose*. If you desire to be a steward of purpose, read on.

STEWARDSHIP PRINCIPLE #1: MAKE IT JOB #1 TO BE THE TORCH BEARER OF PURPOSE

Probably the single most important role of the founder or CEO of an organization is to walk the talk and be a role model for the values that he or she wants the employees to live by.

In every purpose-based organization there is a key leader who carries the torch of purpose and values and ensures that the organizational culture is living it every day. If the people at the top of an organization don't buy into the values and purpose in a meaningful way, it's unlikely to ever take root in a meaningful way throughout the organization.

Colleen Barrett at Southwest Airlines was the keeper of the company culture, making sure that LUV stayed alive and that growth never diluted the culture that made the company famous. She epitomized the warm, down-to-earth, open-hearted human being that she expected her employees to be.

Charles Schwab is the kind of man who can explain everything you ever needed to know about investing over lunch and never make you feel intimidated or confused while doing it. His approachable and no-nonsense persona sets the tone for the entire organization.

Sam Walton used to go to visit his stores, gather his Associates around, get down on one knee, and say, *"I know what I know; now I want to know what you know."* His spirit of relentless curiosity about how to serve the customer better was never ending and inspired his Associates to be on the lookout for better ways to serve the customer, too.

Robert Gates, the former president of Texas A&M and now secretary of defense, espoused a philosophy of servant leadership that he wanted every student who passed through the halls of Texas A&M to emulate. He had an open-door policy that amazed his students. We spoke with literally dozens of randomly intercepted students who had personally plopped themselves down in his office to share a concern while he listened attentively and, when appropriate, took steps to create a solution or empower them to do so.

The key point is you can't delegate the creation of values and purpose to some middle-management function. The leaders at the top of the organization need to unequivocally believe in the values. They need to live them. They need to exemplify them in a way that's visible to employees throughout the organization. And, ultimately, they need to inspire others to do the same. This isn't something that is done once at an annual rally and then checked off the to-do list. It has to be constantly reinforced and lived every day.

And the truth is, without leadership embracing and living the values and purpose, it won't happen. Not only will it not happen without the leadership, but without the leadership embracing the values and purpose, you risk alienating, frustrating, and, ultimately, losing those value-driven people in your organization who would really like to channel their talents and energies toward making a difference.

While leaders must be the ultimate torch bearers of purpose, it doesn't mean they're the only torch bearers. That would be a pretty dim light. They can't do it alone. The fire has to catch on throughout the organization to generate the critical mass and momentum neces-sary to succeed. But ultimately, the leaders will determine whether or not the purpose is fulfilled.

Lead by your convictions. Lead by example. And then let your fire ignite the entire organization.

STEWARDSHIP PRINCIPLE #2:
BELIEVE IN PURPOSE BEFORE PROFIT

In the opening chapter, we discussed how purpose is a path to high performance. We shared the findings from several studies by acade-mic researchers and business gurus proving that purpose-driven orga-nizations significantly outperform comparison companies. Now, the trick to this phenomenon of purpose and values driving profitability is that purpose can't be embraced for that reason. Purpose-driven leaders genuinely believe in the purpose of the organization and the values on which their culture is built beyond any profit-driven motive. They're not doing it because a consultant told them that it would be good for their bottom line. They've built their organizations on values because they couldn't possibly do it any other way. It's in their DNA. There is a passion for solving a problem and making a difference in the lives of their customers that goes beyond any strengths weak-nesses opportunities threats (SWOT) analysis. And their employees and customers are more loyal and engaged with the brand because of that authenticity.

Purpose-driven leaders don't send out company memos describing purpose and values as this year's strategy for driving performance. They spend their time thinking about how to bring the values to life in a way that will be meaningful to their employees and relevant to their customers' lives. They spend their time thinking about the difference they want to make in the lives of their stakeholders—knowing that if they're successful in pleasing their constituents, the money will follow.

Quick example. *Commitment* is one of the values that John Deere lives by. It arises from a genuine understanding of how much their customers rely on the company to care for the land that their livelihood depends on. One of the most successful dealers in the John Deere network took it upon himself to develop a *"Stay on the job till it's done"* mantra embraced by his employees; he developed extended hours to be there for customers during harvest time. He gives bonuses to employees who consistently received high satisfaction marks from customers. He pays for employees to engage in activities that benefit the local community. He writes hand-written thank you notes to every customer and takes his best customers out to dinner to discuss how he might serve them better.

Many companies do some of these things. What makes this John Deere dealer unique is that he "stays on the job till it's done" every day in every way. He leads by example, and it would be hard for his employees not to become inspired by that kind of leader.

John Deere dealers don't need to send out memos to their employees suggesting that "commitment" is the new tactic that's going to help them increase their margins and gain a competitive advantage over the big-box retailer down the street. It's a part of their DNA. The authenticity of their commitment is what makes John Deere the brand that it is. Without that authenticity, it is unlikely that purpose and values will ever deliver the competitive advantage they're capable of delivering.

Let's compare a hotel company that has a sustainable purpose driving everything it does with the typical hotel chain that deploys purposeful tactics (i.e., those tactics do make a real difference) to save the company some money.

Walk into just about any mainstream hotel these days and you're likely to find a little tent card somewhere in the room that says something like, "Because we here at the Halfway Hotel care so much about the planet, we recommend that you reuse your towels so that we save energy associated with unnecessary cleaning costs." Is your first thought upon reading that card, *"Wow, what a wonderful sustainable hotel. I'm going to be sure to stay here again and tell all my friends about this place"*? Or is it something more like *"Hmmm, they're trying to save money"*?

That act, as good as it might ultimately be, doesn't mean a whole lot to a customer who walks into a hotel room that is usually about 68 degrees and is quickly met by the smell of harsh cleaning fluid wafting in the air. The customer walks into a bathroom where he'll use a small bit of product that will result in three or four plastic bottles and a barely used bar of soap being thrown into a landfill each day. Without a genuine commitment to sustainability, that one act won't be an authentic game changer.

Compare that tactic with what one experiences when walking into the recently opened Hotel Terra Jackson Hole, the first in a boutique collection of eco-friendly, luxury hotels developed by the Terra Resort Group. It is one of just five LEED-certified hotels in the country. And you'll not only find that they have a towel reuse program but you'll also find nontoxic paints and carpets; chemical-free cleaning products; 100 percent organic products in the spa, low-flow water fixtures; high-tech air circulation; use of recycled, renewable, and reclaimed materials throughout; native landscaping requiring no irrigation; wind power accounting for more than 35 percent of power purchased for the hotel; energy efficient transportation for guests; sustainable and locally sourced ingredients on the menu items in their main restaurant; and an organic Terra café serving free trade coffee.[1]

They have a corporate director of sustainability, Ashley Morgan, who is responsible for not only sourcing green suppliers for the resort but also investigating the social responsibility of potential partners as well as the legitimacy of their claims to ensure there is no "greenwashing" going on. You can tell that this is a true labor of love based on the extent of her commitment to working with partners who are each making a difference in their own right.

We're doing all natural beds with 100% organic cotton sheets by Coyuchi. I love the work they are doing on the ground in India to make a difference in the lives of their farmers and to promote or-

ganic farming. We're also using Equal Exchange coffee throughout the property in guests rooms and in the café . . . they do amazing things with their growers, like simply making sure they are being paid fairly . . . they can help us actually quantify the impact that our small hotel is making to their farmers.[2]

Do you think the leaders of the Terra Resort Group are engaged in these practices because they think it will make them more profitable? Or is it much more likely that they believe in it so deeply and personally that they are going to create a truly extraordinary experience that people will absolutely love and rave about to everyone they know?

Engage in a mighty purpose because you believe in it. Channel everything you've got into it. And the profits will follow.

STEWARDSHIP PRINCIPLE #3: USE PURPOSE TO CREATE ALIGNMENT AND DRIVE PERFORMANCE

One of the primary jobs of any leader, at any level of an organization, is to ensure that the talent and energy of every employee is being utilized in the most constructive way possible. In *The Power of Full Engagement*, Loehr and Schwartz talk about the unique role of a leader to direct all the available energy toward a common purpose:

Leaders are the stewards of organizational energy. They recruit, direct, channel, renew, focus and invest energy from all the individual contributors in the service of the corporate mission. The energy of each individual contributor in the corporation must be actively recruited. This requires aligning individual and organizational purpose. Alignment drives performance. Lack of alignment significantly restricts the quantity, quality, direction and force of available energy.

As a leader, the energy you have to spend getting people aligned around a purpose is inversely related to the level of awareness that the world has of your purpose. The more the world knows what your organization stands for, the more you will attract individuals who are in alignment with the goals of the organization. John Mackey doesn't have to spend a lot of time holding seminars to train new employees about the principles that drive Whole Foods Market because everyone who has ever set foot in a store or spent five minutes on their Web site knows what the company believes in.

Sam Walton was probably the most legendary leader in this regard. He had everyone in his organization focused on lowering the price of merchandise so that ordinary Americans could save money and afford a better quality of life. This focus directed the energy of Associates, suppliers, supply-chain managers, truck drivers, and vendor-partners, and led to the creation of the most efficient and legendary discount store in America and, now, the world.

The leadership at Wal-Mart makes everyone acutely aware that no energy is to be wasted on things that don't support the core purpose of Wal-Mart.

Despite what many people think about Wal-Mart today, what always struck us over the eighteen-year relationship we had with Wal-Mart was their focus on the customer. "What are we going to do for her today?" was often a question that guided our meetings. *How can we help her in health and beauty? How can we help her send her kids back to school with what they need to thrive? How can we help her serve healthy, fresh food to her family?*

There has always been an unspoken and intrinsically understood notion that any money the company spends unnecessarily is money that could have gone to helping their core shopper save money and take care of her family. Everyone realizes that all available talent, energy, and resources are to be pointed in one direction: helping the customer afford a better quality of life. If you do that, the sales will follow.

STEWARDSHIP PRINCIPLE #4:
KEEP IN MIND WHAT YOU'RE FIGHTING FOR

Competition has done us a lot of good in the last half-century, but one question remains inadequately addressed: "What are we competing for?" Leaders all over the world are now increasingly moti-

vated to deal with that question. There is an increasing, albeit un-spoken, preoccupation with doing the right thing."[3]

After thirty years of helping organizations grow their business, I've sat at the table with a lot of CEOs. Those who talk about winning in terms of financial performance alone are like night and day compared to those who talk about winning in terms of making a difference in the lives of their stakeholders. And, as noted earlier, rarely do those fighting for shareholder value achieve the kind of performance achieved by those focused on making a meaningful difference.

What Are You Fighting For? Escape from Beigeland

We first sat down with Barry Feld, the CEO of World Market, in the spring of 2007. He had recently become the CEO of the company and was looking for a partner that could help him get the brand back on track. The previous leader had looked to the competition for guidance and, despite all inconsistencies with the history of the company and the desires of their customer base, had decided to attempt to increase revenue by skewing the merchandise mix toward expensive Pottery Barn–like furniture items. In the process, he had driven away die-hard World Market shoppers who had loved the brand for the authentic and vast range of items it offered from countries that spanned the globe. Initially, there was an artificial boost in sales from loyal shoppers trying out the higher-priced furniture items but over time, traffic went down dramatically and World Market was becoming a me-too retailer slugging it out to sell more of the same stuff as everyone else.

From our first conversation it was clear that Barry's chief concern was tapping into the history of the brand in order to show American households they didn't have to live in homogenous *beigeland*. He was living in North Carolina when he took the CEO position in Oakland, California. He used the move as an opportunity to see the country. He packed up his family in an RV and headed west. Upon driving into a new town, Barry would make an announcement to his children, letting them know what new town they were about to experience. It didn't take long before his daughter dismissed his announcement of the approaching town with *"Oh, what's the point? All these towns*

*look the same, Dad. The McDonald's will be on the right and the big
box retailers selling the same stuff will be right behind that . . . just
keep going."*

This experience only heightened Barry's dedication to rekindle the
authentic roots of the company that began on Fisherman's Wharf.
Authentic imports were sold for cost plus 10 percent right there on
the docks, and people flocked to the merchandise not only for the savings but for the authenticity and uniqueness of the products. When
Barry talked to us about winning that day, he didn't talk about stock
price. In fact, he knew the turnaround would be a massive undertak-
ing that would take some time before the financial fortunes of the
company would be affected. As he put it, *"We're going to have to sell
a whole heck of a lot of French candles to make up for the $1,500
leather sofa."*

What he was interested in was a desire to show Americans what a
real French candle actually smelled like. He was deeply motivated to
reintroduce Americans to the vibrancy and uniqueness that the world
has to offer. Listening to Barry, you got the sense that he didn't want
to just lead a successful retail outlet; he wanted to start a movement.
He wanted to tell the story of the products. He wanted to tell the stories of the people who made the products. He was interested in finding more ways to support and empower the artisans around the world
who were making the products. He wanted the shoppers to share
their own experiences with World Market goods and recommend
items they'd discovered on their own world adventures. He wanted to
introduce the customers to the World Market buyers who scour the
planet to find unique items and bring them to market before any
other retailer has ever heard of them.

Barry knew what he was competing for. In some ways, he was
driven to provide an alternative to his daughter's observation that
everything seems exactly the same in America. For Barry, "winning"
would happen when people realized that World Market was a portal
for discovering extraordinary things from around the world.

What Are You Fighting For? Freedom

Herb Kelleher, Colleen Barrett, Gary Kelly, and the other leaders at Southwest Airlines are some of the fiercest competitors I've ever met. The airline industry is no place for the faint of heart and we've fought a lot of battles together.

While there's certainly some natural exhilaration that comes from taking on the competition, Herb made sure that everyone inside the company knew what was ultimately at stake: *giving people the freedom to fly*. If we didn't win some of these wars, prices would increase or Southwest would be forced out of the market and individuals all across the country would be denied their freedom to fly. Purpose-based leaders know that in order to win, the objective has to be framed in terms of the reason the war is being waged and not simply in terms of the spoils that come with victory. The spoils of thirty years of profitability and financial stability for his people are the result of 25,000 "freedom fighters" ready to go to battle to deliver freedom to people in America.

Not only were they fighting to give freedom to consumers, in many cases they were fighting for the freedom to compete. In a country built on strong capitalist principles, nothing got Herb angrier than competitive airlines that were trying to restrict Southwest's ability to do business in their territory. Many of the battles fought by Herb were battles for the basic freedom to compete in what's supposed to be a free market society.

While Herb kept his eye on the marketplace, Colleen kept hers on the culture. (Gary now gets to keep his eyes on both.) Keeping costs low wasn't just the key to the freedom they could offer their customers; it was also the key to remaining profitable so that they could take care of their employees. For Colleen, a definition of winning at Southwest Airlines has always included a vibrant culture, driven largely by the Golden Rule, where people truly love to work. Here again, there is an acute understanding of what people are willing to fight for. People are much more likely to battle for a great workplace than they are for a great balance sheet; similarly, they are more likely to fight for the right to deliver freedom to people than they are for the stock price of the company.

If the pursuit of profit had consumed Southwest's leaders, the rich history of the company would never have been written.

What Are You Fighting For? Personal Responsibility

I got my first up-close-and-personal lesson in competition from my first true mentor, my high school football coach Gordon Wood, who at his retirement held the record as the high school football coach with the most wins in the country.

He understood what was really at stake in the highly competitive field of high school football. While I was writing this book, Coach Wood passed away. It got me thinking again about his approach to coaching and to victory. He competed against the best of the best often—if not most of the time—with inferior talent and almost always left the field victorious. Other teams would try to take us down with better talent, better workouts, and more vocal fans. Invariably these same teams would return home limping. The talent and workouts and fans were not the game changers they thought they were. They didn't have a clue that the key factor in making us an unbeatable force was the coach's great desire to make a difference in the lives of his players.

Coach Wood's core purpose was to transform young kids into responsible adults faster than anyone thought possible. While he was drilling us on Xs and Os he was also teaching us to take responsibility for our actions and our grades as high school students. He was in the "personal responsibility" business way before his time.

Coaches from all over the nation, including former legendary NFL coach Bill Parcells, would come to little Brownwood, Texas, to study Wood's program. They would study the films and interview former players. And yet most of them copied everything except the one thing that mattered most: Coach Wood's "invisible" strategy that focused as much on the transformation of the individual as it did on game-winning strategies and tactics.

Enclosed is part of a letter I wrote to Coach Wood's family and subsequently appeared in several major newspapers.

Last night one of the true legends passed away.
His name was Gordon Wood. Or rather, "Coach" Gordon Wood.

He was the High School Coach of the Century by leading more football wins than any other high school coach in his class. Coach Wood was the best of the best—both as a Coach and as a person. His purpose was simple and direct—help young kids become responsible adults. And in the process, win some football games, all of them, if possible. OK—all of them. Period.

We did exactly that in 1965. 14–0. State Championship. Perfect season. No losses. All wins. And I am not just talking about the football games we played and won. For we won before we played any of those games. We won as "kids on the journey to becoming responsible adults." We won by being a team of ordinary boys inspired and challenged to do something special—together.

Coach Wood knew what he was really competing for—he was fighting to transform young, wily, rural teenagers into responsible adults capable of taking on anything. And that's something worth fighting for.

STEWARDSHIP PRINCIPLE #5: USE PURPOSE, NOT JUST PERSONALITY, TO LEAD

The leaders we have worked with have been *very* charismatic—true legends in this arena. What people often miss is that the charisma that inspires people has more to do with the leaders' values than it does their personality or magnetism. They're building organizations that enable people to go to work and find meaning in what they do. Their charisma is born of substance, not superego.

Charismatic leaders like Sam Walton are effective precisely because they are communicating Purpose; leaders who try to inspire by sheer force of character have at best a short-term impact. . . . Leaders are effective to the extent that they express effective Purpose.[4]

Charisma is born out of purpose. And so is effectiveness. A lot of people think that to be an effective leader, you have to get people to do what you want them to do. But truly great leaders don't use their positions to coerce people into doing the work that needs to be done—they inspire commitment by appealing to the fundamental

desire for work that has meaning. The leadership at Southwest Airlines has always sought to inspire commitment to the cause of Southwest rather than cajole or coerce, as noted in the business book *Nuts!*:

> *Leadership isn't some sophisticated technique for getting people to
> do what you want them to do. Leadership is getting people to want
> to do what you want them to do because they share your purpose,
> vision and values.*[5]

Great leaders use purpose to create charisma. We would even take
it one step further and argue that great leaders are born out of the
pursuit of a great purpose.

The leaders we've met didn't set out to become great leaders. They
set out to fight for a cause they believed in, to revolutionize industries,
to make a difference and became great leaders in the process. They
became experts in the art of war, brilliant strategists every one of
them, all in the name of fulfilling the ultimate purpose of their organizations. In telling the full story of Southwest Airlines in *Nuts!*, the
author notes this phenomenon when speaking astutely about the leadership of Southwest:

> *If you study the people who participate in dynamic leadership rela-
> tionships, you will find that the majority of them never set out to be
> great leaders. Rather, they set out to pursue a purpose, a cause, or a
> calling that was worthy of giving it everything they had—in some
> cases, even their lives! Their power is the power of purpose.
> Whether it's chasing an exciting new opportunity or fighting an in-
> justice, their belief in the cause gives them the strength to persevere
> when they come up against seemingly insurmountable odds. In
> their efforts to build relationships and rally people around the
> cause, they are engaging in the act of leadership.*[6]

People often spend a lot of time asking the question, *"How do I
become a great leader?"* All the leadership principles in the world
won't create a truly great leader in the absence of great purpose. Fortunately, some business schools are beginning to realize that. The Yale
School of Management curriculum now includes a leadership development program designed to help its MBA students identify their per-

sonal values and then create or lead organizations that transform those values into new value that benefits society.

So if you want to be a great leader, go ahead and get your MBA, study the principles of great strategy and execution, and hone your sense of humor. But remember that at the end of the day, it's about the values and the meaning that you're creating through the work of your organization that will truly inspire people to do great things.

STEWARDSHIP PRINCIPLE #6:
DO RIGHT BY YOUR PURPOSE

There is nothing less motivating to employees, and more disappointing to consumers, than leaders who are not willing to make the hard decisions that need to be made to fulfill the purpose of the organization in a meaningful way. Doing the right thing requires three things: knowing your purpose, putting your purpose before yourself, and having the courage to do what needs to be done.

I have sat through monthly marketing meetings with Herb Kelleher, Colleen Barrett, Gary Kelly, and the Southwest senior management team for over twenty-five years. I have been a part of historic decisions—some of them seemingly small—that had huge ramifications. I saw firsthand how they used their purpose to cut through seemingly complex issues and do the right thing for the organization.

Let me share with you three great stories about Herb's ability to do the right thing to fulfill the promise of the purpose.

Do Right by Your Purpose—Not Your Competition
Lamar Muse served as the president of Southwest Airlines from 1971 to 1978. He left when the board rejected his plan to expand in Chicago—an expensive plan that could have jeopardized the viability of the airline. By 1982, he was ready to launch his own airline and proudly proclaimed: *"This time I'm not going to get caught between a bunch of knuckleheads who don't know their asses from first base."*[7]

In 1982, Muse Airlines was launched with two Douglas DC-9-Super 80 "comfort cruiser" aircrafts poised to go head to head with

Southwest Airlines on the Houston/Dallas service. Being the humble gentleman that he was, he named the airline Muse Airlines and launched with a campaign that announced: "Big Daddy is Back!" Well, the world wasn't waiting for Big Daddy to come back and frankly didn't think anything with Southwest was broken. But "Big Daddy" Muse thought that he could use certain aspects of the Southwest Airlines business model—fast turn times and open seating—against them. He was determined to trump what he perceived to be the fast-paced cattle-car image and bring elegance and sophistication to discount travel—*"first class service at bargain-basement prices"* was his description of the new airline.

He attacked Southwest Airlines openly and directly in his no-holds-barred marketing campaign. He attacked the highly efficient open-seating model pioneered by Southwest by promoting his company's assigned seating, saying, *"You'll never have to race anybody for a seat when you fly Muse Air. Big Daddy's not into cattle drives, so there's no stampeding to get on the plane."* He attacked the quick turn times that made Southwest the most productive airline in the air and touted the more leisurely experience offered at Muse: *"You deserve more than hurry scurry airline service . . . ten-minute turnarounds with planes leaving the gate while you're still standing in the aisle . . . Muse Air deliberately spends twenty minutes on the ground between flights so nothing's rushed, especially you."* He created a promotion that wouldn't have to be fulfilled until load factors reached 80 percent—which gave passengers in the center seat a bottle of champagne *"from Big Daddy's private stock"* to create an air of affluence on board his flights.[8]

Well, needless to say, this competitive threat from one of the ex-leaders of Southwest Airlines created quite a stir at Southwest. Muse was getting a lot of attention in the press. Employees at Southwest were expressing their concerns about the beautiful, sleek, quiet planes they would be competing with. Many of the leaders at Southwest wanted to respond by making upgrades to their fleet or changes to the operating practices to diffuse some of the wild claims that were being used against them.

But Herb knew two things. One, Southwest Airlines was not in the sophistication and elegance business. Southwest Airlines was in the business of running the most-efficient, high-frequency, and cost-effective airline to get people out of their cars and in the air. If Southwest began investing in these types of upgrades and promotions, it would steer the company off course and away from their purpose. What the people of Texas ultimately needed in their lives was a convenient and cost-effective way to get from point A to point B. They didn't need to be pampered by an airline. If they wanted pampering, they could pay four times the price of the Southwest fare and head over to American Airlines for first-class service and dry chicken.

And two, he knew that *"first class service with bargain basement prices"* wasn't a viable model. All the things that Lamar Muse was railing *against* in his ads were the very things that had to be done to run a successful discount airline. Seating policies and long turn times create inefficiencies, which lead to unproductive airplanes, which, in turn, require higher fares to remain profitable.

So when it came time to put some of the new initiatives proposed to compete with Muse to a vote, Herb was outvoted—but he nixed it anyway. Herb was not about to let the company put sophistication and elegance over their fundamental purpose. He chose to do the right thing. The key takeaway is this: Evaluate each initiative on the table through the lens of the core purpose and you will make the right decision every time.

By the way, Herb was right about the flaws in the Muse model. For three years Muse struggled to stay afloat. Lamar Muse quickly bailed out, leaving the airline to his son to run. And in 1985, Southwest actually acquired Muse Air, changed the name to TranStar Airlines, and tried to run it as a subsidiary company. But when the model still proved to be unprofitable, Herb cited "unacceptable losses" and quickly ceased operations to not burden the rest of the organization. This entire episode turned out to be another example of doing the right thing.

So remember this the next time you're in a meeting and someone says, "well so-and-so competition is doing this so we need to get in that game." If you are a true leader of purpose, you won't simply do what your competitor is doing. You will do what you need to do to fulfill your own purpose. You'll do the right thing.

Do Right by Your Purpose—In Little Decisions that Are Made Every Day

It's not just the massive war games, like battling with Muse Air, that test your mettle. In business, there are little things every day that provide an opportunity to do right by your purpose.

We were at our monthly marketing meeting with Herb, discussing our expansion into the world of long-haul travel, which is essentially any flight in excess of two or three hours. I was arguing passionately about the need to give people something to eat: *"For God's sake Herb, people are passing out in the aisle."* (Granted, I took a little dramatic license to help make my case.)

"Roy, people don't fly an airplane for food and besides what's wrong with our peanuts?!," Herb shot back emphatically.

I yelled back, *"Herb, damn it, give the poor people a Snickers bar to bump up their blood sugar so they won't pass out and sue us!"*

Herb got up and began pacing and smoking. One is in serious trouble when Herb paces and smokes. If he just smokes without pacing, that's OK. When he paces without smoking, things are tense but not in the orange alert zone. But when he smokes and paces, the red zone not only lights up—it flashes.

"Roy, let me share a simple thought since it seems that simple is all that you can understand. Here is a pack of peanuts. It cost 12 cents a pack to give out. Here is a Snickers bar. It cost 38 cents to serve—not counting the overhead bin space that Snickers would take up over peanut bags, which I will get to in just a minute if you can follow this tiny little logic trail. So there is a 20 cent difference between a bag of our gourmet peanuts and a lousy Snickers bar. But what is 20 cents to an ad man, one might ask? Well to you it is only 20 cents—to us it is twenty cents times 3 million customers, and that is $600,000 PLUS the overhead bin space and the extra weight which will cause us to burn more fuel and god knows how much that would be!" He sat down and lit up.

After a moment of reflection, he then said, "OK, we will start handing out two bags of peanuts *but* only if we see that a customer is starting to pass out."

Everyone went into hysterics as we often did. But the point was made: Don't violate your core purpose for a Snickers bar. There are probably countless opportunities for dumb ideas to be summarily dismissed by examining them through the lens of your core purpose and simply doing the right thing.

Do Right by Your Purpose—Even When It Hurts

Southwest Airlines entered the Denver market to the great joy of its customers and the total euphoria of its employees. It's one thing for Southwest employees to fly for free to say Lubbock to see the Buddy Holly memorial and quite another to fly to Denver and have access to the slopes.

Southwest Airlines was not actually a tenant of Denver at the old Stapleton airport—it subleased space from other carriers. Despite that fact, Denver sent Southwest Airlines a bill to contribute to the cost of the new airport to be built some years down the line.

Herb was not pissed. He was apoplectic. Bazooka. He was pacing, smoking, and cussing. He was beyond the red zone. *"We're not even a lessee of theirs. Billing a nontenant for a hypothetical new airport, which we might not serve, is not going to happen on my watch. Here is what we are going to do. We are going to pull out of Denver,"* he said with utmost resolve.

The room was quiet. Then someone spoke up and said, *"Herb, we can't pull out of Denver. We have invested way too much in money, time, and energy."*

Herb listened as he always does, then stated in a very calm yet firm way: *"Denver will poison the entire airport system around the country. If we let them just arbitrarily charge us fees we don't owe then there will be a real domino effect. I will give them two weeks to reverse the decision and if they don't we will pull out by the end of the month."*

Southwest is in the business of democratizing the skies, not subsidizing the new Denver airport.

Denver, believing that Southwest was bluffing, did not reverse its position and Southwest pulled out within that very same month. Was it hard to do the right thing when so much had been invested in Denver? Absolutely. Was it the right thing to do to ensure that a precedent wouldn't be set that could cripple the whole organization? Absolutely.

STEWARDS OF PURPOSE

Make It Job #1 to Be the Torch Bearer of Purpose
Great leaders recognize that without their support and commitment, the core values and core purpose of the organization will not flourish. Evangelizing the purpose is always on their to-do list.

Believe in Purpose Before Profit
Great leaders genuinely believe in the pursuit of purpose over profit.

Use Purpose to Create Alignment and Drive Performance
Great leaders use purpose to channel the collective talent and energy of the organization toward an inspiring goal worthy of their efforts.

Keep in Mind What You're Fighting For
Great leaders know what they're fighting for and inspire employees to fight for the same.

Use Purpose, Not Just Personality, to Lead
Great leaders know that the real secret to inspiring the troops is appealing to their core human values and need for fulfilling work.

Do Right by Your Purpose
Great leaders look at every decision, big or small, and ask whether it will support or subvert the core purpose of the organization.

PURPOSE-BASED

LEADERSHIP PRINCIPLES

In addition to being stewards of the purpose and values, purpose-based leaders have a tendency to live by certain principles discussed in this chapter.

PROTECT THE TROOPS

Protect the troops and they will win the war. The only way to protect your employees and your stakeholders—in other words, your troops—is to never put your company at risk. There is a huge difference between taking a calculated risk and putting your people at risk. Herb taught me this lesson over and over again: when he refused to enter a new market if the demand wasn't a sure thing; when he pulled out of Denver when the powers that be engaged in unfair practices; when he quickly sold off Muse once he learned it was a money-losing situation; when he wouldn't carry the damn Snickers bar on long-haul flights because it would raise costs—all of these decisions were made with the troops in mind. Every decision that might put his people in jeopardy always came down to a careful calculation of risk versus reward.

The other valuable lesson that Herb taught me was to put your employees first. Protect your troops from being demoralized or abused by bad customers. Contrary to popular opinion, the customer is not always right. Sometimes the customer is drunk and unruly and shouldn't be allowed on a plane. Sometimes a customer is incapable of being satisfied. Just watch an episode of *Airline*—a reality show featuring Southwest Airlines—to see what Southwest's employees have to endure on a daily basis.

Everyone at Southwest loves to tell the story of how Herb took care of one particularly dissatisfied customer. She was a regular flier who always ended each flight by sending Southwest Airlines a letter complaining about some element of the service—no first class, no assigned seats, no food, unruly atmosphere, etc. After endless futile attempts by their customer relations folks, it was sent up to Herb. "In sixty seconds, Kelleher wrote back and said, *'Dear Mrs. Crabapple, We will miss you. Love Herb.'* "[1]

Siding on behalf of your employees is a way of protecting the morale of your organization. If your people feel like you've got their back, they'll go the distance for you in return. This approach almost always results in generating the type of satisfied customers that most leaders strive for in all kinds of ways that often don't take into account the satisfaction of the employees.

Protect the troops. They will protect you.

PREPARE YOURSELF TO BE LUCKY

I love the *Farmer's Almanac*. Since 1818 it has predicted the weather and a great deal more. It has also provided astronomical tips—as in, when certain activities will be more fruitful based on the phase of the moon and its relation to the ruling signs of the Zodiac. It has also offered general advice on all sorts of things related to gardening, fishing, conservation, and a host of random human interest pieces. No one knows how the predictions are made or who is behind them, but readers apparently attribute 80 to 85 percent accuracy rate to its predictions.

Before modern irrigation, the true farmers knew full well that they could not control the weather. What they could control was the preparation for the weather that was likely to happen. They prepared the land for luck. The successful farmers were the farmers who were ready for a downpour or a drought.

Sticking with the farming analogy, the leaders of John Deere prepared that company to overtake International Harvester as the world's leading producer and seller of farm and industrial tractors and equipment—a position they have been "lucky" to hold on to since the 1960s. The kind of luck that's required to become not only the unquestioned leader in a key category, but also one of the great American icons of all time, took a great deal of preparation. Beginning in 1837, John Deere has had only eight CEOs in the 170-year period in which it has done business. Each CEO prepared the John Deere brand to become the legend that it is today.

It started with John Deere's first innovation—a new method that kept soil from sticking to the sides of the plow—and continued with research that got farmers off their feet and onto a seat with something called the Gilpin Silky Plow. Then William Butterworth, the third CEO of Deere & Company who led it from 1907 to 1928, had the brilliant insight that machines might outperform horses so it might be a wise idea to get in the tractor business (which led to the acquisition of Waterloo Boy traction engine company). Later Charles Deere Wiman, the fourth CEO who led from 1928 to 1955, recognized that there was more to equipment than pure functionality. That's when he brought in New York industrial design consultant Henry Dreyfuss to help produce the famously successful Model B—a beautiful blend of aesthetic and function. Bill Hewitt, the fifth CEO, who led from 1955 to 1982, built upon the form and function formula by adding power to the equation and created a "New Generation of Power Tractors" that were unveiled at a Neiman Marcus department store in Dallas.

It was the preparation and foresight of each of these leaders that helped John Deere to overtake International Harvester in the mid-1960s and become the reigning king of the category—a position it enjoys to this day. Was there a heavy dose of luck involved with the ultimate reception of these innovative new products among American farmers? Absolutely. But without the preparation and investments in innovation carefully cultivated (no pun intended) by each leader, that luck never would have had the possibility of striking.

Current chairman and CEO Bob Lane is preparing to build some of the "smartest" combines the world has ever seen—from global satellite positioning that guides equipment down the most productive path to seeding technology that dramatically improves efficiency.[2] This is the kind of innovation that will ensure the company's streak of good luck doesn't end any time soon.

Preparation doesn't always require millions of dollars in R&D and major innovations to affect your product offering. There are a lot of ways that you can prepare yourself to be lucky.

We had a work session with a group of John Deere's top-performing dealers—the Who's Who of the John Deere dealer network. One of the things you have to realize about the John Deere brand is that the product is only half the story. While corporate headquarters does its part to prepare the company for success, the dealers are ultimately responsible for the success of the relationship with customers. So how do they prepare themselves to be lucky in relationship-building?

Here's one small example that emerged in our time with these dealers. One of the dealers really wanted his customers to know that not only did he care about the performance of their John Deere equipment, he also cared about their livelihood. He had taken it upon himself to develop a customer outreach program that was based upon all the possible scenarios his customers might experience that year: drought, flood, crop damage, seed shortage, bee shortage (yes, bee shortage—apparently the population of bumble bees that do some pretty critical pollination work has dramatically declined lately . . . who knew?), you get the idea. He had developed a series of proactive responses that were triggered based on whatever event the customer encountered. This often included a personal visit to the customer, a handwritten letter from the dealer/owner, and a special offer that related to the event in question. This type of preparation meant that he could respond on the spot to news affecting each customer—who, not surprisingly, often pledged their loyalty to John Deere in return.

It's surprising how rarely this type of scenario planning is actually done. In almost every industry, there is a general idea of the basic

range of scenarios that might affect one's customers or key constituents. How many organizations take the time to care about these
scenarios and proactively develop programs that are ready when and
if those situations occur? In our experience, not many. By preparing
for any number of scenarios that might happen to your customer
base, you'll be the "lucky" recipient of their affection and loyalty
while your competitors play catch-up by convening their first meeting
about what they are going to do in the face of a scenario they had
never considered.

BE CURIOUS

Norman Brinker is the father of the modern casual sit-down restaurant. He brought Chili's, Romano's Macaroni Grill, and a variety of
other concepts to middle-class America searching for a place to eat
with their families. He taught me what curiosity looks like in action.
He would personally check out every competitor on every corner of
the earth. He taught us to look beyond the obvious, to learn and
question everything about the competition, and to learn and question
everything about our customers.

Norm believed: *Curiosity never killed the cat, it kills the
competition.*

Jim Collins once told me a story about a gentleman who gave him
an apple before his interview (with Collins) as a metaphor for the type
of student-teacher relationship he was hoping to find if he got the job.
While most academics would have been flattered by this gesture, Jim
was immediately turned off. As Jim puts it, he wants curious chimps,
not obedient, apple-bearing students. He wants to be questioned,
challenged, and proven wrong by those around him. It's only by sur-
rounding himself with other equally curious chimps that he's able to
hone his thinking and develop the type of insights that have set him
leagues apart from all the other business strategy gurus out there.

The Art of War teaches us to reward the "scouts"—those individuals who are sent out on the front lines to evaluate the terrain, assess
the threats and opportunities, and help the generals create a plan
based on the situation on the ground.[3] The scouts are the ones who

will help you and your teams to win. The scouts are the curious ones seeking to find out the truth. As a leader, it's your job to encourage, recognize, and reward acts of curiosity throughout your organization.

One of the leaders at John Deere does just that in a very simple yet powerful way each day with the employees on the front lines—employees who are overlooked by many organizations as sources of innovation. One of the core values of John Deere is, in fact, innovation. This dealer didn't want curiosity and innovation to be the domain of R&D in the corporate office. And he firmly believed that it's the men and women on the front lines who have the firmest grip on reality, including those problems that require immediate attention. This dealer had developed a very simple tactic to encourage curiosity. Anyone who discovered a problem and thought he had a better way of doing something was empowered to try out his solution. Some companies empower their workers in similar ways but do not follow up or offer any incentive for their people to innovate. John Deere is different.

That dealer had a simple process that ensured the employee was rewarded and the whole dealership could benefit. After the employee tried out his new idea, he simply had to describe it in a paragraph or two and submit it to the office manager. In return, that employee would automatically get a $25 "curiosity bonus" added to his next paycheck. It didn't matter if the idea worked or not. It was the willingness to observe, create, and try out something new that mattered. A constant flow of new ideas is the reward of having this simple mechanism in place. Great leaders don't just encourage certain behaviors, like curiosity; they think about ways to make them happen consistently and inspire people to participate.

One last thought on curiosity: Process can be the killer of curiosity. There is a time and a place for process. But when process becomes too prescriptive, bureaucratic, or inflexible, it actually undermines curiosity. It essentially says to your people, don't think about new ways to do something; go through the motions and management will be mollified. What kind of incentive is that for a bright, intelligent individual (presumably the type of individuals you want to attract and hire)? The great leaders we've worked with know when to apply process and when to let go of the reins and give people the freedom to be curious, question the status quo, and take the organization to new and greater heights.

The leadership at BMW, for example, not only lets go of the reins, they put their designers in the driver's seat and give them the freedom to chase down radical new ideas. Because they're an independent company (with no parent company to report to), they're unencumbered by the processes and bureaucracy that plague many of the mega-automotive groups. Their independence has drawn some of the best designers in the business to their doorstep—all eager for an environment that supports creativity, curiosity, and risk-taking.

FOCUS ON THE JOURNEY

There were no destinations on the Sam Walton train. It was always a nonstop journey. Mr. Sam taught us to use destinations as benchmarks, not as resting places. He used to say that destinations are a blink on the timeline of life, especially in business. No doubt that setting destination goals motivates an organization to go faster, harder, and higher. But, as important, once that goal was achieved, Mr. Sam always set another impossible goal and challenged the organization to achieve that new goal as quickly as it could.

For example, if a buyer met some seemingly impossible goal of lowering the price of an already low-priced item, that was fantastic! Everyone celebrated for five minutes and then it was time to move on to the next thing.

Under Lee Scott's leadership, Wal-Mart recently worked to reduce the cost of a key item that had a profound impact on the lives of millions of their customers: It reduced the copay on hundreds of prescription drugs to $4. When we talked with Wal-Mart shoppers, particularly the elderly on fixed incomes, there were literally tears in their eyes when they described what this meant to them. To go from spending $200 a month to $40 a month on prescriptions meant more food on their table, more gas in their cars, and more presents for grandchildren, etc. Wal-Mart had plenty of reason to celebrate, and there were celebrations. But those celebrations really served to remind Associates what Wal-Mart could do for people and quickly translated into a renewed commitment to come up with that next great idea that would delight their customers.

On the flip side, Wal-Mart has been the target of much criticism in recent years. Whoever said all PR is good PR is an idiot. It's never good to have your company openly criticized in the media, especially when it's talking about harm that you are allegedly doing to the communities in which you operate or the Associates you employ. It causes sleepless nights for leaders and can sabotage the morale of your employees. If you let your organization get fixated on bad headlines, you can quickly find your organization careening down a black hole of negativity. Purpose-based leaders take criticism seriously. They investigate, create solutions if necessary, communicate what's being done, and then move on down the road.

Several years ago, Wal-Mart was being frequently attacked for poor environmental practices. From salmon farms that were ruining the oceans to packaging that was filling up the landfills, Wal-Mart was making an impact on the environment and it wasn't a good one. Lee Scott took these criticisms very seriously, and his leadership is beginning to turn the sustainability story around. *Fortune* magazine recently reported:

> The scope of Wal-Mart's activities is impressive, especially around environmental issues. It is buying solar power, making its trucks more efficient, selling organic food and cotton, reducing its waste, trying to bring more sustainable practices to industries as diverse as gold mining and packaging, and going beyond legal requirements to get potentially hazardous chemicals out of the products on its shelves.[4]

When Lee Scott talks about the new commitment to sustainability, he talks about it not as an earth-loving tree hugger, but as the leader of a company dedicated to reducing costs so that their customers can afford a better quality of life. For example, increasing the fuel efficiency of their trucks lowers prices for the customer. Reducing and simplifying packaging lowers prices. Selling compact fluorescent light bulbs saves customers money. Developing energy-efficient stores saves money that can be passed on to the customer. Sustainability is not a destination for Wal-Mart. It is one more path that it has taken on its never-ending journey to lower prices for its customers.

So whether you have something to celebrate or something to overcome, great leaders keep everyone focused on the journey—always moving the organization ahead.

PRACTICE THE GOLDEN RULE

Great leaders tend to be great practitioners of the Golden Rule. Their application of the Golden Rule goes far beyond just being nice to one another. The Golden Rule can be an amazing catalyst for change—righting injustices and moving the entire organization forward.

Corporate social responsibility is a long-overdue concept that is getting a lot of attention lately. The simple premise is that corporations should take responsibility for the impact they have in the world—the impact they have on the communities in which they operate, the impact they have on the lives of their employees, and, ultimately, the impact they have on the environment.

A leader who has built his organization in a socially responsible way is a leader who believes in the Golden Rule. He's looked at his organization from the perspective of the employee, the local community, the vendor-partner, and the generations that will follow, and asked the simple question: *Is this how I would want to be treated?*

To answer this question in its entirety requires an awareness of the effect of your actions. If you don't know the full effect of your actions on key constituents, stop what you are doing and make a concerted effort to understand the full effect of your actions on the community, the planet, etc. With that knowledge in hand, you can then thoughtfully consider whether or not you would want to be on the receiving end of it—whatever "it" happens to be. In the past, many leaders could plead '"ignorance." Now that's not acceptable. Understand the impact of your decisions and then put yourself on the receiving end of those decisions. If you would feel good about them, great, you're living by the Golden Rule. If not, you've got some work to do.

Increasingly, successful organizations have to look at the whole system in which they operate. They can't just serve one stakeholder (e.g., the customer) and damn all others. In other words, you can't just live the Golden Rule with your customers, but not live by the Golden Rule with your employees or vendors or any other key stakeholder. It's not a pick-and-choose-when-you-want-to-live-by-it kind of principle. Universal principles are tricky that way.

Wal-Mart has always done a phenomenal job at lowering the price of goods for their customers and their customers have historically loved Wal-Mart for it. They're constantly putting themselves in the shoes of the working-class family making $40,000 a year and trying to think about what it can do to help them achieve a better quality of life. And that family truly appreciates Wal-Mart for that. But those low prices can't come at the expense of their Associates or at the expense of the planet. Wal-Mart has to apply the Golden Rule to all of their key stakeholders to become a truly great brand. And, as we have noted, the company is well on its way to becoming a great brand while not abandoning their core purpose of saving customers money. The more effort they spend improving the quality of life of all of their stakeholders, the sooner they will restore their reputation as a good company.

The Golden Rule is one of Southwest Airlines' core values, and arguably it's the one at the top of their priority list. It's at the root of everything they do. One of the unique features of Southwest Airlines is their Culture Committee. The Culture Committee was developed to ensure that the Southwest Spirit was alive and well throughout the entire organization. It's made up of Southwest employees who are appointed to the committee because they represent the values and spirit of Southwest. It's considered a high honor to be appointed to the Culture Committee, and the members take their volunteer duties as a spirit evangelist seriously. Essentially, the Culture Committee travels around spreading the LUV—helping out wherever needed, serving lunch, hosting happy hours, recognizing people who have gone above and beyond, whatever is needed. In our more-than-twenty-five years with Southwest, committee members have come to the agency dozens of times to do nothing more than show their appreciation for the work we've developed together. They've hosted cookouts on our back lawn, served drinks for an all-agency happy hour, held ice cream parties, thrown our agency anniversary party, raffled off free tickets for our employees—you name it, they've done it. And what's the return on investment, you might wonder? Well, we would do just about anything we can for them in return. There's no us and them, it's truly just us.

How many vendor-partners do you have that feel that way about you? How often have you reached out to your vendor-partners and let them know how much you appreciate them? I'm guessing there's a correlation between the answers to those two questions.

And it almost goes without saying that the more the Golden Rule is applied at the personal level, the happier life you're bound to have. This is a critical thing to keep in mind as a leader doing all you have to do to make it to the top. If you trample over too many people on your way up, you're going to find yourself awfully lonely, alienated, and rightfully paranoid when you arrive. It's a lot more fun to get there with alliances that will hold you steady and friends that will make it all worthwhile.

So when you think about the Golden Rule, please don't dismiss it as a trivial ditty you heard in Sunday school that means saying please and thank you. All the world religions wouldn't have agreed on it and held it up as a central tenet of a life well lived if it wasn't a powerful idea that could be used for something as lofty as the transformation of the individual. It can transform how you do business in the world, how you relate to your stakeholders, how you treat your employees, and how you feel when you ultimately reach the top.

OBSESS OVER DETAILS

If you have never been to a Wal-Mart shareholders' meeting, you have missed the only truly authentic and unparalleled revival in corporate America. The first one I went to was in an unair-conditioned basketball gym in Fayetteville, Arkansas. Sam started the meeting at 5:30 in the morning and everyone came: Associates, shareholders, vendors, and, yes, the Wall Street investment crowd. It was hysterical. Here they were in the front row in folding chairs, all dolled up in Armani suits. They were sweating their butts off, trapped inside this unair-conditioned gym, not exactly sure what to expect of Sam Walton and his magic yellow tablet.

I was riveted. I took detailed notes on everything he was saying even though I had no idea what half of it meant . . . EDLP, Correction of Errors, Ten-foot rule, The sundown rule, Just in Time Inventory, etc., code words for running the most competitive business in America.

Ten thousand people packed into the gym. There were microphones all over the gym for people to ask questions—not set-up or staged questions, but real questions like:

"Why is it that the women's restrooms in Dayton Ohio aren't clean?" asked a shareholder from that area.

"Bob," Sam called out in front of ten thousand people. *"Please get me the assistant store manager of that store on the phone."*

Bob did and put the phone up to the mike that Sam was holding. *"Hi Joe, this is Sam Walton at our shareholders' meeting. There is a lady . . . what's your name again? Betty. OK, Joe, Betty shops at your store there in Dayton and says that our women's bathrooms aren't clean. Would you do me a huge favor and ask one of the women Associates to go to the restroom and check it out . . . no-no we will hold . . . all of us."*

"Mr. Sam. This is Joe again. Carey just went into the women's restroom and said it was not very clean—but it is now," Joe said, stumbling along.

"Joe. Why do you think we should have clean restrooms in our stores? Is it because it is our Wal-Mart policy to always have clean restrooms or because the customers would rather use clean restrooms than dirty ones? Think about it, Joe. And by the way I am going to give Betty here my private phone number so she can call me direct if there are any more problems. Is that OK with you, Betty?"

Crowd goes nuts!

Sam goes on and on for five hours, not one person bored or smug, except, of course, the sweating Wall Street bunch who still could not believe that they were there but had nevertheless been as mesmerized by Mr. Sam as the rest of us.

By noon, as Sam was wrapping it up and just before he was about to let everyone go, his son Robb Walton whispered something in his ear.

Sam said, *"Oops. My son Robb has informed me that I have been talking for 5 hours and I forgot to mention the 'money thing.' You know the profits. Well, we made 1 billion dollars this year. Is that OK with everyone? [Huge applause.] And I think we ought to split the stock again. Is that OK with everyone?"*

The ten thousand screaming Wal-Mart fanatics went berserk. Yes, even the Wall Street bunch were up on their feet doing the Wal-Mart cheer, which proves that money can make converts of even the most cynical.

While most CEOs would have spent the five hours focusing on the incredible revenues and profitability of the company, Mr. Sam never lost sight of the details. He knew that if you obsess about doing right by the customer at the most basic, detailed level, *the money thing* will happen.

Does your organization obsess about the details? Why not? Do you think it doesn't matter as long as you take care of the big stuff?

In this day and age when so many aspects of business are cost of entry (quality, service, value), it is often the details that make the difference. Those details will not get attended to without a workforce that's truly passionate about the customer. Obsession over the details is what separates the great companies from the not-so-great: the Nordstrom from every other department store, Whole Foods from every other grocer, and Southwest from every other airline, to name but a few examples.

FESS UP WHEN YOU MESS UP

Purpose requires accountability. With a purpose in place, an organization rallies its talents and energies in the service of that purpose. That amount of commitment is predicated on the belief that the leaders of the company will *protect the troops and do the right thing.* When mistakes happen or bad decisions are made and the troops are placed in jeopardy, people will stay the course if their leaders fess up to the situation and outline a course to correct the errors. In the absence of a mea culpa, a feeling of betrayal and cynicism can quickly erase any feeling of loyalty the troops may have had before the episode. And once loyalty is lost, it is very difficult to get it back.

The leaders who we have seen make mistakes usually make errors of the mind, not of the heart. And there's a big difference. We all have made mistakes when we had the best of intentions. In those instances, it's time to assess what went wrong, learn from it, share the lesson with your people, and move forward.

If you're making mistakes of the heart, driving the organization forward based on your own lust for power, control, or greed, then you've got some personal fessing up to do. Great leaders put the good of their organization ahead of their own every time.

DUMP THE GARBAGE

It's really difficult to lead an organization into a bright future if you're carrying around the garbage of the past. Gerald Mann founded Riverbend church in 1979, a church that now has more than eight thousand members and was recognized as one of the ten fastest-growing churches in America in the 1990s. He also served as the official chaplain of the Texas legislature for two decades and is rather famous for his one-line "zinger prayers" that he often delivered to them, such as *"Lord, help us to lead such lives that when we die, even the undertaker will be sorry."*

He's retired now, but he used to deliver a sermon every January called **Dump the Garbage.** The message was simple and yet somehow it was always new and poignant:

> My friends, it's a new year and you cannot start out this new year, you cannot make right decisions about tomorrow, if you are carrying the garbage of the old year—the garbage of yesterday.

Leaders of purpose have garbage to dump, too: grudges, guilt, greed, mistakes, losses, remorse. Holding on to those feelings will only create more of it. Whatever is on your mind will show up in your organization and in your life.

Dump the garbage. Do it early and often.

HELP PEOPLE BELIEVE IN THEMSELVES

My last observation of great leaders is how they enable other people to live up to their potential and fulfill their own dreams.

It was 1971. We had just started our company and we needed capital. So we went down to the largest local bank at the time, City National Bank, and met with a loan officer named John Oliver. We sat down with John in his big-time, intimidating bank. There I was in a brand-new tie-dyed T-shirt and a freshly washed ponytail.

John stared at us and then asked, "So what do you need?"

I said, "We need to borrow $5,000."

He asked, "What's your business plan?"

I said, "Making money. What's yours?"

So with a new tie-dyed T-shirt, a freshly washed ponytail, and a smart-ass attitude, I received a loan for the five grand. Or at least that was what I thought until a few years ago when I found out through a longtime friend the real story of that loan.

Robert Sneed, a highly respected Austin lawyer, became my first real mentor outside my Brownwood family. He was never too busy or impatient to listen to me. He taught me so many things, most of which centered on the values of integrity and a strong work ethic.

But back to the loan. Several years ago I was visiting with a friend who knew us in the early days, and he said, "Roy, remember that $5,000 loan you got from City Bank?"

I said, "Of course. I laid out a brilliant business plan they couldn't possibly turn down."

He said, "Did you know that Robert Sneed guaranteed that note under one condition?"

I was stunned and stumped as well. Stunned that I didn't know anything about Sneed's involvement and stumped as to what the one condition was.

He said, "The condition was that *no one could know.*"

No one could know? In other words, while banks and lenders were demanding a first born as collateral, Robert Sneed was demanding that no one know he was backing the loan.

Robert never told us. He wanted us to believe that we got that loan on our own. He wanted us to believe in ourselves and not be burdened with a feeling of obligation to what someone else might want in return. In the process he taught us the power in believing in others. We paid him back a few weeks ago.

PURPOSE-BASED LEADERSHIP PRINCIPLES

Protect the Troops. Great leaders protect the troops by never putting the organization at risk and always putting the interests of their employees first.

Prepare Yourself to Be Lucky. Great leaders do what needs to be done to prepare the organization for what's on the horizon. They anticipate possible scenarios and prepare accordingly.

Be Curious. Great leaders encourage curiosity—recognizing and rewarding the curious "scouts" in their organization who disrupt the status quo and propel the organization forward.

Focus on the Journey. Great leaders keep everyone focused on the journey of fulfilling the purpose of the organization rather than stopping too long at any one destination along the way.

Practice the Golden Rule. Great leaders look at their actions from the perspective of their employees, their customers, the communities in which they operate, their vendor-partners, and the planet and ask, *is this how I would want to be treated?*

Fess Up When You Mess Up. When mistakes happen, assess what went wrong, learn from it, share the lesson with your people, and move forward.

Dump the Garbage. Whatever is on your mind will show up in your organization and in your life. Dump the garbage that may be getting in the way of moving forward.

Help People Believe in Themselves. Great leaders enable other people to live up to their potential and fulfill their dreams—without seeking acknowledgment in return.

PART III

Are You a Leader of Great Purpose?

The following survey is intended to gauge the extent to which you are behaving like a purpose-based leader. Many of the questions assume that you have a basic understanding of the purpose of your organization. If you do not have a purpose, we suggest you work on identifying what your purpose is and then come back to this survey when you've begun to work with it on a regular basis.

Question	Yes	No
1. Do you truly believe in the purpose of your organization? In other words, do you believe it is a worthy pursuit independent of any *profit* motive?	____	____
2. Do you have all the talent and energy of your workforce aligned around the purpose of the organization?	____	____
3. Have you given your people a clear sense of what they're fighting for—beyond money and market share?	____	____
4. Are you using the language of purpose (rather than the cult of personality) to guide and inspire your employees?	____	____
5. Do you personally spend a good deal of your time and energy dedicated to evangelizing and ensuring that the purpose of your organization is well understood and actively being served?	____	____
6. Are you willing to make hard decisions based on dedication to your purpose? (versus navigating based on the actions of your competitors)?	____	____
7. Do you consider the risk to your stakeholders—both financially and emotionally—before making any major decisions?	____	____

Question	Yes	No

8. Are you preparing your organization for multiple scenarios that you might face in order to be "lucky" when the time comes?

9. Are you encouraging, recognizing, and rewarding acts of curiosity throughout your organization?

10. Do you keep the organization moving forward at all times—resting only for a moment to celebrate victories or address problems?

11. Do you live by the Golden Rule with all your stakeholders—employees, customers, community, vendor-partners, and the planet?

If you answered yes to the majority of the questions, congratulations, you have what it takes to be a purpose-based leader. You believe in your purpose and are willing to do what it takes to support it. You align your workforce around the purpose and give people a clear sense of what they're ultimately fighting for. You've made it a personal responsibility to carry the torch of purpose, and you inspire others with that purpose rather than managing on sheer personality. Your leadership is a key ingredient to building a successful purpose-based organization.

If you answered yes to roughly half of the questions, you've probably got some issues around truly embracing your purpose. Try to identify the barriers to leading on purpose that may exist within your organization. Is there a lack of belief in or alignment around the core purpose of the organization? Do you have your own doubts about the viability of purpose over profits? Are there competing agendas that stand in the way of recruiting the talents and energies of the organization toward fulfillment of the purpose? Does your calendar have all your time and energy channeled toward general management activities? Find the roadblocks. Tear them down. And commit yourself to leading on purpose in *all* of the ways that we've identified.

If you answered yes to only a handful of questions (say, a third or less), you may need to really evaluate how you are spending your time, energy, and talent. Review the questions pertaining to purpose that were outlined above. It may just be that you really don't know what the true purpose of your organization is yet. If you're spending all your time

on strategy and execution and none on purpose, values, and philosophies, you may need to seriously reevaluate what's on your "to do" list.
As we discussed earlier, strategy and execution is important, it's just not
everything.

BRINGING YOUR PURPOSE TO LIFE IN THE MARKETPLACE

FULFILLING THE PROMISE
OF THE PURPOSE

What brands do you love? Take a moment to think about the brands that truly move you. Think about the brands that you would really miss if they ceased to exist. Do you have two or three in mind? Now, what is it about that brand that makes you love it? As the founder of an advertising agency, it breaks my heart to say this, but I'm guessing that there's more to those brands than great advertising.

The great brands of today don't rely *exclusively* on advertising to communicate who they are and what they stand for, certainly not to the extent that commodity brands do. Why? Because great brands are the result of every experience a customer has with the brand.

The Southwest "brand" is built every time a Southwest employee tells a joke, every time a plane leaves on time, every time someone takes a flight that they wouldn't have otherwise taken, and every time someone is able to redeem his Rapid Rewards without any hassles. That is what creates "the brand."

The Wal-Mart "brand" is built every time someone walks in the store and fills up her cart with more goods than she thought she could afford.

The Norwegian Cruise Lines "brand" comes to life as soon as someone boards the ship and experiences the freedom to do whatever she wants, whenever she wants, however she wants.

The AARP "brand" is built every time someone sees a piece of legislation passed in favor of an issue facing an aging population.

The John Deere "brand" is built every time someone drives across this great land and sees the green and yellow tractors tending the earth. It's built when you walk into a dealership and see and feel the John Deere values in every employee you meet.

The Kohler "brand" is built every time one of their designers transforms an everyday commodity item into an inspired work of art. It's built whenever someone turns on one of Kohler's faucets or takes a bath in one of its tubs.

The BMW "brand" is built the moment someone sits in the driver's seat, turns on the engine, and takes off. The Google "brand" is built every time someone does a search and finds what she's looking for. The Starbucks "brand" is built with every morning sip of a two-pump, extra-hot, no-whip Mocha.

The more an organization understands its purpose, the more it can create products, services, and experiences that will create a strong brand in the marketplace. Truth be told, advertising is very far downstream in the process of building truly great brands.

But many companies still operate under the delusion that you can manufacture a great brand out of thin air. You just have to do something funny enough or outrageous enough, and you'll develop the cache necessary to drive your business. And, I suppose, if you find yourself in the unfortunate position of selling a 100 percent commodity-type product or service with nothing to differentiate it from competitors, then advertising really is your only shot at creating interest—but boy is that a long shot! My heart goes out to the agencies that find themselves in the position of making something out of nothing and then being fired because it ultimately does not work.

The simple fact of the matter is this: Great brands are born out of great leaders who have created great organizations that create something that actually matters to people.

That simple observation has driven us to seek out clients that are trying to make a difference and, as a result, have created something worth talking about. Honestly, it's like giving your agency a precious gift when you've actually paid the price to build an organization with an authentic purpose. As marketers, it's our job to develop solutions that will help you fulfill that purpose and grow the business.

We've developed purpose-based branding as a powerful tool to:

- tell the world what you stand for;
- attract and inspire employees who share your values;
- guide the creation of products, services, and experiences that matter to people; and
- face the realities of the current market situation and address them with powerful and persuasive messaging.

Here's how we go about it.

PURPOSE DISCOVERY: *WHAT BUSINESS ARE YOU REALLY IN?*

Sometimes we are approached by organizations that already have a clear articulation of their purpose, and we can get right to work bringing it to life in the marketplace. Other times we have to do some work to help identify and articulate a purpose that is clearly present in the organization but, for whatever reason, has never been articulated. And sometimes an organization may come to us with really no idea what its purpose is but the leaders express a genuine desire to work with their authentic assets and passions, identify a purpose, and move forward with it.

The key takeaway is this: You have to first identify and articulate the purpose of the organization to have a meaningful starting point to build a brand.

We outlined in chapters 2 and 3 how to go about discovering and articulating a purpose. The following case studies will share in-depth examples of the discovery process.

POSITIONING BEYOND DEFEAT: *WHAT DO WE HAVE THAT PEOPLE WANT THAT THE COMPETITION CAN'T DELIVER?*

It is a great privilege and honor to work with purpose-driven organizations—that privilege brings with it a feeling of responsibility and obligation that's rarely found when working with clients purely out for profit. We want our clients to win. For if they win, that means someone's life is altered for the better. Someone gets to take a flight she wouldn't have otherwise taken (Southwest Airlines). Someone is able to save money so he can live a little better (Wal-Mart). Someone's able to experience the joy of driving (BMW). Someone's able to nurture not only his body but the planet, too (Whole Foods). Someone gets to move, shape, and enrich the land he lives on (John Deere). America remains safe from air, space, or cyber attacks (Air Force).

So how do we ensure that our clients fulfill the promise of their purpose in the marketplace?

Brilliant positioning. Unlike purpose that never changes and is part of the organizational DNA, your positioning strategy is developed based on the realities of the current marketplace and can evolve over time. We have to recognize the barriers to the fulfillment of your purpose and then use the power of marketing to begin to change the attitudes and behaviors that stand in the way.

We like to consider ourselves practitioners of *The Art of War*, written by Sun Tzu, a Chinese military strategist, during *sixth century* B.C. One of his most basic strategies is called *positioning beyond defeat,* and it is accomplished by knowing everything you can about your competition, yourself, and the terrain where the battle will take place.

> Know your opponent, know yourself and know the terrain:
> one hundred challenges without danger;
> not know the other but know yourself; one for one:
> know not the other or yourself: every challenge is certain peril.

Anchored in purpose, it is our job to study everything we can about ourselves, the competition, and the consumer terrain to develop a positioning strategy that will ensure our clients win in the marketplace. In many ways, this work mirrors the behavior of most purpose-based leaders. Strong leaders tend to be masters of the art of war and have studied the market in much the same way to protect their troops and discover the opportunities to advance their organization forward successfully.

We use a triangle to illustrate this simple, yet often overlooked, positioning discipline:

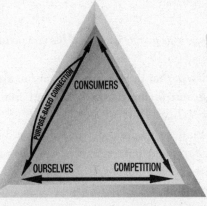

The triangle provides a simple framework to answer the question: what do we have that people want that the competition can't deliver?

Ourselves: We start with a brutally honest assessment of the brand's strengths and weaknesses. How is it better/similar/worse than the competition? What are the most compelling proof points to the purpose? What constraints might hinder our ability to compete? What do our customers like/dislike about us? We look at anything and everything that might be relevant to the story we're able to tell in the marketplace based on genuine, authentic strengths of the organization.

Competition: This is where we determine what stands in our way of success. Is it a strong, well-funded, established competitor? An attitude that needs changing? A trend that's working against us? An overcrowded category? Negative publicity? We try to identify every possible barrier in our way. If you don't understand what you're up against, you'll never be able to position your organization beyond defeat.

Consumer: We want to know everything we possibly can about the people we are trying to reach? What are the priorities in their lives? What marketplace forces are shaping their decisions? How do they make decisions about our type of product/service? What are their needs/frustrations, likes/dislikes with our brand in particular? What are their unmet needs that our brand needs to address today? And, most important, what difference do we make in their lives?

At the end of all of that exploring, we want to be able to answer the question:

What do we have that people want that the competition can't deliver?

If we can answer that question, we're on our way to creating demand for the brand in the marketplace and fulfilling the purpose along the way.

In the case studies that follow, you'll see the discoveries made at each point of the triangle that led to positioning strategies that helped fulfill the promise of each purpose.

BRINGING IT TO LIFE

OK, so we're anchored in purpose and we have brilliant insights about what's going on in the market and what must be done to win. Now it's time to create the visionary ideas that will move the business forward.

Get Your Employees on Board

You have to bring the purpose to life inside the organization. If your employees aren't clear what you stand for or don't know what you're preaching to the world, look out! Your customers will be in for some frustrating experiences when their expectations aren't held up by interactions with the company. Your employees need to be as inspired as your customers. Think about all the ways you could inspire your workforce and put as much energy into those initiatives as the ones you create for your customers.

In the Southwest Airlines case study you'll read about a Freedom

Manifesto that went out to every employee from Herb Kelleher, an event where all employees were deemed Freedom Fighters. An employee Freedom campaign was launched with HR in conjunction with the launch of an original purpose-based branding campaign we launched to the public. It not only creates a more consistent experience for the customer, it also gives employees something to rally around.

Prioritize Brand-Building Experiences

Before you jump into the creation of a traditional advertising campaign, stop and look at the way your customer experiences the brand. In doing so, you might find a host of highly influential moments that affect how your brand is perceived. Those influential moments should be at the top of your marketing to-do list.

Figure out what really matters to people and develop marketing solutions accordingly. Sometimes the best way to improve perceptions of your brand might be to update your retail experience, fix your customer service policy, redesign your Web site, or enhance your social-responsibility practices. Knowing what really matters to your customers will help you spend your marketing dollars most effectively.

Fulfill Your Purpose Everywhere You Can

A lot of marketers approach "integration" as an exercise in ensuring that the visual identity of the brand is consistently expressed throughout all mediums. That's a good thing to do. But purpose takes the idea of integration to another level. It transforms integration from an exercise in consistency to an exercise in creation—it's about looking at everything as an opportunity to deliver another dimension of your purpose.

Think about all the initiatives on your to-do list. How many of them are helping to contribute to the overall purpose of the organization? How many of them are contributing to the story of your brand in the marketplace? How much more powerful would your brand be if everything you were putting out in the world was attempting to fulfill the promise of your purpose in some new and exciting way? Purpose is the great uniter. If your marketing efforts aren't being developed with the overall purpose of the organization in mind, you're likely to have a whole lot of messages resulting in a whole lot of nothing in the market.

The case studies in the following chapters will show how we developed promotions, loyalty programs, retail experiences, service models, and more to further deliver on the purpose of the organization.

Don't Be an Uninvited Guest!

Years ago my partner Tim McClure and I were driving back from San Antonio after meeting with a client who really didn't like the work we had presented that day. *It happens.* The client said something like, *"If that ad came on my TV, I'd be in the kitchen making a sandwich before it was over."* His feedback really hit a nerve. It hurt our feelings to think that all the hard work we had put into creating this ad was dismissed as an intrusion in this man's evening activities. On the drive back to Austin, Tim couldn't let it go. *"What makes some ads riveting . . . and others irritating, intrusive, uninvited guests in people's homes?"*

And then and there he started to craft what's come to be known as our **Uninvited Guest Creative Philosophy:**

> *Advertising is an **uninvited guest** in people's homes, cars, and some of the most private moments in their lives. We must **intrigue** them—captivate them with the way we look, the things we say. We must **entertain** them—encourage them to laugh, or at least smile, to cry, or at least feel empathy, and sometimes, simply to think. We must **persuade** them—convince them that what we have to offer is genuinely unique and valuable. Otherwise, it is unlikely we will be invited back. Successful advertising becomes an **invited guest.***

This was true back then and holds even truer in the modern era when people have more control than ever before over who they let in and who they keep out. Between satellite radio, TIVO, and direct mail and telemarketing blocks alone, brands that don't provide any real value don't stand a chance of breaking through and being invited into the lives of the people you are trying to serve. The gut reaction of many advertisers is try to find more intrusive and unavoidable methods of reaching people—so you end up with a logo plastered across a tennis court during the U.S. Open that you can't possibly avoid. Does this in-your-face work-around really endear the brand to the fans? Last time I checked, the only feeling this kind of approach generated was irritation.

The point is not to spend even more money chasing eyeballs or finding sneakier ways of forcing people to fixate on your brand. The point is to create *ideas* that are so intriguing, so entertaining, so persuasive and relevant to the people you are trying to reach that you are invited into their lives with open arms. With a little luck, they might even seek you out.

In the chapters that follow, we will let you in on the journey of bringing to life the purpose of some of the world's most notable organizations.

CORPORATIONS

HOW PURPOSE

CAN TAKE YOU HIGHER

Giving people the freedom to fly.

We've shared a lot of behind-the-scenes stories about what Herb Kelleher and his band of brothers and sisters did (and continue to do) to create the wildly successful airline that is Southwest Airlines. Southwest Airlines is a great example of a brand that was built through visionary leadership, an industry-shattering operational system, and a culture that's become legendary. You would think that the advertising should have been a slam dunk. But despite all that we had to work with, for many years prior to discovering Southwest's purpose, we did what most advertising agencies do: We looked at the benefits Southwest offered to customers and cleverly packaged them in compelling and creative themes. We talked about the low fares. We talked about the frequent flights. We showcased the friendly people. All good things to do but, ultimately, not adding up to the brand that Southwest had the power to be. We found ourselves constantly susceptible to moment-in-time parity claims from aggressive competitors who were hell-bent on taking the wind out of Southwest's sails.

By spending enough and being creative enough, we were able to fill the planes. But filling the planes and building the brand in a way that would give us a long-term competitive advantage are two fundamentally different things.

When we finally recognized that all those attributes actually laddered up to giving people the freedom to fly, we took off out of tactic land and headed toward blue skies.

> One day Herb said to us: "I think we've built a great company with a great culture that we should all be thankful for but I'm worried about the brand." He told us that when airports measure noise pollution they measure the take-off and landing noises of individual planes as well as the collective noise generated by all of the activities occurring at that site. He thought we had done a superb job managing the individual noise—but he was worried about the collective noise. What did it all add up to?

Many organizations come to us trapped in tactic land. If you have good things to talk about, you can do some pretty good work in that space. But what we want to show you is how our advertising for Southwest Airlines went from "good" to "great" once we understood their purpose and began telling that story to the world. We didn't leave the tactics on the tarmac. But we laddered them up to a much more powerful place of purpose which enabled us to fill the planes and build the brand at the same time.

THE EARLY YEARS: *BUILDING A BRAND IN TACTIC LAND*

Just Say When

When we became their marketing partner in the early eighties, Southwest Airlines was building the most robust flight schedule you could imagine between key business destinations in Texas and charging the lowest fares anyone had ever heard of. The combination was so powerful that Texans traveling for business actually changed their mode of intrastate travel en masse, swapping the highway for the skyway. It was just too convenient and inexpensive not to. We heard business people say that their productivity soared because of the switch. Southwest had made Texas a smaller place, making it possible to go to a morning client meeting in Houston and still put in an afternoon of office work back in Dallas. The flights were so plentiful that many people showed up at the gate without reservations confident that there'd be a flight around the corner. The tagline "Just Say When" capitalized well on this schedule strength.

As long as Southwest was talking to customers in a mature market where they had this schedule advantage, it was a great message; but the moment they moved into a new market where competitors flew more often, they had a scheduling disadvantage that made the tagline positioning platform fall flat on its face.

Next: The Company Plane

In the late eighties and in the face of plans to grow, grow, and grow more, we realized that we needed to change Southwest's communication to something that would be effective in both mature and immature markets. For customers, the Southwest advantage was truthfully more than schedule frequency. It was a combination of frequency *and* fare *and* customer service—the sort of customer service that was extraordinarily rare and oddly inimitable (even to this day.) Because businesspeople were using Southwest so frequently, the flight attendants began to know their customers' names, much like a private pilot knows who's on board. The attendants and pilots began to know what business the customers were in and where they preferred to sit. They began to learn what drinks they would order, and in some cases they'd even introduce a customer to other customers who had similar businesses.

The experience of flying on Southwest was not only convenient, it was personal. And so "The Company Plane" campaign was born. And just like "Just Say When," "The Company Plane" was good communication. It did what it was supposed to do for the business travelers it was intended to reach. But—it wasn't great. It too outlived its usefulness as legacy carriers promoted business-class amenities and lounges that were never going to be matched by Southwest because they were never going to fit into the Southwest business model. Southwest found itself in a battle of attributes again, trying to justify their "company plane" status. So we moved Southwest's communication forward again, on to another attribute that we thought we could hang our hat on. (Are you beginning to see the problem pattern?)

Just Plane Smart

By the early nineties, Southwest was no longer just a regional airline. It was coming on strong and posing serious threats to the legacy carriers. To avoid another pitfall of positioning the brand around any one of its attributes, Soutwest decided to hedge bets and describe the breadth of the Southwest offering as "Just Plane Smart." This communication celebrated all the reasons why Southwest was a smarter choice for air travel than the competition—low fares, on-time arrivals, frequent schedules, friendly people—the whole package. But again people were quick to point out reasons why it might be smart, in some situations, to fly on other airlines—a better schedule, a market Southwest didn't serve, a nonstop flight might all arise as "smart" reasons to fly the competition. This well-intentioned idea inadvertently set up Southwest for direct comparison with competing airlines in a battle of attributes (again)—and that's a precarious battle to fight.

These campaigns were all successful insofar as they communicated the basic features and benefits of flying Southwest Airlines. And, coincidentally, Southwest was doing very well as an airline. So the obvious question arises. *If these campaigns (despite some minor drawbacks) were good and Southwest was experiencing profitable growth, what was the real problem?*

The problem was, Southwest Airlines was a great airline and deserved a great brand. How much better might Southwest have done had we discovered their purpose earlier, unified their marketing efforts accordingly, and began telling the market what Southwest really stood for sooner? When we began working with the airlines' purpose, we saw a dramatic increase in the traction we were able to get in the marketplace. We were able to develop marketing programs that defied the traditional tactical battlefield because we were operating on a higher plane.

Think about your own marketing efforts. Are you constantly fighting with the competition over the right to own this attribute or that attribute? You may do very well engaging in those fights, but each and every day you've got to wake up and fight them again. By understanding the difference you make in the lives of the people you serve, you may discover a competitive advantage that lifts you above the fray. Let me share with you how we rose out of that space and into a much more fruitful territory.

SOARING TO HIGHER GROUND

Maybe we were exhausted from a decade and a half of trying to build a brand in tactic land. Maybe we were frustrated that every year we had to spend more money to get our message to register. Maybe we instinctively knew that Herb had created something revolutionary and the brand needed to embrace what it had done. But there came a day when we stopped talking about the brand and started listening to our customers who were able to shed some light on the real power of the brand.

People began telling us about the freedom Southwest had given them. People began telling stories about trips they had made that they wouldn't have made were it not for Southwest. We began hearing entrepreneurs talk about matching their own business expansion to Southwest's expansion because it assured them reasonable travel costs for the many trips that would be required to build a successful business. We began hearing about families getting together more often, college students going home more often, and families exploring the country more often. The stories we were hearing were the stories of individuals who, in their own words, had been given the freedom to fly. Once we stopped trying to explore the attributes that made Southwest Airlines different, and instead let people tell us what difference Southwest Airlines made in their lives, we began to see the real power of the brand.

No matter what aspect of the business we focused on—low fares, frequent flights, friendly people—it all laddered up to freedom. Low fares made flying affordable, which gave people the freedom to take a trip. High-frequency schedules gave people a level of flexibility and customization that gave them the freedom to come and go at a moment's notice. Friendly people took the stuffiness out of the elite domain of flying and made everyone feel welcome and free to take to the skies no matter who they were or where they came from. And one day a woman we were interviewing in San Antonio during some routine brand-positioning research just came out and said it, *"because of Southwest, I've been given the freedom to go, see and do more things than I ever thought possible."* And presto—that sealed it—it was time we lifted Southwest Airlines out of the airline business and put them in the freedom business. We officially articulated its purpose in the simple phrase:

Southwest Airlines' purpose is: To give people the freedom to fly.

I remember the day we told Herb and Colleen that we wanted to make Southwest Airlines a symbol of freedom and claim its rightful position as the great "democratizer" of the skies. While they had never thought about who they were in exactly those terms, the second they heard it they knew we had nailed it. Herb had fought for the freedom to compete in the industry. He had fought for the 85 percent of the market that had never had the freedom to fly. It was time for the brand to evolve from focusing on what made us different (fares, schedule, people) to focusing on what difference we were making (freedom).

Once we had discovered Southwest's true purpose, we began the process of purpose-based branding. What follows is an overview of how we took Southwest Airlines out of the airline business and put them in a whole new category: the freedom business.

Starting on the Inside: *When you're building a brand on purpose, it's important to begin by making sure that all your employees are crystal clear on the purpose of the organization.* After all, they are the people responsible for making it happen. If you've nailed the purpose correctly, it really shouldn't come as a big surprise to your employees when they hear it. It should give language to what they instinctively know to be true. If they hear it and it's a big head scratch that needs repeated explanation, you probably need to go back to the drawing board.

The first thing we did to seed the idea of FREEDOM inside Southwest Airlines was draft a letter from Herb to all his employees that we called the **Freedom Manifesto** that went something like this:

IN THE PAST, THE SKIES BELONGED ONLY TO A FEW. ONLY THOSE WHO ACHIEVED STATUS ACHIEVED FLIGHT, BECAUSE ONLY THE ELITE COULD AFFORD THE FREEDOM TO GO, SEE, AND DO AT A MOMENT'S NOTICE. YOU WORK FOR A COMPANY OF PEOPLE WHO CHANGED ALL THAT. YOU WORK FOR A COMPANY WHO BELIEVED THEN, AS IT DOES NOW, THAT FLIGHT SHOULD NOT BE LIMITED TO THE WELL-TO-DO, BUT THAT IT SHOULD BE AN OPPORTUNITY FOR ALL: THAT PEOPLE SHOULD HAVE THE FREEDOM TO FLY. ▪ OUR BATTLE FOR THIS FREEDOM BEGAN NEARLY THREE DECADES AGO. AND WHILE OUR MAIDEN FLIGHT MAY BE CREDITED TO ONLY A FEW, OUR GALLANT MISSION BELONGS TO YOU. YOU MAKE THAT FREEDOM POSSIBLE.

FOR THOUSANDS OF PEOPLE TO GO, SEE, AND DO, YOU MAKE THAT FREEDOM POSSIBLE. ▪ BY KEEPING OUR COSTS LOW, YOU MAKE THAT FREEDOM POSSIBLE. BY DOING RIGHT BY A CUSTOMER, YOU MAKE THAT FREEDOM POSSIBLE. BY WINNING A FARE WAR OR BATTLING OTHER AIRLINES WHO'D RATHER SEE US GO THAN COME, YOU MAKE THAT FREEDOM POSSIBLE. ▪ IT IS YOUR SPIRIT AND TENACITY THAT HAVE MADE SOUTHWEST AIRLINES A SYMBOL OF FREEDOM. BECAUSE OF YOU, TODAY, SOMEONE HAS VISITED A GRANDCHILD, EXPLORED AN OPPORTUNITY, OR JUST TAKEN A TRIP FOR NO MORE REASON THAN TO SEE WHAT'S OUT THERE. ▪ BECAUSE OF YOU, TODAY, SOMEONE HAS THE FREEDOM TO FLY.

TO MY HEROES, FROM MY HEART. HERB KELLEHER. A DEDICATION.

SOUTHWEST AIRLINES
A SYMBOL OF FREEDOM

Freedom was launched with a letter from Herb to all Southwest Airlines employees.

"In the past, the skies belonged only to a few. Only those who achieved status achieved flight. Because only the elite could afford the freedom to go, see, and do at a moment's notice." It goes on telling the story and closes with the line: *"Because of you, today, someone has the freedom to fly."*

Employees were no longer just employees. They were now officially anointed Freedom Fighters. Employees received a **freedom video** that brought the freedom story to life along with T-shirts emblazoned with either: *"Go more places," "See more people,"* or *"Do more things,"* which became a part of employee uniforms.

Southwest has always been regarded as a "great place to work" and people have always loved working at Southwest Airlines. Their culture is legendary. But when employees were given such a crystal clear understanding of the difference that their talents and energy were making in the lives of the people who flew Southwest, they were beyond enthusiastic. As the saying goes, they went "nuts." (*Nuts!* was the title of the first published book describing Herb Kelleher's Southwest Airlines.) They were fired up to liberate, rather than merely launch, new markets and went gung ho leading freedom parades down main streets shouting to the rooftops that the skies had now been democratized! The Southwest employees embraced freedom and proudly became Freedom Fighters.

Another thing you want to consider when bringing your purpose to life is to imagine how your employees can also be beneficiaries of that purpose. For sure, Southwest Airlines employees are also given the freedom to fly with free travel benefits. But we wanted to take it further than that. We worked with the director of their People department to develop a series of **Employee Freedoms** that ensured that every employee got his or her own special taste of freedom: *Freedom to create financial security. Freedom to pursue good health. Freedom to travel. Freedom to work hard and have fun. Freedom to learn and grow. Freedom to make a positive difference. And freedom to create and innovate.* This last employee freedom is held near and dear to everyone's heart and is responsible for many of the on-board jokes,

The freedom to be yourself is the freedom to be your best.
Log on for great career opportunities at www.southwest.com.

You can't help but smile when you work for a company that knows how to play as hard as they work — like Southwest Airlines. Because we believe people do their best work when they have the freedom to be who they are. We reward our Employees with great benefits like free travel, 401(k), profitsharing, and more. Of course, we get just as much back from the hardworking people who helped us rank as one of the top five companies to work for by Fortune® magazine.

If you're looking for a great career opportunity, log on to southwest.com. You can even create and submit a résumé online. Or fax your existing résumé to 214-792-7015. And get ready to land the career of a lifetime at Southwest Airlines.

SOUTHWEST AIRLINES®
A SYMBOL OF FREEDOM

Freedom was offered to potential employees in recruitment advertising.

regulation parodies, and legendary customer service moments that the airline is famous for.

When you've laddered up to a higher purpose, you want to be sure that you're recruiting employees who share your values and are ready to fight for your purpose. Southwest uses the freedom to express yourself as a powerful recruiting tool. Unlike other jobs that many of Southwest's candidates might be considering, "At Southwest Airlines, you are free to be yourself"—in essence, free to carry on the Southwest Spirit through your own unique talent and personality.

BRINGING FREEDOM INTO THE MARKET

Once we had our Freedom Fighters fired up and ready to go, it was time to launch freedom externally. Because we had done so much work over the years generating awareness of the attributes that enabled Southwest to claim that it was in the freedom business (e.g., low fares, frequent flights, and friendly flying), we weren't shy about shouting the freedom message.

Inspired by our San Antonio customer, the campaign theme was: *Go. See. Do.* We were really trying to inspire people to take advantage of Southwest and take to the skies to pursue whatever they had dreamed of doing. Our employees became freedom evangelists, all our advertising (outdoor billboards, radio, and television) became calls to action to go, see, and do more than you had thought possible; and every touch point throughout the experience celebrated the freedom that Southwest offered people. The peanut bags, ticket jackets, in-flight napkins, cups—all reinforced the message of freedom in appropriate ways.

CREATING PURPOSEFUL PROMOTIONS

Truth be told, most ad agencies wince when it comes time to do promotional advertising. It's typically not viewed as a meaningful way to build a brand. But if you are able to create demand-building promotional ads that are directly linked to the fulfillment of your purpose, you can tear down the wall between brand advertising and promo-

tional advertising and create the kind of work that does both effectively. We've never done so-called pure branding. Every spot builds the brand *and* every spot is intended to fill the planes or create some form of engagement with Southwest. *And let's face it—there is no brand without demand.* In the case of Southwest Airlines, you can only give people the freedom to fly if you've got a low fare or a great schedule or some other liberating element to talk about.

To give you a sense of what I'm talking about, we developed the workhorse campaign, *Wanna Getaway?* in 1998. It uses promotional price points to drive home the idea of freedom and it filled the planes at the same time. The concept of the campaign is driven by the simple insight that there are times in life when you just wish you could get away, right that very instant. The payoff: With Southwest Airlines low fares and/or frequent flights, you can.

If you haven't seen the *Wanna Getaway?* ads, you must not own a television. The campaign has been running for over ten years and has been cited in the *World's Funniest Commercials* and recognized by *USA Today* readers as one of their favorite spots. But more important, it's filled the planes, built revenue, and given people the freedom to take trips they wouldn't have otherwise taken. They're funny. They're effective. And they've inextricably linked the brand to the idea of freedom to travel.

BRINGING FREEDOM TO LIFE
IN A LOYALTY PROGRAM

We helped Southwest launch a loyalty program in the early eighties. It was called The Company Club, to match the tagline in use at the time. And looking back, it was screaming freedom conceptually, even then. Because of the short-haul nature of the airline, The Company Club counted your one-way travel segments, instead of your overall miles, and it sent you a free ticket in the mail whenever you flew enough of them. How's that for immediate gratification—a ticket in hand, without even asking for it? The ticket was easily used. If there was an empty seat, you could have it and what's more, the free ticket was easily transferred to whomever you chose if you had too many of them, which many people did because they flew so often. Here again, freedom provided a much more compelling way to talk about the benefits of the program to our fliers.

And just think about how difficult it is to use your frequent flier rewards on other airlines.

Therein lies the beauty of Southwest's system. It's the ultimate in freedom. There are so many restrictions and blackout dates on other airlines that it's extremely difficult to ever actually use your rewards. And what good is a reward if you don't have the freedom to use it?

The freedom direction did provide us with an opportunity to enhance the frequent flyer program, too, adding new partners and multiplying the ways for customers to get segments without even flying. Why might a company create a way to give away its product without requiring *any* purchase? *Freedom.* And that created loyalty. This sort of methodology is not unique now—many airlines do it. But it is only truly valuable when it is combined with the ease of use that Southwest has made famous. What Southwest created was a more rapidly rewarding program with more rapidly useable rewards. And so it is no surprise that the new name soon became Rapid Rewards. Southwest had the will to create a loyalty program that truly gave people more freedom to fly, which gave us another powerful freedom story to tell in the market.

Freedom to actually use a frequent flier reward became the cornerstone of Southwest's loyalty program Rapid Rewards.

DELIVERING FREEDOM WHILE
MEETING SPECIFIC BUSINESS GOALS

Southwest Airlines came to us in 2004 to help with a very specific business objective: Drive more online bookings. Southwest had 57 percent of its bookings coming through southwest.com and wanted that percentage to increase. At first blush, that may not seem like a very purpose-based goal.

But just about any business objective can be met while also fulfilling your purpose if you approach it with that end in mind.

To think about how we might solve the challenge, we pulled together a brainstorming session that included Southwest marketing and interactive people, the GSD&M creative team, and some folks from Camelot Communications (the media group that's worked with Southwest for decades).

The challenge we put to the group was to develop ideas that would deliver more traffic to the site—breaking through the 57 percent plateau we had reached in online revenues—*and* deliver more freedom to our customers.

On any given day of the week Southwest has great low fares that go unused. Unlike a product on a shelf that can be sold tomorrow if it is not sold today, a seat on a plane is lost revenue never to be profited from once that plane takes off. This was a lose-lose situation: The customer lost a great opportunity to fly and Southwest Airlines lost revenue. So the question was: *How could we create awareness of the hot deals that were available online in order to increase online bookings?*

In the course of brainstorming ideas one team came across an example of how a company had managed to generate immediate awareness of a "hot deal": It was the Krispy Kreme "hot doughnuts now" Red Light. If you're driving down the road and you see that red neon light shining in all its glory, there's a very good chance that you will pull off to grab one of those hot doughnuts making its way through the sugar glaze waterfall. This led the team to wonder: Could we create a Krispy Kreme red light to alert our customers to the hot deals that were available for a small window of time? Fortunately, we had Brad Newcomb, senior director of online operations at Southwest, in our group. With his strong background in IT, he immediately started thinking about what was possible. Within about thirty minutes we had drafted the concept for DING!—a downloadable desktop icon that notifies Southwest customers when Southwest's hottest deals are available at southwest.com.

Within six months, Brad and his team had created the application, and by February 2005 we were ready to launch it in the marketplace.

Here's how DING! works: Customers navigate to southwest.com and download the application directly onto their desktop. Once installed, a small little plane tail icon appears permanently in their toolbar. The icon emits an audible "ding" whenever a new deal is available.

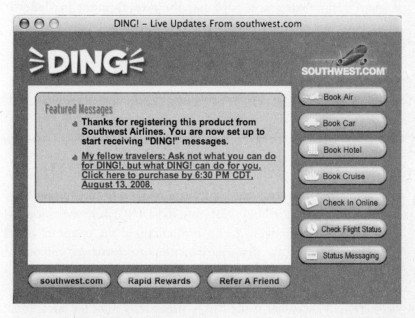

Ding! is a downloadable desktop icon that gives people the freedom to travel by alerting them to Southwest's hottest deals.

This clever idea delivers a load of freedom never before given to customers. It provides nearly instantaneous fare availability. As soon as the special online fares are loaded into the system by Southwest Airlines, customers are gently alerted. It is like having a personal assistant constantly scanning fares for you. And customers love it.

We heard countless stories of DING-inspired trips that transformed uneventful weekends into fun-filled adventures to a new destination—or, conversely, a spontaneous return to a beloved destination. The more people get DINGed, the more they begin thinking about taking a trip they wouldn't have otherwise taken. As one DING user noted on a Yahoo message board shortly after the product was launched: "I got dinged a few times over the last week and realized that I am now actively thinking about traveling, somewhere/anywhere if the right offer comes along. . . . And with those low prices, you figure 'Why not?' " This product not only inspires people to think about taking more trips, but also gives them the freedom to do so by taking full advantage of Southwest's lowest fares.

The advertising work that was created to promote DING! tapped into the thrill that we heard in people's voices as they described the value of a trip that they wouldn't have otherwise taken. We captured the urgency of the deal and the exuberance of the customers in a campaign that called upon people to drop everything when they hear the "ding."

DING! helped southwest.com surpass its goal. By October 2006, Southwest reached 72 percent in online revenues, had over one million active DING! users, and had generated more than $150 million in sales from this new tool. Not only did DING! help meet Southwest's business objectives, it also revolutionized the customer relationship by creating the first-ever direct link to customers' computer desktops. As a competitive weapon, it represents a channel that bypasses all the competing channels or online travel sites that a customer would encounter if she had to proactively hunt for fares. In a sense, it had created a new distribution channel for marketing—a channel that people personally invited into their lives, a channel we could use to efficiently and affordably deliver our best deals to our customers. But the greatest testament to DING! is its ability to stimulate travel that would not have happened otherwise—it gives people

the freedom to go, see, and do more than they would have done otherwise.

CALLING ON FREEDOM TO SET LOVE FREE

One of the last stories I'll share is a story about the fight for the right to deliver freedom in Southwest's own backyard. Southwest Airlines started intrastate service in 1971 out of a small downtown airport in Dallas called Love Field. It was the only airport in that area at the time. Then in 1974, Dallas/Fort Worth (DFW) International Airport opened its doors promising nirvana for air travelers. Most airlines relocated their operations to the new airport. But for Southwest to move to DFW would be tantamount to abandoning its business model. DFW was a big, expensive, hub-modeled airport, which spelled expense and inefficiency for an airline known for its ten-minute turnaround of its planes. So Southwest chose to stay at Love Field and continue to build its increasingly robust intrastate business.

By 1979, Southwest announced their plans to provide interstate service from the downtown Love Field location. And that's when all hell broke loose. The powers-that-be at DFW International Airport and Jim Wright, a Fort Worth congressman, were scared. They knew what Southwest's low fares at Love Field would do to business at DFW if Southwest competed on longer routes and they feared that Southwest would pose a serious threat to the viability of DFW if they were allowed to expand their service. So Wright and DFW succeeded in passing an amendment to restrict Southwest to flying only intrastate and contiguous state routes out of Love Field. If a passenger wanted to go any further on Southwest, he would have to deplane at one of those permissible destinations, collect his luggage, and buy a brand-new ticket to continue on to another destination in Southwest's network.

Well, by the 1990s, anyone who had the misfortune of flying through DFW noticed that the system was bursting at the seams—annual air traffic had literally exceeded capacity. By then there was no longer the possibility of Love Field posing a threat to the viability of DFW. The time to repeal the Wright amendment was long overdue.

So we set out to finally unshackle the company from this anticompetitive, anachronistic amendment. And in the name of freedom, we launched a campaign called:

WRIGHT IS WRONG
JOIN THE FIGHT AT SETLOVEFREE.COM

People were directed to www.setlovefree.com to read about efforts to repeal the Wright amendment and were encouraged to sign a petition that would give them—guess what?—their freedom to fly. We made our case for freedom on the opening page:

> *After 27 years, the Wright Amendment is an anti-competitive relic. Once passed as a federal law designed to protect a fledgling DFW International Airport, it has clearly out-served its purpose. It now deprives the people of Texas from enjoying the wide variety of low fares that other cities take for granted. Southwest prides itself on being the premier low-fare carrier, giving people across America the "Freedom to Fly." Southwest Airlines revolutionized the airline industry by giving millions of Americans access to affordable air travel through its cornerstone of everyday low fares.*
>
> *Southwest Airlines is a Company of proud Americans, being profitable for the past 33 years, and it is the only consistently profitable carrier since 9/11. We were founded on the premise that all Americans deserve the ability to enjoy affordable air fares, no matter where they fly. Southwest Airlines believed in giving you this freedom in 1967, and 39 years of court battles, blatant anti-competitive maneuvers, criminal charges against those seeking to prevent Southwest's service, protectionist congressional legislation, and name-calling has not dimmed Southwest's passion for North Texas and those who visit our area. We will not give up on you now! North Texas deserves affordable air travel and a choice of airports. It's time to recognize Southwest's determination to provide affordable air service to all Americans instead of forcing it to fly with one wing tied behind its back. It's time to repeal the Wright Amendment!*

Shortly after we launched our appeal to give the citizens of North Texas the freedom to fly, DFW and American Airlines launched their counterattack: *Keep DFW Strong*. Their main argument against giving Southwest the freedom to carry more passengers is that it would force airlines operating out of DFW to lower their fares. So keeping DFW strong really meant keeping fares high so that DFW airlines could remain profitable.

Hmmmm . . . if you were a resident in Dallas and could either support the profitability of DFW carriers or support an airline that was trying to give you the freedom to fly more places, which would you be in favor of? Well, Public Opinion Strategies conducted a poll during this battle and found that 82 percent of the Dallas/Ft. Worth Metroplex residents wanted the Wright amendment repealed.[1] And on June 15, 2006, the shackles finally came off and a repeal of the Wright amendment was announced. All the citizens who had signed the petition received an e-mail with the subject: *Love Has Been Set Free: Wright Amendment Reform Act Becomes Law.*

We've shown how we brought the idea of freedom to life in employee communications and policies, in advertising, in promotions, in the Rapid Rewards loyalty program, in the DING! application, and even in launching a movement to repeal an amendment. Each one of those initiatives is making a difference by giving people freedom, in some form or fashion, and building brand equity for Southwest Airlines along the way.

INTEGRATION = FULFILLING THE PROMISE OF YOUR PURPOSE EVERYWHERE YOU CAN

Once you've discovered your purpose, it creates a whole new perspective on the concept of *integration*. Integration often amounts to nothing more than design consistency. For example, if all the advertising is printed in the right shade of blue, uses the right font, and ends with the right tagline and logo, then it's integrated. We hope these examples show that when we landed on the idea of freedom, we did much more than just slap "a symbol of freedom" on everything we did. We actually integrated the very idea of freedom into every employee program, loyalty program, online tool, product innovation, and, yes, advertising message that we could. Integrating the idea means embodying and delivering the idea—actually using each assignment as an opportunity to deliver another dimension of freedom to our constituents. That's what makes integration exciting and ultimately valuable to the brand.

WINNING ON PURPOSE

When it comes to touting the success of the Southwest Airlines brand, we could refer to the high levels of awareness, likeability, and consideration tracked in conventional advertising brand trackers—and they are very high. Or we could list all the awards received over the years from industry associations—and there have been many. Or as an agency, we could try to take some small credit for the phenomenal financial success that Southwest has had—which is considerable (as in, the only profitable airline in the industry for thirty-six years in a row). And we certainly have a legitimate right to claim spoils in the victory for helping them achieve dominant market share in the markets they serve—by a long shot.[2]

But when you are a partner in purpose, your real measure of success is determined by the fulfillment of the stated purpose. In this case, how many people were given the freedom to fly? Over our twenty-five-year history with Southwest Airlines, we've seen the flying population expand from 15 percent to 85 percent. And every market that we've helped "liberate" has experienced the benefits of "the Southwest Effect," a phenomenon first identified by the U.S. Department of Transportation back in 1993.[3] Simply put, when Southwest enters a market, average fares decrease significantly and the number of passengers increase significantly. Let me share some examples:

> One year after Southwest Airlines opened service between Providence and Baltimore/Washington, average fares between the two cities dropped by 73 percent and passenger traffic soared by 782 percent, with more than a half million people flying this route. In fact, Rhode Island's T.F. Green Airport became

the fastest-growing airport in 1997 after Southwest started service there. Overall airport traffic leaped 88 percent during Southwest's first year of service.

[Another] study, focusing on Southwest's arrival in Philadelphia, proved that not only did fares fall in the majority of short-haul, medium-haul, and long-haul markets, but also that the passenger traffic significantly increased in markets served by Southwest. Fares between Philadelphia and both Manchester and Providence fell by more than 80 percent and ten times more passengers boarded these flights than ever before. Passenger traffic on flights to Los Angeles increased by 69 percent and the fares decreased by 36 percent. Air travelers in Philadelphia paid fares that were 20 percent above the national average before the arrival of Southwest Airlines. Now those same travelers, less than a year after Southwest entered their market, enjoy fares that fall well below the national average.

Mission accomplished! DING! *You are now free to move about the country* is a powerful brand idea because . . . you really are. When you are truly trying to make a difference in the world, the only real measure of success is whether or not you actually made the difference you set out to make.

HOW PURPOSE
CAN MAKE YOU BETTER

To save people money so they can live better.

The history of brand-building at Wal-Mart follows a similar trajectory as Southwest Airlines. Wal-Mart spent decades building their brand with a strong set of core attributes—the lead being *Every Day Low Prices*. Then came a new generation of marketing leaders who had both studied and admired the transformation that took place at Southwest Airlines when they got out of the *low fares and frequent flights business* and laddered up to the *freedom business*. They were ready to discover and bring to life Wal-Mart's purpose as well.

THE TRADITIONAL RETAIL BRAND-BUILDING MODEL

Retailers tend to build their brands on the backs of the 3Ps: products, pricing, and promotion. Because Wal-Mart shunned sales promotions in favor of *Every Day Low Prices* and Sam Walton believed so deeply in the Associates, Wal-Mart's 3Ps were products, pricing, and people—with a heavy focus on pricing.

For years the brand was built with work that celebrated *"Every day low prices on the brands you trust. Always." Always* was one of the most recognizable taglines in America, and it served to reinforce the trust that Wal-Mart shoppers had in the brand. They knew they would never be ripped off or given a raw deal—quite a valuable promise in the world of bait-and-switch promotions and 24-hour sales. That kind of blocking and tackling helped make Wal-Mart a hugely successful company. When we began working with Wal-Mart in 1986, they had sales of $8.5 billion. By 2004, their sales had grown to $315 billion. Not a bad run!

Moving from What You Sell to What You Stand For

But there came a day when Wal-Mart's remarkable ability to drive down costs and save their customers money began to be demonized in the media. People no longer seemed to understand what the company really stood for—beyond low prices. Wal-Mart, still recognized for great value, was seen as devoid of *values*. And as Doug Smith, management consultant and author of *On Value and Values,* notes: "*Organizations that promote Value without Values, ultimately hollow out and sicken the collective soul.*"[1]

If you work for a corporation whose esteem is in peril (for whatever reason), it's important to discover or rediscover the true value of your organization in the world. Your purpose won't excuse you from righting legitimate wrongs or fixing things that are broken. However, it will explain your fundamental reason for being in a way that should restore the pride and reignite the momentum you need to move forward from a position of strength rather than weakness.

It was time for Wal-Mart to embrace and add a fourth P to their branding formula: purpose.

Like Schwab, Southwest, and a host of other clients discussed in this book, we didn't have to manufacture a purpose. The leadership at Wal-Mart had always been focused on making a difference in the lives of their customers. Their business model had revolutionized and democratized the accessibility of merchandise around the world. It was time to develop a deeper understanding of the impact of the brand in the lives of Wal-Mart customers to create a brand that was as purpose based as the organization. Following Sam Walton's famous adage, we began by turning to the customer for answers.

When you get confused go to the store, the customer has all the answers.

—Sam Walton

It's important to recognize that Wal-Mart is not just an economic necessity for their shoppers—although many shoppers do credit Wal-Mart with helping them make ends meet. There are also many more who choose to shop at Wal-Mart because of the difference it makes in their life. Wal-Mart shoppers (and keep in mind that two thirds of America shop at Wal-Mart on a monthly basis) proactively choose to shop at Wal-Mart because the money they save translates into a better quality of life—a life with less financial stress, more opportunities, and the ability to say yes more often. It might mean sending their child to school with their head held high, taking a longer vacation with their family, feeding their family more organic foods, putting more presents under the Christmas tree, or saving for a college fund.

Whether you're talking to an upper-income shopper, a member of the striving middle class, or a low-income shopper, each will be able to tell you how Wal-Mart enables them to live better:

Shopping at Wal-Mart makes me feel like I'm a good caretaker of our funds. With four children and four college educations to pay for down the road, saving money matters.
    —Wal-Mart shopper with $400,000 household income in Plano, Texas

Here's what I do. I go to the expensive stores and get all of the ideas and a sense of the look that I want. Then I go to Wal-Mart to pull it off for less.
    —Wal-Mart shopper with $65,000 household income in Austin, Texas

The reality is that we're trying to keep a roof over our kids' heads, trying to feed them, trying to clothe them, trying to let them be proud when they go to school in the clothes they are wearing . . . and Wal-Mart helps us not bury ourselves under a load of bills to do it.

    —Wal-Mart shopper with a $30,000 household income
    in Alameda, California

Highly engaged Wal-Mart Associates who are proud to work at Wal-Mart understand the role that Wal-Mart plays in the lives of their customers. Every day they see firsthand how people are affected by Wal-Mart. They see mothers able to say yes to their children more often, retirees able to afford all their prescriptions, and first-time homeowners able to outfit their homes with everything they need.

> *I love coming to work and seeing the looks on people's faces when they realize that they're able to afford something they've been wanting . . . or looking shocked when they get their receipt and realize that they haven't blown their budget. It makes you feel good to be a part of that.*
>
> —Wal-Mart store manager

Finally, the leaders had always instinctively understood the purpose of Wal-Mart. In fact, one of the last public statements Mr. Sam ever made included a simple, profound explanation of what Wal-Mart could accomplish for the world:

> *If we work together, we'll give the world an opportunity to see what it's like to save, and have a better life.*
>
> —Sam Walton (in an acceptance speech for the
> George H.W. Bush Medal of Freedom)

We needed to capture the richness of what we learned from the customer, the passion we had heard from the very best Associates, and the simplicity of Sam Walton's observation about Wal-Mart's role in the world. And we needed to express it in a way that could be easily understood by every stakeholder involved: Associates, customers, suppliers, and communities.

With all that in mind we articulated Wal-Mart's core purpose very simply:

> *Saving people money so they can live better.*

The simplicity and authenticity of the purpose ensured that it could take root and flourish throughout the company. With two million Associates, a surprising number of whom knew Mr. Sam personally, the purpose had to be consistent with their experience and his vision for it to gain any traction in the organization. Today it has infiltrated the thinking of the entire company—from store-level Associate to buyers to marketing and all the way up to the CEO.

BRINGING IT TO LIFE

What brought it all together was Wal-Mart living the mission of saving people money so they can live better.
—Lee Scott, Wal-Mart Stores, Inc., president and chief executive officer
(2008 Annual Report and Proxy to Shareholders)

Once we went back and grounded everything we did in our company's purpose, the advertising became easy.
—Tony Rogers, vice president of advertising, Wal-Mart

With the purpose in focus, the branding began to reflect the *ultimate value* of the low prices that Wal-Mart delivered to their shoppers. For example, when Wal-Mart helped to drive down the cost of prescription drugs to $4 for hundreds of the most common generic prescriptions, we featured an elderly customer whose life had been greatly enhanced thanking Wal-Mart for the difference it had made in her life *("I just want to say, Thank you. From the bottom of my heart . . .").*

When summer rolled around and gas prices hit record levels, we created a humorous ad about the compromises people were making to take a vacation (e.g., a family camping trip that had to take place in the vacant lot across the street from their home) and let them know if they saved money at Wal-Mart, then high gas prices didn't have to spoil their summer fun.

With a corporation this large, the language of purpose needed to infiltrate much more than the advertising to begin to turn the tide of public opinion. It needed to frame all the communications coming out of Wal-Mart. And has it ever.

From the 2008 Annual Report:

To a sustainability Web site with the URL: savemoneylivebetter .com

To company fact sheets framed with the language of purpose:

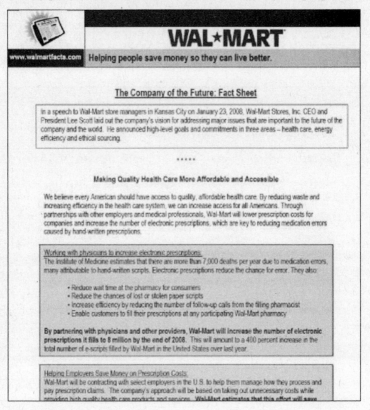

You'll even find *Save Money. Live Better.* emblazoned across the top of every Wal-Mart receipt emerging from cash registers across the land.

FULFILLING YOUR PURPOSE IN MORE WAYS

In the process of rediscovering, articulating, and focusing the energies of the entire company around the true purpose, Wal-Mart has begun to think about how they can help people save money and live better in all sorts of new ways. Lee Scott has committed to ramp up environmental efforts, to invest more in the communities where the stores operate, and to renew their commitment to helping Wal-Mart Associates live better lives, too.

Initially there were some Wall Street naysayers who feared Lee Scott had become a tree hugger who was distracting the company from making a profit with his high-minded vision of saving the planet. But Lee Scott didn't view sustainable investments as a distraction at all. Having mastered traditional supply-chain management to become the irrefutable low-price leader, sustainable practices represent the next frontier of eradicating inefficiencies from the system. In so doing, Wal-Mart can continue to lead the way in saving people money and do so in a way that takes "living better" to a whole new level.

For example, improving the fuel efficiency of their trucking fleet by 15 percent and eliminating unnecessary packaging (which ends up in landfills) are both smart sustainable practices that lower costs and can be passed on to save the customer money *and* help them live in a better, cleaner environment.

Developing a personal sustainability project that has helped Associates lose 184,315 pounds and helped 19,924 Associates quit or reduce their smoking helps Wal-Mart save on long-term health-care costs and absenteeism while also helping those Associates live better lives.

Wal-Mart has made a big effort to lower the cost of more energy-efficient and eco-friendly products. Leading with their purpose, Wal-Mart always celebrates the savings or personal benefit to the shopper and then gives a nod to what the collective buying power of Wal-Mart shoppers can do for the planet.

Two current television advertisements bring to life the purpose.[2]

To promote a GE compact fluorescent lightbulb a Wal-Mart shopper explains:

> This is a GE compact fluorescent lightbulb. It didn't cost a lot because I got it at Wal-Mart. It can save me $47 dollars in electricity costs. Forty-seven dollars just by changing a lightbulb. But here's the really neat thing. If every Wal-Mart shopper, all two hundred million of us, used just one bulb, it would be like taking over eleven million cars off the road. That's a pretty big deal for a little lightbulb.
>   Voice-over: Budget friendly prices. Earth friendly products.
>   Wal-Mart. *Save Money. Live Better.*

To promote a water filter, another Wal-Mart shopper explains:

> This is a pure water filter. Got a great deal on it at Wal-Mart. It can provide as much as 3,200 bottles of water, which can save me up to $600 a year. And if every Wal-Mart shopper, all 200 million of us bought one, we could keep billions of plastic bottles from ending up in landfills every year. Now that's refreshing.
> Voice-over: Budget friendly prices. Earth friendly products. Wal-Mart. *Save Money. Live Better.*

PURPOSE: A WORK IN PROGRESS

Wal-Mart issued a sustainability progress report in 2007 cataloging the progress they've made as a company, in its communities, with Associates, and for the planet.

Wal-Mart is looking at ways to reduce waste and increase efficiencies in the health-care system so that customers, Associates, and even other employers can save on health-care costs. They're finding ways to bring energy-efficient products to market affordably to help their customers save on energy costs. They've committed to working only with suppliers that comply with ethical and environmental standards which ensures that only high-quality products are delivered to the customer.

What purpose has enabled Wal-Mart to do is approach corporate responsibility in a way that naturally builds the brand. If Wal-Mart is in the *saving people money so they live better* business, it requires the company to take a look at all the areas where the quality of life is threatened due to high costs (health care and energy, for example) and put the Wal-Mart model to work to fix it. In so doing, Wal-Mart can fulfill its obligation to behave responsibly and fulfill the promise of the purpose at the same time.

BUILDING YOUR PURPOSE VERSUS
BEHAVING RESPONSIBLY

Be careful not to mistake corporate social responsibility practices for your brand, if it's not in fact the core reason for your being. We see a lot of companies that are beginning to use their corporate social responsibility practices to do just that. But if those practices aren't linked to the authentic core purpose of the organization in a meaningful way, it's unlikely that it will be seen as anything more than wanting to take credit for behaving responsibly—something all people now expect from the companies they do business with.

BMW has created an amazing high-performing luxury vehicle fueled by hydrogen. Does it now use this remarkable innovation to position the brand around environmentalism? No. The headline it uses to tell the story of the Hydrogen 7 reads: *Driving pleasure is the motivation. Hydrogen the drive.* BMW focuses on how this vehicle has all the driving performance of a BMW but with zero emissions. The story becomes another proof point to the idea that BMW is a company where brilliant ideas become ultimate driving machines that are a joy to drive—now even more joyful because they have zero impact on the environment.

So it is with Wal-Mart. The more they support sustainable practices and make ecofriendly products affordable for more people, the more they will be able to help their customers live better lives.

As Lee Scott states in the sustainability progress report: *"Like everything we do, sustainability begins with our customers. From the day that Sam Walton opened the doors of the first Wal-Mart store in 1962, our mission has been to save people money so they can live better. Today that mission extends to sustainability. . . . We make no claims of being a green company. . . . But what we are saying is we're doing sustainability in a way that's real and right for Wal-Mart and is touching the lives of millions of people around the world."*[3]

WINNING ON PURPOSE

Read any case study of Wal-Mart's success and it will surely be attributed to Wal-Mart's pioneering work in supply-chain management and pricing strategy. And to be sure, they wouldn't have become the number one retailer in the world without doing so.

But the reason for their success is much deeper than that. That business model has enabled them to make a profound impact in the lives of the 176 million people in 13 countries who shop at Wal-Mart stores each week. The purpose is the reason for their success and it's pushing Wal-Mart to become an even better company in the future.

> *I am optimistic about our future because I know that customers everywhere will continue to depend on Wal-Mart to save them money so they can live better.*
> —Lee Scott, president and CEO, Wal-Mart Stores, Inc.
> (2008 Wal-Mart Annual Report)

HOW PURPOSE
CAN ACCELERATE
YOUR MOMENTUM

Enabling people to experience the joy of driving.

When BMW came to us in 2005, they were a very successful company. They had a good understanding of their purpose already in place. The BMW people told us they weren't in the automotive business; they were in the *joy* business. And with a little wordsmithing we articulated BMW's purpose as: *Enabling people to experience the joy of driving.*

BMW also came to us with a history of great advertising. *The Ultimate Driving Machine* is probably one of the best known taglines ever written. And, at first blush, it seems to be a wonderful description of a vehicle that enables people to experience the joy of driving.

BMW also came to us with phenomenal vehicles to sell. The *Ultimate Driving Machine* was not an empty promise. The industry ratings were stellar, and the moment we began test driving the cars we all personally realized how much fun it really could be to drive.

So, great purpose, great tagline, great vehicles, what was the problem? As fun and focused as BMW's purpose was, as memorable as its tagline was, as great as its vehicles were, the joy of driving a BMW wasn't fully appreciated in the marketplace. In 2005, there were 1.9 million luxury performance vehicles sold in the United States. Of all of the people who bought a luxury performance vehicle, 75 percent of them had never even considered buying a BMW.[1]

Sometimes, the biggest impediment to the fulfillment of a purpose is a lack of understanding in the marketplace. If you've got a great purpose at the heart of your organization that drives everything you do, you might be able to accelerate your momentum by telling people about it! Turns out, BMW was spending too much time talking about what it sells, and not enough time talking about what they stand for.

The Problem: Not Understanding What BMW Stands For

After much research into why BMWs weren't being considered by more people, it became very clear that people didn't really know anything about the company behind the car. They knew that BMW made high-performing, luxury vehicles that tended to pass them on the highway. They knew that BMWs were status symbols. But since they didn't know what BMW, the company, stood for, BMW was often reduced to a luxury badge they didn't relate to. It was time to let people know what BMW stood for as a company.

BMW: A Company of Great Ideas

Since its inception, BMW has been an independent car company, beholden to no one. Because top management is not bound or gagged or beholden to any parent company, they're able to take risks and invest in innovations that would never see the light of day at other car companies. Their independence has enabled them to ladder up from a company of great performance to a company of great ideas. Here are some of their best ones:

Ideas like inventing the category of sports sedan. In 1968 BMW shocked the automotive world when it introduced the BMW 2002 and proved that performance and sedan could coexist in the same concept.

Ideas like night vision. In 2006, BMW was the first to allow drivers to see almost a thousand feet ahead of them in complete darkness.

Ideas like battle-testing every one of the 20,000 BMW components in extreme laboratory environments. BMW is the first manufacturer to record the data from the Nurburing race track and create a Nurburing Simulator that subjects axles, wheels, and tires to the world's most grueling racing conditions at speeds up to 160 miles per hour, 24 hours a day. Every mile on the simulated test track equals 20 miles on a customer road.

Ideas like designing a hydrogen car with near zero emissions. BMW has created the world's first automobile propelled with liquid hydrogen that emits essentially water, thereby reducing pollution and greenhouse gases and creating a solution for a more sustainable fuel. Beyond its cars, BMW is investing in solar, wind, and hydropower to generate the electricity needed to realize fully the potential of hydrogen fuel. And the company currently has plans under way to build twenty-four hydrogen refueling stations throughout California.

Ideas like turning vehicles into works of art. Alexander Calder painted a French racing drivers' BMW 3.0 CSL back in the seventies, and since then artists such as Frank Stella, Roy Lichtenstein, David Hockney, and Jenny Holzer have all used actual vehicles as a canvas to create works of art—known as BMW Artcars.

Ideas like hiring a world-class architect to build a revolutionary new manufacturing plant. BMW hired Zaha Hadid Architects of London (who went on to win the coveted Pritzker Architecture Award) to create a unique space that brought together office space with the factory floor, assembly workers with managers, products with processes. The space offers total transparency throughout so everyone is aware of how their jobs influences others.

Ideas like building a plant that runs on methane gas from a local landfill. The BMW plant in Spartanburg was designed with a 9.5 mile pipeline running from the plant to the Palmetto landfill, which provides 50 percent of the plants' total energy.

The list of remarkable ideas that BMW has pioneered goes on and on. At the heart of the company we found three core values that helped explain the depth of ideas we had found:

Independence. Innovation. Authenticity.

As an independent company, BMW has the latitude to pursue ideas they believe in—ideas that result in breakthrough innovations, ideas that are born out of an authentic passion for driving. Throughout the organization, we found a refusal to compromise on any investments that needed to be made to ensure that they truly are delivering The Ultimate Driving Machine.

Once we understood what the company stood for, we set out to find an audience who shared those same values.

FINDING THE PERFECT AUDIENCE: THE IDEA CLASS

We began our search for the ideal target audience by exploring segments of the population that would naturally share BMW's core values of independence, innovation, and authenticity.

Carmen Graf—our media guru in audience profiling—began to find attitudinal and behavioral statements to identify a segment of the population that not only valued ideas and creativity, but also shared a passion for driving, a love of great design, an appreciation for independent thinking, and, most important, earned the income to afford a BMW. By the time it was all said and done, Carmen had identified a segment of the population that we called the "Idea Class." It was 23 million people strong, and it turned out that these people tended to live in the top twenty BMW volume markets.

Ideas are the currency of the Idea Class—it's how they make their living and it's the source of their joy. By telling the story of the ideas that had been born, cultivated, and brought to market by BMW, the Idea Class began to experience a newfound joy and appreciation for BMW. They had no idea what a BMW was really all about—and no real idea what went into creating the Ultimate Driving Machine.

It was only when they began to understand the latitude that BMW has as an independent company to push ideas to their limits—in everything they do—that they began to appreciate the full experience of driving a BMW. By telling the full story of the organization, the

BMW brand suddenly got a lot more interesting. We heard Idea Class members say things like:

> *I always saw the BMW logo as a symbol of conspicuous consumption . . . now it seems more like a symbol of great thinking that culminated in this machine.*

> *I always thought of "the ultimate driving machine" as just driving really fast . . . but they seem like they're thinking of the ultimate performance of everything they do—workers in the plant . . . every component of the car . . . the efficiency of their manufacturing . . . it's a lot more than just cornering at 100 mph . . . interesting.*

> *Knowing more about the company would make me think differently about BMW owners—less status conscious, more progressive.*

PUTTING IT ALL TOGETHER

The market needed to understand what the company stood for in order to take this already successful brand to the next level. To that end, we articulated BMW's positioning strategy in the following manner:

> **BMW is a company of ideas.** We believe that ideas are everything. And because we are an independent company, we have the freedom to make sure innovative ideas live on to become the Ultimate Driving Machine.

We essentially transformed BMW from a car of great performance to a company of great ideas. The brand work that we created began to tell the story by contrasting the independence of BMW with a competitive field plagued with conventional thinking and hindered by parent companies that tend to compromise ideas. This work brought a new dimension to the BMW brand—a dimension that was needed for people to appreciate fully the experience of driving a BMW.

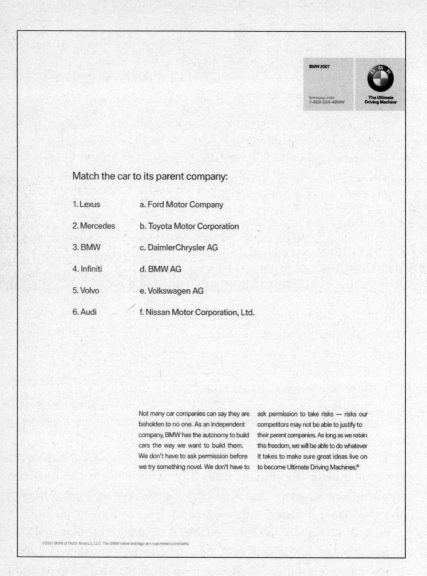

Match the car to its parent company:

1. Lexus   a. Ford Motor Company

2. Mercedes   b. Toyota Motor Corporation

3. BMW   c. DaimlerChrysler AG

4. Infiniti   d. BMW AG

5. Volvo   e. Volkswagen AG

6. Audi   f. Nissan Motor Corporation, Ltd.

Not many car companies can say they are beholden to no one. As an independent company, BMW has the autonomy to build cars the way we want to build them. We don't have to ask permission before we try something novel. We don't have to ask permission to take risks — risks our competitors may not be able to justify to their parent companies. As long as we retain this freedom, we will be able to do whatever it takes to make sure great ideas live on to become Ultimate Driving Machines.®

We took people behind the scenes to see how BMW was using the power of visionary ideas to help save the environment.

We're using a landfill to make our plant cleaner.

When you're an independent company, you have the autonomy to do things differently. Take our Spartanburg plant, for instance. It gets more than half its energy from a nearby landfill, using waste methane for power instead of natural gas. As a result, the atmosphere is spared thousands of tons of greenhouse gases. And our commitment to reusable energy extends far beyond one plant in South Carolina. For instance, our hydrogen car is no mere concept car; it already exists. In fact, one of the main reasons we don't make every BMW hydrogen-powered is that we're waiting for the industry infrastructure to catch up. We believe if a car company is truly interested in doing things differently, it shouldn't stop at the cars they make. It should permeate every facet of the organization. At BMW ideas are everything. And we make sure great ideas live on to become ultimate driving machines.

Now take a second to think about how the "joy of driving" might be interpreted differently once you're made aware of these types of innovations. Think about the joy that comes from being affiliated with a brand that is on the cutting edge of environmental design, architectural design, art and culture, and just a general commitment to celebrating and cultivating great ideas. Think about how these ideas influence what it means to be the Ultimate Driving Machine.

By leveraging the values of the organization and telling the story of the great ideas that were able to live on and become Ultimate Driving Machines, we created a much more intriguing and appealing brand that the Idea Class could embrace.

As a brand ambassador for innovative ideas partnerships BMW provides great opportunities to further cement its corporate purpose and positioning in the marketplace. The right partnership can signal to the market what you believe in and what you're trying to do. We wanted to align BMW with an event that was known for the celebration of visionary ideas. Enter TED (Technology, Entertainment, Design).

The TED Conference extends an invitation to a thousand great

We celebrated the visionary thinking and independence that enabled BMW to build the architecturally renowned Leipzig plant.

thinkers to discuss innovative ideas that are shaping the world we live in. People like Malcolm Gladwell, Jeffrey Katzenberg, Bill Gates, and Al Gore lead the dialogues. The contents of these conferences had never been made available to the public. BMW changed all that by sharing the wisdom and inspiration from TED with the rest of the world via podcasts available only on the BMW Web site or through iTunes.

The company also used the event to showcase the Hydrogen 7 vehicle to this influential group of visionary thinkers—a wonderful example of the visionary thinking coming out of BMW. By aligning the brand with the greatest innovative and independent minds of the modern era and showcasing BMW's revolutionary Hydrogen 7 vehicle in that environment, the company let the members of the Idea Class know exactly what BMW was all about. Now to the selling part.

THE X3: THE ANTIDOTE TO THE SUV.
ANOTHER GREAT IDEA FROM BMW

In 2006, we were tasked with relaunching the X3—a smaller, more compact version of the sport activity vehicle (SAV) embodied by the X5. We were targeting empty nesters and new families within the Idea Class. These conscientious and creative individuals needed the functionality of an SUV but were fearful of the stereotypes associated with these behemoths. They did not want to be affiliated with the "soccer mom" segment or labeled an "environmental enemy." In this day and age, members of the Idea Class are increasingly frustrated with the lack of fuel efficiency and the impact on the environment associated with SUVs. Many express a frustration with the lack of innovation on this front: *"It shouldn't be that hard to create a vehicle that serves your needs without costing a fortune to fuel and being a blight on the environment . . . geez!"*

And that's just what the X3 became—an antidote to the lumbering, bloated SUV that litters every highway. An antidote for everyone that has ever winced at the thought of sacrificing what they believe in for the functionality they need. As an antidote to the growing anti-SUV ideology, the X3 became another example of a great idea from a company of ideas.

We took the competition head-on with the bold proclamation that "This is not an SUV." Poking fun at the excess and flaws of SUVs enabled us to highlight the design integrity and innovation represented by the X3. In thinking about how to bring this to life in the most dramatic and compelling way possible, our creative people and our media team came up with the brilliant idea to make the media the message. We went out and literally found large, lumbering, oafish vehicles—cement mixers, city buses, armored cars—and turned them into media channels.

The medium is the message: Large, lumbering vehicles were turned into media channels to disrupt conventional thinking in the category.

Street teams followed the vehicles and handed out literature explaining that the X3 was emphatically "not an SUV." In tandem with this effort we worked with our partner agency Dotglu to develop and launch a microsite (nobehemoths.com) that compares SUVs to everything from a ship to a box to white bread, listing their negative traits (bland, sluggish, precarious, etc.) and offering up the X3 as the antidote.

We created colorful print ads that featured SUV "rants" and, again, presented the X3 as the direct opposite of what the typical SUV has to offer.

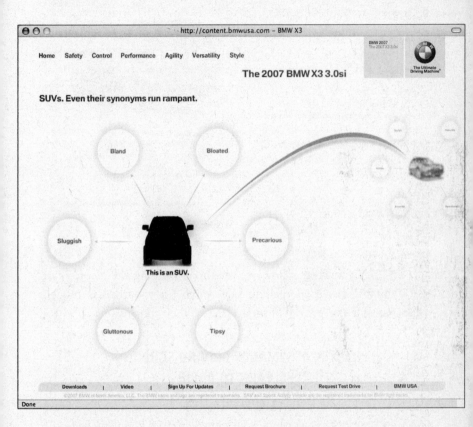

The Idea Class citizens we were trying to reach were absolutely thrilled with what the X3 represented. It represented a philosophy as much as it did a feat in engineering. It represented an idea that they wanted to be affiliated with and created a newfound affinity and interest in BMW. The result: Consideration increased, dealership visits increased, and we achieved sales that not only met the goals set by BMW (which, by the way, are always high to begin with), but exceeded them by 10 percent.

This is not an SUV.

SUVs have poor manners.
They put their elbows on the table and
wipe their mouths with their sleeves.
They do not floss.

They are boxen.
Large beasts with huge egos and small brains,
a significant percentage reek of vinyl.
They are top heavy.

They laugh too loud
and ask people to feel their biceps.
They are full of cruft.
They are bloated and have seventeen cupholders.

If it weren't for bad style, they'd have no style at all.

This is not an SUV.

This is the new BMW X3 SAV.®
Lean as a sprinter, a powerful 260-hp engine and the exclusive xDrive
all-wheel-drive system give this Sports Activity Vehicle uncanny
driving ability in any situation. Its interior has been completely
redesigned, featuring available 16-way adjustable leather seats and
real wood trim, all under a massive panoramic moonroof.

To learn more about the BMW X3 SAV, visit noBehemoths.com.

©2006 BMW of North America, LLC. The BMW name and logo are registered trademarks. SAV and Sports Activity
Vehicle are the registered trademarks for BMW light trucks.

The X3 demonstrates how we go about weaving the ideology of the company into a compelling sales pitch for a particular model. That's become our proven approach for all their models.

BMW PERFORMANCE DRIVING SCHOOL— RELEARN TO DRIVE

The last example I want to share was a little assignment we were given for the BMW Performance Driving School. If you want to find a place that is totally dedicated to enabling people to truly experience the joy of driving, this is it. And yet it was a grossly underleveraged asset in the brand-building arsenal.

The driving school is a $12.5 million driving facility with two miles of pristine track, a team of professional driving instructors, and a stocked fleet of BMWs. The school enables drivers to improve their driving skills and experience challenging road conditions in a safe environment while pushing BMWs to their limits. With a small marketing budget, little to no support from the dealers, and minimal prominence on the BMW USA Web site, it's not surprising that awareness of the facility was low among BMW owners and driving enthusiasts at large.

We thought this was a shame. Sometimes seemingly small assets can provide powerful proof points to the promise of your brand—and the driving school proved to be one of those little diamonds in the rough.

When we were interviewing one of the driving instructors about what difference he was trying to make in the lives of the students that came through the driving school, he said something that really struck a chord with us: *"Our job is to undo the bad driving habits that people have learned over the years and teach people how to drive again. Once they understand how to handle a car, they can rediscover the joy of driving."* Undo the bad driving habits . . . that was an interesting thought.

When we turned to our prospective audience we found that most of them didn't think they had any problems driving—that's a problem if you're trying to get people to sign up for a driving school. However, armed with the insight from the driving instructor, we really pushed people to share with us any bad habits or questionable skills they might have been taught early on that might possibly be interfering with their driving ability. We soon had people telling us hilarious stories of uber-aggressive gym coaches regaling them to drive as if they were an offensive linesman, older sisters who advocated shifting and applying mascara at the same time, and Sunday school teachers who believed in the power of prayer to get you safely from point A to B.

Over time it became evident that whoever taught you how to drive most likely wasn't qualified. It was a simple human truth that everyone could relate to. And that was the insight that led to the big idea: *Relearn to Drive.*

We created an unbranded campaign that portrayed nine archetypal "driving instructors," one of whom you're bound to have encountered. When you interact with these "instructors," you're directed to a Web site: relearntodrive.com. Once we had people nodding in recognition of driving mentors they may have experienced, they were prompted to "Undo the Damage" and taken to the branded "Performance Driving School Content."

We seeded the campaign in the market by sending a link to any automotive media outlet we could think of and, not surprisingly, it started spreading like wildfire. We had a great partnership with *The Onion*. *The Onion* created the perfect content tie-in with a video spoof titled "Traffic," which promoted a mock U.S. Department of Transportation press conference suggesting honking as a solution to clearing congestion on America's highways. This campaign turned out to be *The Onion*'s most successful ad campaign to date.[2]

Overall, the campaign was wildly successful in terms of meeting any objectives set by the BMW Performance Driving School—call volume to the center was up 50 percent and classes were 100 percent booked for 2007 shortly after the campaign had launched.[3] But whether or not you actually enrolled in the driving school, this asset became another powerful, substantive example of BMW's commitment to helping people discover the joy of driving.

> We were first introduced to the driving school when BMW invited the four agencies vying for their business to Spartanburg, South Carolina. BMW decided to pit each agency against one another in a timed lap race. Two of the agencies were from New York. We figured they couldn't drive so we could easily beat them. I'm happy to report that I did in fact have the best time of all the drivers from all the agencies. We couldn't help but recommend to BMW that it might behoove them to pick an agency that can actually drive a car. I believe that was our first step toward real kinship with BMW.

WINNING ON PURPOSE

So what was the result of this shift toward more purpose-based branding—branding that focused as much on the ideology and values of BMW as it did the performance of the vehicles that they sell? Unaided brand awareness, consideration, and likability have all significantly increased since "A Company of Ideas" was launched in the marketplace. We've helped to generate significantly more traffic to both the Web site and to the dealerships. As a result, in 2007, BMW experienced the best sales result in the history of BMW North America in a flat market.

A final thing to note on BMW's success is that it accomplished these remarkable sales goals with significantly *less* marketing spend per vehicle than the competition. Most luxury automotive brands spend anywhere from $1,500 to $2,500 per vehicle on marketing. BMW spends less than $600 per vehicle.[4] The more purpose driven you actually are—in other words, the more people who believe in what you stand for and relate to your values—the less spending you have to do to convince people of your value. The right message, in the right places, to the right people will go a very long way.

13

NORWEGIAN CRUISE LINE®

FREESTYLE CRUISING®

HOW PURPOSE
CAN SET YOU FREE
FROM THE SEA OF SAMENESS

Defying cruise convention to deliver a liberating experience for all.

If you are part of an organization that has never formally articulated a set of core values driving your culture or a core purpose explaining your reason for being, the prospect of doing so may seem overwhelming. Norwegian Cruise Line (NCL) is a great example to show that sometimes the key to unlocking your values and purpose is right under your nose. Sometimes an innovative product or service you've developed may be indicative of underlying institutional values and a purpose that have never been explicitly expressed. When you explore the underlying beliefs behind the innovation, you may soon discover a rich set of values and a clear pathway to your purpose.

Norwegian Cruise Line came to us in 2005 with a request to help build awareness for a little something that they had developed called Freestyle Cruising. Freestyle Cruising was developed in response to customer complaints about the regimented approach to dining that's standard in the cruise industry. This means having to sit next to the Plotnicks from Long Island or the Winkles from Cleveland every night at 5:00 P.M. every day of your vacation. Freestyle Cruising obliterates scheduled dining times and preassigned seating and offers over half a dozen restaurant options that guests are free to frequent whenever and with whomever they please.

Freestyle Cruising also does away with strict dress codes that most cruise lines have for different events—the logic being, maybe people would like to wear whatever they want when they're on vacation.

Before we produced any work to build the brand, we wanted to get inside the company and identify the values and purpose behind the creation of Freestyle Cruising. In doing so, we could not only create better advertising and marketing materials down the road, we could also help to focus the organization on creating more innovative products and services that would support and enhance the brand in truly meaningful ways.

We asked all of NCL's best employees (the star performers) across a wide variety of functions the following questions: *What core values do you personally bring to work every day that are nonnegotiable for the work that you do? What core values are supported, rewarded, and critical to the success of NCL?*

This is what we heard from those we asked:

Innovation rose to the surface very quickly. "NCL is the innovator. We created Freestyle, homeland cruising, NCL America. . . . We're constantly looking for new and exciting ways to improve the industry." Turns out that NCL has a history of firsts in the cruise industry—Freestyle Cruising just happened to be the latest manifestation of that.

Freedom and Flexibility were also values that went hand in hand with the innovation value. NCL employees felt that the NCL culture gave employees the freedom and flexibility they needed to do their jobs and, not surprisingly, they were creating products and services designed to give their customers more freedom and flexibility on their ships.

Teamwork is another value that emerged that's indispensable when pulling off the gargantuan task of turning ships around as efficiently and flawlessly as NCL does every weekend in ports all over the world.

And finally, the value of **fun**. People at NCL don't take themselves too seriously. They love their jobs and have a lot of fun exploring ways to delight their guests throughout the experience.

Resorts don't tell people what to wear, when and with whom to eat, and where to go after dinner. . . . We have to match resorts in their ability to offer an unstructured, casual, attentive atmosphere in which to decompress from everyday life.

—Colin Veitch, NCL president and CEO, *Chicago Tribune*, January 21, 2001

We articulated NCL's values in the following way:

Innovation: Constantly pushing for new and better ways to delight people at sea.

Freedom and Flexibility: Whatever it takes to get the job done.

Teamwork: We're all in this together.

Fun: Let's have some!

Core values don't have to have any direct connection to the core purpose of the organization. But, in this case, they did. When we asked people what they were really passionate about, their answers would invariably come around to the idea of *innovating* in order to deliver a new and better guest experience than what conventional cruising could offer. When we asked what NCL could truly be the best in the world at, employees said things like giving people more freedom and flexibility than anyone else in the industry. In fact, when we looked at the history of innovations that had come out of NCL, many of the most notable ones were designed to give people more choices, flexibility, and freedom than had previously been available in the industry. When we asked what the world would lose if NCL ceased to exist, employees spoke passionately about the industry losing a pioneer: *"It would be like a reverse back in time . . . the industry would lose the innovator, the cruise line that goes out on a limb to try new routes, new programs, new ports of call."*

And they also spoke passionately about the freedom, flexibility, and choice the customer would lose: *"Customers would be limited to more cookie-cutter cruises . . . it would put people back in the cattle herd experience most cruise ships offer."* All their answers pointed us in the clear direction of an overarching purpose for NCL, which had never been articulated but was nevertheless alive and well in the organization:

> Defying cruise convention to deliver a liberating experience for all.

So much of NCL's drive to innovate was directed at the conventions of the industry that actually inhibit the freedom, flexibility, and escape from the demands of daily life people are seeking when they go on vacation. By understanding the values and purpose of the organization, all of a sudden Freestyle Cruising became much more than a feature that we needed to increase awareness of—it became compelling proof of a larger purpose that could help us tell a more meaningful story about the brand.

POSITIONING BEYOND DEFEAT

The next step is to figure out how to best position the brand in the marketplace to bring the purpose to life in a way that resonates with customers and differentiates you from the competition. To that end, we have to answer the question:

What do we have that people want that the competition isn't giving them?

Americans are some seriously overworked, overtired, overscheduled, and stressed-out people. They work 49.5 weeks a year, which translates to 499 more hours than Germans, 260 more hours than Brits, and 137 more hours than the Japanese! They feel burdened by their commitments to what can feel like everyone but themselves—their bosses, their children, their community endeavors. Now the good news is, all that stress means that people need vacations that liberate them from the tyranny of their frenetic lives. They need an opportunity to take care of themselves for a change. The word leisure, from the Latin word *licere,* actually means "to be permitted." And that's just what people want—to be permitted to do whatever they want, whenever they want, in pursuit of their own personal interests.

What surprised us was just how overlooked this fundamental driver of vacations is in the marketplace. It's true that there is a broad range of things that people say they need out of their vacation—you should be able to relate to these if you're a human being in need of a vacation:

- Need to escape > Freedom from pressure and responsibility
- Need to do nothing > Freedom from "shoulds"/space to do nothing
- Need to pursue personal interests > Freedom from serving everyone else's needs
- Need to indulge > To be treated like royalty/to get pampered
- Need for novelty > Freedom to try something new
- Need for stimulation > Freedom to go on an adventure/explore /learn

Now think about which one of those is at the top of your priority list for your next vacation? If you're like most Americans, far and away the most frequently mentioned need is the need to be free from the pressures and stresses of everyday life. While they may want sprinkles of indulgence, novelty, and stimulation, what they really want is freedom from the regimentation and demands of daily life and the freedom to do whatever they want for a change.

So far the fundamental purpose of NCL seemed to be right in the strike zone of what people want in a vacation. So we needed to understand what kind of competition NCL really faced in terms of satisfying this fundamental desire that people have.

Despite the fairly obvious fact that what most people want out of a vacation is the chance to unplug, unwind, and do their own thing, not one of NCL's direct competitors was positioning their brand to fulfill that need. Carnival (the Fun Ship) and Royal Caribbean (the thrill-seeker/Adventure ship) position their brands to appeal to a desire for adventure and excitement—a far less frequently mentioned need and one that is frankly better fulfilled by land vacations.

Holland America and Celebrity position their brands around premium, luxury experiences in an attempt to overturn the stigma of mass-market mediocrity that often hinders companies in this category. But the fundamental motivation for taking a vacation wasn't really being addressed by anyone in the category—certainly not in any overt or focused manner. So it seemed that we were sailing right into uncharted waters (pardon the pun).

The real threat to claiming this position emerged from exploring consumer attitudes toward cruising in general. Quick. When I ask, what do you think of when you think of taking a cruise? What pops into your mind? Do you immediately see it as a solution to your overstressed, overscheduled, overcommitted life? Probably not. If you're like many people, you might just envision loads of people being herded around a ship from one meal to another, looking at their watch for when the next scheduled activity might begin. Many people who have experienced conventional ships complain about the loss of control over how they spend their day, when and with whom they'll be able to eat, and what and where they can dress down. These are all factors that greatly undermine the sense of freedom, escape, and stress-free experiences they're ultimately seeking.

This was a perceptual challenge that we could really sink our teeth into thanks to the work done by NCL to create Freestyle Cruising. Freestyle Cruising provided a unique opportunity to overturn negative perceptions of cruising and deliver the experience that people are ultimately seeking from a vacation experience.

With Freestyle Cruising, each individual is liberated from the oppression of the clock and is given the freedom to do exactly what he or she wants to do. It gives people a level of freedom that's hard to find on land and unexpected at sea, and that's a clear competitive advantage over the direct competition. At its best, Freestyle Cruising from NCL delivers ultimate freedom from the demanding and stressful lives that Americans lead and provides the freedom to create an experience on their own terms.

We expressed NCL's positioning as:

"Go Your Own Way" Freestyle Cruising from NCL frees you from the demands of daily life and gives you the opportunity to go your own way.

FINDING FREESTYLERS

Part of positioning yourself to win includes finding the perfect audience that will be most receptive to your message. We start with the basic demographic profiling of individuals who take cruises—adults over age 45, household incomes of $50,000 plus, educated, family oriented . . . the very basic profiling of the type of people typically engaged in the category. But we try to find people who not only fit the category but also fit the brand. We wanted people who cared about personal freedom and choice, who valued flexibility, and who were comfortable with an "anything goes" environment. We found a psychographic segment that agreed with statements like *I'm open to new experiences, I like to do things my way, I prefer vacations without organized activities or set schedules.*

It turns out that there are forty-four million people in America who fit the cruising profile (whether they've cruised or not) *and* share these attitudes, and they happen to be highly concentrated in about eighteen key markets in America. This degree of customer concentration allowed us to be very efficient with our media spending. We called this group of people Freestylers, and they became the focus of our marketing efforts.

Launching Our Story with a Rebellious Little Fish

FREESTYLE CRUISING®

When it came time to build the brand around the purpose and positioning, a very young creative person developed a simple little icon that came to be known as the *rebellious fish,* which probably tells the brand story as powerfully as anything can. We've used it to express the spirit of Freestyle to employees, to the travel agents who are critical influencers in telling the brand story, and to potential and current guests. And if it isn't obvious by simply looking at it, we've told the story of the rebellious fish to our employees and to the trade this way:

> *We are the fish that swims in the opposite direction. This is our brand. It's not our logo or a mascot, but it stands for our idea of what cruising should be. It stands for Freestyle Cruising. As you know, Freestyle Cruising means our guests are off the clock. They don't have to plan their day around a set dinner time where you're forced to make small talk with the Wurtzels from Baltimore. They can follow their fancy. Sleep in. Eat late. Linger on shore. Whatever they want. It's their vacation, isn't it?*

It also provides a very quick read in environments where people are moving along rapidly and are highly unlikely to stop and read long copy in an advertisement.

Calling On All Employees to Become Rebellious Fish

Employee Guide to Freestyle Cruising distributed to all employees prior to launch of campaign.

As always, the first people you need to get on board with the purpose, values, and positioning are the employees. We created a very whimsical little book that captured the spirit of Freestyle and explained in colorful language what NCL was all about:

> *At NCL we do our own thing. We throw the industry rules out the window.*
>
> *We enjoy our own code. Plainly stated, our Purpose is:*
>
> *Defying cruise convention to deliver a liberating experience for all.*
>
> *We defy the industry by being innovative in everything that we do.*
>
> *. . . you become the little rebellious white fish with us. And we're going our own way—together.*

If NCL is truly going to deliver a Freestyle experience on board, that means NCL employees must not only understand it but also embody it in their own unique way. Every employee should be able to play a role in fulfilling the promise of the brand in some way. For shipboard employees, that means their responsibility is to ensure that the guests are free to *go their own way* throughout the experience. Employees are encouraged to *just say no to no.*

Those other cruise lines say "no, you can't come into this restaurant wearing that!" *We say, "Yes, you can eat in your resort casual clothes, and the special tonight is mahi mahi."*

They say, "No, you can't dine at 4:15; you must dine next to the Plotnicks from Albany at table 8 for the 6:30 seating." *We say, "Yes, you can dine when you're good and hungry."*

When they say, "No, you can't sleep in on disembarkation day." *We say, "Yes, you can hit the gym, have brunch or read a book on deck on disembarkation day, but why don't you sleep in first, oh King of the Karaoke Bar."*

They say, "No, you can't stay longer on the beach if you want to make it back for your 6:30 seating." *We say, "Yes, you can stay longer. But you could use a little more SPF 30."*

With a very simple little booklet, we were able to communicate the brand to our employees in a way that was easy to grasp and gave clear direction on the "liberating" form of service they should be providing to guests.

Making Sure We Stood Out from the Crowd with Travel Agents

With employees on board, it was time to inspire the trade, namely, travel agents who still represent a significant amount of cruise-ship bookings. They're selling all the ships. And in many ways, the ships have similar features and services. But how NCL liberates guests to experience those features and services is what sets it apart. We didn't want that point to be lost on travel agents so we created a fun, interactive Freestyle activity book that invited them to rebel against the category with us. We wanted to make sure they appreciated what NCL had to offer the customers who walked into their travel agencies. Activities included a host of things like:

Mantra: I will help give my clients at least one week where they can do what they want, when they want, wearing whatever the heck they want. I'll help them do it with Freestyle Cruising aboard NCL.

What to Wear: Match the correct attire with the correct activity. Answer Key: There is no wrong answer.

Freestyle Vocab Scratch-off Activity: Agents were instructed to scratch off "nasty" words like Late, Work, Schedule, Rush, Conform, Regimen, Rules, Agenda, Clock; and find the Freestyle vocab underneath that included: Relax, Play, Free Will, Whatever, Whim, Carefree . . .

Watch Covers: A selection of stickers with the instruction: Since you don't need your watch on an NCL cruise, why not cover it with one of these attractive designs?

We also wanted to introduce the trade to our unique Freestyler audience so they would be able to spot Freestylers when they walked into their travel agency, sat down in front of them, and asked, *"which cruise should I take?"* In this way, we've helped the travel agent help their customers find the ship that will be perfect for them. Win-win for everyone involved.

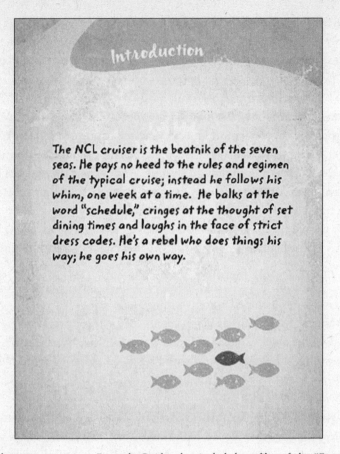

Introduction

The NCL cruiser is the beatnik of the seven seas. He pays no heed to the rules and regimen of the typical cruise; instead he follows his whim, one week at a time. He balks at the word "schedule," cringes at the thought of set dining times and laughs in the face of strict dress codes. He's a rebel who does things his way; he goes his own way.

Travel agents were given Freestyle Guides that included profiles of the "Freestyle" cruiser.

When it comes to building your brand in the market, a little creativity goes a long way. How much direct mail do you immediately pitch in the garbage? The feedback we got from travel agents was overwhelmingly positive—they understand what NCL is all about, they could explain Freestyle Cruising to their customers, and they had a fun time arriving at that understanding.

With employees and travel agents all geared up to support the *"You're free to whatever"* experience, it was time to let overworked, overstressed, overcommitted people know that they now had a vacation option that would give them the liberation they were seeking.

We knew we had to overturn perceptions of the category and clearly differentiate NCL from the rest of the pack, and we held nothing back. After all, when you're working for a company that has created something with the potential to really make a difference in the lives of their customers (even if it is just a week of being unplugged), you want to do everything in your power to make sure people take advantage of it. We had to let people know that cruising wasn't what they thought it was—and that NCL provided a unique alternative that could give them what they were looking for. To that end, we made direct comparisons between the freestyle way of life and the regimentation found on other ships with headlines like:

Dinner will be served promptly at whatever o'clock.

You must board. You must disembark. Thus ends the list of "musts."

Our dress code: Wear Something.

GOING OUR OWN WAY

When you're not the biggest spender in the category, you have to get creative to be heard. Find opportunities to communicate your message where you have no competition because no one else is advertising there. And more important, think about opportunities to make the medium reinforce the message you're trying to get across. For example, our media folks came up with the idea of creating an entirely new medium that would be an absolutely perfect place to communicate our antidress-code dress code: dry cleaner garment bags. They read: *Whatever this is, you can wear it on board.*

We also wanted to give people a taste of what we were talking about so we partnered with MonsterVision to create an interactive experience that brought the Freestyle idea to life in a really engaging way. MonsterVision created wall and floor projections that people can physically interact with. As people interact with the images, a tracking system reads their body language in real time and responds instantaneously. We created a game where baseball fans at Angel Stadium in Anaheim could smash clocks to end the tyranny of the over-scheduled life. On the other side of the country we let theatergoers at the New World Stage Theatrical Complex in Manhattan select ensembles that included everything from a blue bikini to a little black dress for virtual NCL guests to wear to dinner that evening.

Interactive experiences enable potential cruisers to get a taste of Freestyle Cruising.

How much more likely is our Freestyle message to sink in with an individual who accepts an invitation to participate physically in an activity that brings our message to life than someone who merely hears about it while sitting on their couch channel surfing?

WINNING ON PURPOSE

Some of the success of this story resides in the intangible transformation that happens when an organization shines a light on a set of values and a purpose that has been operative for a long time but never fully appreciated or clearly articulated. The focus that it brings to developing new on-board activities, features, partnership strategies; the direction it provides to thousands of on-board employees; the clarity it brings to the development of differentiating communication is really incalculable.

We began to see the marketplace understand the brand in a way that it never had before. Third-party reviewers began to tell the NCL story in a way that clearly set NCL apart from the sea of sameness in the category.

Erica Silverstein, a critic from Smartertravel.com, appealed to non-cruisers to not give up on cruising just yet. "If you've seen *The Love Boat* or *Titanic* and decided formal dinners and forced socialization are not for you, try Norwegian Cruise Line before you give up on cruising. Norwegian's 'Freestyle Cruising' concept aims to give cruisers more choices and freedom."

In another review by Matt Hannafin on Frommers.com, Norwegian Cruise Line was applauded for "not being afraid to change up the paradigm." The freestyle way of life creates "a childlike urge to jump in and play—which is pretty much exactly the effect a cruise ship should have."

In addition to this kind of third-party reinforcement that has emerged to further differentiate the brand, we have also experienced some tangible proof to the power of this purpose in the marketplace. Some of the results include:

- Twice as many first-time cruisers intend to cruise with NCL since the launch of the campaign
- Traffic to NCL.com increased over 120 percent in the first six months of the campaign
- And NCL revenue is up 15 percent

Going forward, NCL wants to measure how they are doing against truly delivering a liberating experience for their guests. If you can truly make a measurable difference in addressing the fundamental needs people have when it comes to their precious leisure time, the money will follow.

MEMBERSHIP
ORGANIZATIONS

14

HOW PURPOSE
CAN MOVE YOU FROM
DISCOUNTS TO WHAT COUNTS

*To champion positive social change that will enhance
the quality of life for all as we age.*

One of the defining moments in getting older is the day you open your mailbox and find an envelope with your name on it from AARP. While we would like to report a level of joy felt by millions of baby boomers at the opportunity to join this mighty organization, what we often witness is more akin to indifference or worse, irritation.

When you work for a membership-driven organization, it's absolutely critical that the potential members you are trying to reach have a crystal clear understanding of the purpose of your organization. What are you asking them to become a part of? What difference will it make if they join? When people join organizations—whether it's a political party, a religious denomination, or a charitable organization—those organizations contribute to one's sense of identity. It says something about what they stand for. Letting them know what you stand for is therefore essential.

When baby boomers look at that AARP envelope sitting in their mailbox, many of them only see access to some discounts that they may or may not have any use for. The only identifiable trait uniting members of AARP is age and possibly a penchant for saving money—certainly not a very strong basis for a high level of engagement with the organization. For all they know, the purpose of AARP is to secure discounts for "greedy geezers." We set out to change that.

FROM DISCOUNTS TO WHAT-COUNTS

AARP needed to reveal its true purpose in a way that would cast the organization in a new light and create a meaningful basis for a relationship with members. Uncovering AARP's purpose turned out to be less heavy excavation and more "open your eyes and see what's right in front of you." Talk to any of the leaders in the organization and the conversation quickly turns to the work they are doing to create social change that will improve the quality of life for Americans as they age.

> *AARP is an organization about social change . . .*
> —Bill Novelli, CEO and president

> *The AARP brand is built on the foundation of the collective power to make a difference. The AARP identity is defined by our ongoing actions to promote positive social change.*
> —Emilio Pardo, chief brand officer

> *AARP's most important role is to be a catalyst for creating social change . . . we need to use our power and resources in a socially responsible way to benefit the public at large.*
> —John Killpack, Director, Advocacy Resources,
> AARP government relations and advocacy

The articulation of the core purpose practically wrote itself:

To champion positive social change that will enhance the quality of life for all as we age.

Now that is a purpose with the potential to resonate with the 78 million baby boomers who would soon be receiving those AARP letters in their mailboxes. The trick was positioning the organization in a way that spoke directly to the sensibility of boomers. Successful positioning always arises from the intersection between the organizational purpose and a keen understanding of the needs and desires of the audience you are trying to serve.

MARRYING THE POWER OF THE ORGANIZATION WITH THE HEART OF ITS MEMBERS

The baby boomer generation has gone through life with an innate and committed desire to reinvent society on their terms. As they head into the over-50 segment of life, they're not going to let up. There's a lot they want to see "fixed"—not only for their own personal benefit but for the benefit of future generations as well.

As passionate as they are, they look at the magnitude of the issues that affect the quality of life as you age (Social security, health care, elder care) and recognize the need for a powerful force behind them to truly make an impact on these issues. When we enlightened them to the true purpose of AARP (championing positive social change), they began to look at AARP in a new way. They saw the potential to infuse the power and "muscle" of a huge organization with the values and "heart" of 35 million baby boomer members. Together, they had the power to make things better. And that became the positioning platform that has begun to reshape AARP as one of the most influential brands of our time.

The Power to Make It Better.

Now when baby boomers open their mailboxes and see that AARP envelope, they have begun to see an organization they want to belong to because membership represents the opportunity to make a difference in the quality of life as you age.

BRINGING IT TO LIFE

The key to delivering this message effectively lies in paying homage to the values of the boomer generation. Recognize boomers' good intentions to make a difference and then position AARP as the partner that empowers them to get the job done. In this way, AARP can become a highly relevant and valued partner in the life of its members. We close each portrayal of our members on a mission to make a difference with a line that adds firepower to their intention: *"If one person could do it alone, the world wouldn't need AARP."*

One commercial opens on a husband and wife preparing for a seemingly modest dinner party in their home. Then we see a place card being set on the table that reads, "Senator Jordan."

WIFE: Senator Jordan here. Salad on the outside, honey.
HUSBAND: OK.
The doorbell rings.
WIFE: They're here.

She walks to the front door and opens it to let in three influential politicos who take a seat at the dinner table whereupon we hear the woman address the group in a very casual manner:

WIFE: Thanks for coming to my prescription drug summit. Before we leave today, I want us to get an affordable drug benefit in Medicare. Everybody on board?
They all nod in agreement.
WIFE: Let's eat!
ANNOUNCER: If one person could do it alone, the world wouldn't need AARP. AARP. The power to make it better.

In another ad designed to address Social Security, we see an everyday guy carrying a big jar labeled "Save Social Security." We hear him shouting enthusiastically: "Help save Social Security! . . . Donate to Social Security!" We see him asking for donations at a ritzy polo match where polo enthusiasts willingly donate wads of cash to the jar. We see him at a black-tie ball where a woman takes off her huge, diamond necklace and puts it into his donation jar. We see him at an art gallery opening where the artist willingly removes a valuable painting from the wall and gives it to him. We see him knock on the window of a limo and a hand emerges with two silver candlesticks to donate to the cause. Finally, we hear a voice-over say: If one person could do it alone, the world wouldn't need AARP. AARP. The power to make it better.

KNOWING WHAT REALLY MAKES A DIFFERENCE CAN MAKE ALL THE DIFFERENCE

If you are an organization that has a mighty and ambitious purpose, understanding the priority issues that will ultimately make the greatest difference to the overall purpose of your organization is absolutely critical. It enables you to build credibility among the audience you are trying to serve while building momentum around the purpose of your organization. When your purpose is very ambitious, as is AARP's, tackling high-profile, marquee issues can provide powerful, tangible proof to the purpose. Social Security is one of those issues for AARP. Social Security is the lynchpin to a good quality of life for millions of elderly Americans. So it has been one of the issues we have tackled that has helped cement AARP as a powerful and relevant brand in the lives of its members.

In 2005, the Bush administration began to push for the establishment of private accounts where the contributions of each worker would be managed by the individual as a solution for Social Security solvency. The establishment of these private accounts would require that money be taken out of the existing Social Security surplus or funded through additional debt—at a cost estimated at *$2 trillion* ($2,000,000,000,000). With companies reducing pensions, healthcare costs rising and personal savings rates at an all-time low, Social Security's stable, defined benefit has become the primary source of retirement income for most Americans. Jeopardizing this increasingly important source of retirement income would have dire consequences on the financial stability and quality of life of millions of retiring citizens.

While there are many solutions that need to be considered to fix this complex system, the privatization of Social Security was akin to tearing down a house to fix the kitchen sink. And that's the message that AARP voiced in the marketplace to combat this approach that could have jeopardized millions of aging Americans.

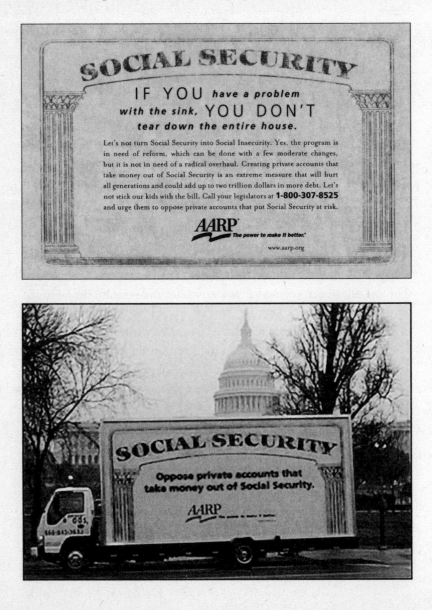

We surrounded Beltway influentials with messages like: *Private accounts would turn Social Security into Social Insecurity,* and *Oppose private accounts that take money out of Social Security.*

We also wanted to communicate that the move toward privatizing accounts hurt not only those in retirement, but also the generations to come.

A PURPOSE-BASED WIN

This campaign was cited as one of the contributing factors to the abandonment of the push for private accounts by the administration. In a postmortem by Social Security overhaul proponents (as reported in CQ (Congressional Quarterly) Today on February 24, 2006):

> *"The opposition was far more aggressive than the White House anticipated it to be."*
>
> *During the meeting, participants watched a recording of a now-famous television ad AARP produced that likened Bush's Social Security proposal to tearing down a house in order to fix a clogged sink.*
>
> *"The impact of that ad during the debate was so pronounced,"* a participant said.
>
> **"AARP, they kicked our butts, basically."**

WINNING ON PURPOSE

Since we began building the brand based on the purpose of the organization, we've seen key brand measures of familiarity, favorability, and relevance increase, as well as membership engagement measures like "intent to join" and "intent to renew" trend upward. Consequently, membership has grown by over 2.5 million individuals and is nearing the 40-million-member mark.

But the ultimate measure of success for AARP lies in their ability to create positive social change that improves the quality of life as the population ages. Day in and day out the organization helps make meaningful progress in improving Social Security and lifetime financial security. They help in the development of antiage discrimination practices in the workplace. They work with state and federal legislators to protect citizens from predatory lending practices and they help to secure affordable, reliable utilities for the elderly in need. They advocate for affordable health-care coverage for all. And they pioneer thinking in the area of livable communities uniquely designed around the needs of an aging population.

True purpose-based organizations look at the difference they make in the world as the ultimate measure of their success.

NONPROFIT
ORGANIZATIONS

15

HOW PURPOSE
CAN CREATE COMMON GROUND
ON HIGHER GROUND

Empowering people in America to perform
extraordinary acts in the face of emergency situations.

You might wonder why a nonprofit, philanthropic organization whose only function is to make a positive difference in the world would need to go through the process of discovering their purpose. Shouldn't their purpose be obvious? Especially if the organization is one of America's most trusted, most recognized, and most supported philanthropic organizations? Well, if you work for an organization that has multiple lines of business, all seemingly different and yet equally important to the people impacted by those services, you might be able to empathize with the challenge faced by the American Red Cross.

When your house is seemingly divided, it's hard to stand on solid ground. A large part of our work with the American Red Cross has been finding the common ground upon which all lines of service can be built. In so doing, we can help create a brand that is greater than the sum of its parts. If you're working in an organization with numerous business units operating in silos, you might think that coming up with a common, unified purpose is an impossible task. I am happy to tell you that there might be far more common ground than you think.

THE SEARCH FOR COMMON GROUND

Currently, the American Red Cross has about five core lines of service:

- **Disaster Relief:** they respond to more than seventy thousand disasters, including house or apartment fires, hurricanes, floods, earthquakes, tornadoes, hazardous materials spills, transportation accidents, explosions, and other natural and man-made disasters.
- **Preparedness Health and Safety Services:** they teach citizens to be prepared for emergencies by assisting people in creating an emergency kit, making a plan, and being informed about appropriate steps to take. They prepare people to save lives through health and safety education and training. They help citizens with everything from first aid and CPR to swimming and lifeguarding.
- **International Services:** They help vulnerable people around the world prevent, prepare for, and respond to disasters, complex humanitarian emergencies, and life-threatening health conditions.
- **Biomedical:** they collect nearly half of the nation's blood supply.
- **Services to Armed Forces:** They send communication on behalf of family members who are facing emergencies or other important events to members of the U.S. Armed Forces serving all over the world.

With all these services supported by the Red Cross, it was becoming increasingly difficult for people in the organization to answer the seemingly simple question: *What is the purpose of the American Red Cross?*

If you were to try to answer that question from the "lines of service" perspective, you might hear five very different answers. And if you assembled the leaders from each one of those divisions into a room together to talk about the American Red Cross brand overall, you might find great difficulty arriving at a definition that everyone could embrace. You might end up developing individual marketing campaigns to support each business unit and, in the process, miss out on the opportunity to build a very powerful brand that is more than the sum of the parts. And that's exactly what was happening.

Our job was to dig deep into each one of these lines of service and uncover the common ground that could transcend the specific line of service and explain the overarching purpose of the American Red Cross.

DISCOVERING THE CORE PURPOSE
OF THE AMERICAN RED CROSS

To discover your core purpose, you have to understand the difference that you make in the lives of the people whom you serve. The American Red Cross is unique because it makes a difference not only in the life of the person receiving the help, but also in the life of the individual who provides aid to someone in dire need of assistance.

Let's start with a look at the more obvious beneficiary—the people in the midst of a dire emergency. We learned that no matter what line of service we're talking about, the American Red Cross makes a difference by transforming a life in some form of crisis to a life with some form of hope. That hope can come in many forms depending on the service—life-sustaining blood, a shoulder to cry on, short-term resources, or critical information—but all offer some form of substantive help that empowers the individuals to carry on. All these lines of service have an almost immediate and obvious transformative effect on the beneficiary.

But more enlightening was the transformative effect that the American Red Cross had in the life of the *donor*. When we talked to the people who had stepped up to write checks, donate blood, take a course, volunteer, or prepare for an emergency, we discovered another powerful transformation occurring:

- The act of writing a check to help a life in crisis transformed the donor from a passive/apathetic individual to an empowered/compassionate humanitarian.
- The act of donating blood—literally giving a piece of your life away—transformed someone from an average individual to a potential life-saving hero.
- The act of preparing for a disaster transformed people from average householders to responsible parents and citizens capable of protecting loved ones.
- The act of getting trained in CPR or first aid transformed a person from a passive observer of an emergency situation to an empowered lifesaver.

The idea of transforming individuals from *ordinary Joes* to *extraordinary heroes* was and is a very powerful idea. At the end of the day, people have an innate desire to demonstrate their humanity—their worthiness as a human being. They want to step up to the plate when called upon and deliver help to those in need. The revelation in understanding this transformation is that the relevance of the American Red Cross is rooted more in the ability to facilitate humanitarian instincts than it is in providing any particular line of service.

What makes the American Red Cross such a beloved and relevant organization is that it facilitates this humanitarian instinct by empowering individuals to make a difference in the lives of people who are in some form of crisis. It is not so much *how* they do it but *that* they do it that matters.

And this bodes well for the organization, especially from the perspective of more efficient and effective communication. We could waste a lot of money trying to make people care about the lines of service that the Red Cross is engaged in. But people don't wake up thinking about natural disasters or the nation's blood supply. They do, however, care about being good human beings. They want to go to bed at night knowing that they did their part to use their talents, gifts, and resources to make a difference in the world. With this understanding, the lines of service merely become the ways in which people can make a difference—they are a means to a much nobler end. They can change over time (and have) in response to the emergencies facing the public.

At this point you might be saying, "well, that's a great insight about human motivation but why can the Red Cross serve that need better than any other philanthropic organization?" There are two unique aspects of the organization that answer the question.

The Nature *of High-Impact* Emergency Situations Provides a Gratifying Experience

The American Red Cross is inextricably associated with emergency situations, which the public defines as any situation that meets one or more of the following criteria:

- Requires an immediate response
- has an element of immediacy *(or else)*
- a moment when circumstances exceed preparations
- near impossible for an individual to handle on his or her own
- is life altering (a life is impacted in a dramatic way)
- potentially a life-or-death situation

Compared with ongoing societal issues upon which many organizations can spend a lifetime attempting to make headway, the American Red Cross deals with emergency situations that demand immediate action and, consequently, provide immediate gratification—for all parties involved. People like seeing the difference they made—a life is saved, a family is sheltered, a heart attack victim is saved, a military family is reunited. There is no question of "making progress." This is a critical appeal of the American Red Cross in a world where people can be easily overwhelmed at the prospects of making progress on issues that may take a lifetime to solve.

The American Red Cross Provides More Opportunities for Fulfilling Humanitarian Instincts in *Highly Visible, Highly Personal* Ways over the Course of a Lifetime

The vast majority (70 percent to 90 percent) of engagement with charitable organizations involves check writing to aid in a cause where you may never have a sense of the difference that was made by your contribution. When you write a check to the American Red Cross, however, you can turn on CNN and visibly see that money being used to help someone in the midst of a disaster. *When I see the Red Cross truck pull up and starting passing out water and blankets, I feel like I'm the one that put that blanket around their shoulder.—American Red Cross financial donor*

But beyond check writing, the American Red Cross provides people with a lifetime of options through which they can express their humanitarian instincts. Whether you're taking a class, giving blood, getting prepared, volunteering, or writing a check, you're expressing your desire to be ready to make a difference in the event that an emergency strikes.

If you're a mother of three with no time to volunteer, you can go online at night and learn how to prepare your home for an emergency. If you're a college kid short of money, you can give blood. If you can spend two days learning CPR, you can be ready to save a life if anyone ever needs you. Whatever life situation you happen to be in, the American Red Cross will have some opportunity for you to express your humanitarian instincts and make a difference in the life of someone in crisis.

Given the similar transformation we witnessed in each line of business and the new understanding of the difference the organization makes in the lives of *all* people touched by the organization, we determined that the ultimate purpose of the American Red Cross is:

> *Empowering people in America to perform extraordinary acts in the face of emergency situations.*

ACTIVATING THE PURPOSE THROUGH POWERFUL POSITIONING

The next question we had to answer was: *How do we activate it in the marketplace? How do we position the organization in the most effective manner to drive people to give their time, money, or blood?*

To answer that question effectively, we have to understand what's keeping people from taking action presently. Unfortunately, when they seek channels for their altruism, they often feel like they can't make a meaningful difference. Most organizations just want their money, and most donors don't have a lot of faith that their donations will make much of a difference.

However, the American Red Cross gives people a direct sense of making a difference because of the high-impact, high-visibility, direct nature of the work. Both parties lives are enhanced by the interaction: you give blood/a life is saved; you donate/a life gets back on its feet; you prepare/your family is kept safe; you get trained/an individual gets saved—making the life-changing, transformative nature of an interaction with the American Red Cross the first key to effectively positioning the brand and driving action.

We also found that there was an unintended consequence of complacency when a philanthropic organization takes too much credit for the good deeds done by the organization. It leaves people feeling that "the organization" will take care of it. One of the most remarkable aspects of the American Red Cross is the volunteer army that makes it run. If ordinary people do not rise to the occasion to help those in the midst of a crisis, the work of the American Red Cross will not get done.

With that in mind, we developed the following positioning strategy:

Be part of a life-changing experience. When emergency strikes, lives can suddenly take a different path. When you rise to meet the challenge, everyone's life begins changing for the better.

BRINGING IT TO LIFE

By recognizing that the American Red Cross is a conduit for the humanitarian instincts of the volunteers and donors, the communication between the organization and its constituents immediately began to change. The Red Cross shifted its narrative from a 'look what we're doing" to "look what you've done." The messaging expanded to include not only the difference that was being made in the lives of Red Cross beneficiaries, but also the difference that was made in the life of the donor or volunteer.

Sometimes this kind of not-so-subtle change in tone can make a significant difference in the quality of engagement with your constituents. Consider the following "One Minute Update," the monthly e-mail newsletter from the American Red Cross:

E-Mail Update
Subject: Have Pride in Your Life-Giving Work • One Minute Update • February 2008

> You Make a Living by what you Get, But you make a life . . .
> by what you Give!   —Sir Winston Churchill

Dear Haley,
Every day at the American Red Cross we are privileged to witness the truth of Churchill's stirring words. In a society, where so many are focused on what they get, I am proud of the volunteers at the Red Cross who focus on what they give. And what they give is truly life giving:

- Blood
- Shelter
- Clean Water
- CPR
- Aid to the Military and their Families

The miracle of giving is that when we give these basic necessities of life to another human being, we receive a gift too . . . the gift of life! What we give comes back to us 100 fold . . . what goes around comes around. We receive the benefits of our own giving in the joy we see in the renewed lives of people in need whose lives were saved by our gift.

These are challenging times at the Red Cross and in our troubled and broken world where natural disaster and violence occur every day. This is a time for all of us to step up and give the gift of life . . . and in so doing, we receive life ourselves! Thank you for your incredible generosity to the Red Cross. As you continue to give time, dollars and the necessities of life to others, may you discover the truth of Churchill's words: "You make a living by what you get . . . but you make a life by what you give."

With pride in your life-giving work,

Bonnie McElveen-Hunter
Chairman of the Board, American Red Cross

This letter eloquently captures the desire for a life well lived that drives donor and volunteer involvement across all lines of service. If you lead a membership organization, does the communication you send to your members speak to their needs—or yours? Do you fundamentally understand their attraction to your organization? By recognizing how your organization is uniquely suited to fulfill deep-seated needs of your members, you can begin to develop relationships with them that are much more rewarding for everyone involved.

CHANGE A LIFE, STARTING WITH YOUR OWN

The purpose and the positioning provided a home for all the various lines of service to "live in." Working together, they tell a much more intriguing and compelling story of the American Red Cross than any one of them could accomplish alone.

Each piece of communication is designed to celebrate the actions taken by ordinary individuals that made a big difference in the lives of others. Each piece of communication closes with an affirmation of the transformative effect on both individuals: *Change a life, starting with your own.* We invite people to explore "life-changing opportunities" at the American Red Cross—giving them the freedom to find the right opportunity to express their humanitarian nature among any line of business that suits their situation or interest.

Yvonne donates
to give back.

When Roger lost everything,
she gave him back his hope.

Give to the Red Cross and change a life, starting with your own.
Call 1-800-RED CROSS or visit redcross.org.

American Red Cross

H20400

The American Red Cross gives people a direct sense of making a difference because of the high-impact, high-visibility, direct nature of the work. This campaign demonstrates how both lives are enhanced by the interaction.

Natassia gives blood to feel like she's making a difference.

Josh is living proof that she is.

Donate blood today and change a life, starting with your own.
Call 1-800-GIVE LIFE or visit givelife.org.

American Red Cross

H20396

WINNING ON PURPOSE

Finding the common ground upon which all lines of Red Cross service could build was rewarding for us and productive for them. Now we are helping to create a brand that is more vital to its constituents and truly greater than the sum of its parts.

The ultimate measure of success will be to track an increase in the number of people engaging in humanitarian action through the American Red Cross. We want to see a world where we turn "good intentions" into meaningful action. We want to see the American Red Cross become the partner that empowers people with the know-how and the wherewithal to stretch their humanitarian muscles and make a difference.

16

HOW PURPOSE

IS ACTIVATED

THROUGH INSIGHT

*Building a world where young people
reject tobacco and anyone can quit.*

If you work for a nonprofit organization, you probably have a very clear understanding of what you're fighting for and the difference you're trying to make in the world. What you often need to focus on is the psychology of the audience you need to influence. What do they believe and how does that detract from the fulfillment of your purpose? By being crystal clear about the problem that stands in the way of fulfilling the purpose of the organization, you can focus all your energy on developing relevant solutions that get at the heart of the problem.

The American Legacy Foundation was established in 1999—the result of the master settlement agreement with the tobacco industry (the largest civil litigation settlement in U.S. history). Tobacco companies agreed to pay forty-six states and five U.S. territories billions of dollars in yearly installments to compensate them for taxpayer money that was spent on patients and family members with tobacco-related diseases. The agreement also created and funded the American Legacy

Foundation whose core purpose is *to build a world where young people reject tobacco and anyone can quit.*

We were tasked with helping the foundation fulfill the latter part of its purpose: *building a world where anyone can quit.*

The question became what could we do to break an addiction so strong that less than 5 percent of smokers are able to successfully quit smoking in any given year.

FROM THE LAND OF FUTILITY
TO THE LAND OF POSSIBILITY

Nonprofit organizations are often tasked with trying to make a difference in areas in which making a difference can seem impossible. Without a keen understanding of the audience you are trying to serve and the will to do whatever it takes to address the real issues affecting progress, fulfilling the purpose of the organization can feel like an exercise in futility.

We see nonprofit organizations with the most noble and worthy purposes you can imagine stuck in the land of futility because they haven't positioned themselves in a way that addresses the true barriers to progress. Often they develop work that's preaching to the choir. Think of all the antilitter campaigns you've seen over the years. Crying Indians. Give a hoot don't pollute. Keep [such-and-such town] Beautiful. These campaigns make people who don't litter feel great and have no impact on the people throwing fast-food bags out their window on the highway. *Don't Mess with Texas* came at this issue based on an understanding of the psychology of the audience we were trying to reach. We tapped into the pride of Texans, not the idealism of environmentalists. You have to see the world through the eyes of the people whose behavior you are trying to affect. That's what we did with smokers to help fulfill the purpose of the American Legacy Foundation.

WHAT'S PREVENTING PROGRESS?

There is a long history of campaigns that have alerted smokers to the fact that smoking is dangerous. The vast majority of smokers are well aware of the consequences of smoking. In fact, 70 percent of smokers want to quit and a full 41 percent will attempt to quit in the coming year. But sadly, only about 5 percent of them will quit successfully. The rest will fail in their attempt—usually in the first seventy-two hours.

What's going on? Why the enormous gap between the intention to quit and successfully quitting? The answer to that question would become the foundation for creating a solution that could begin to fulfill the purpose of the organization.

When we talked to smokers who were planning to quit and asked them how they were going to approach it, their response revealed the root of the problem: "cold turkey." Most smokers were going to rely on "sheer willpower" to quit an addiction that's been a fundamental part of their lives for years. They're physically, socially, behaviorally, and psychologically addicted to a drug as addictive as heroin or cocaine. Everything from the coffee they drink in the morning, to stress relief in times of trouble, to socializing with friends, talking on the phone, and finishing a meal is linked to smoking. It is highly unlikely that people will be able to *will* themselves through an addiction this powerful.

Studies have proven that smokers are more successful in their quit attempts when they analyze where they are likely to get tripped up and then develop strategies to cope with those situations. It became clear that in order to *build a world where anyone can quit,* we needed to create a smoking cessation system that would help people through the process of recognizing and overcoming the triggers most likely to sabotage their quit attempt(s).

We created such a system and we branded it EX. We positioned EX based on the insight that preparation leads to success. If we can get people to take stock of why they smoke, we can prepare them to relearn life without cigarettes.

BRINGING IT TO LIFE

A Day in the Life of a Smoker

If you truly want to make a difference in the lives of a particular audience, you have to walk a mile in their shoes. You have to know where to reach them when it counts. That's the only way you can ever be invited into their lives and stand any real chance of making progress. Thinking through a day in the life of a member of your target market can provide you with more insight about how to effectively reach your audience than all the "new media" seminars in the world. And that's just what we did to develop our creative and media strategy for this effort.

It's 7:00 A.M. Our smoker wakes up in the morning and prepares to have a cigarette with the morning coffee. He turns on the Weather Channel to see what his day will look like and the following commercial appears:

> A man falls out of his bed on to the floor, attempts to cook an egg without a pan, and puts his pants on backwards. We hear a voice-over that says: *When you're used to always doing something with a cigarette, it can be hard doing it without one. But if you can relearn how to start your day without cigarettes, then you can relearn to do anything without cigarettes. Introducing EX—a new way to think about quitting.*

The commercial caught his attention because he usually does spend much of his morning getting ready with a cigarette in hand, but he's never really thought about it as a fundamental part of his morning ritual.

It's 8:00 A.M. and on his way into work, he stops for coffee—and a cigarette—to help keep his energy up for the day. When he reaches for his cup of coffee, he sees a sleeve around the coffee cup that reads:

A coffee cup wrapped with this message reaches someone during a highly influential moment.

The sleeve reinforces the idea that coffee is a trigger and asks him to make a note of other morning triggers right on the coffee sleeve. It also invites him to visit BecomeAnEX.org to learn ways to relearn how to do these things without smoking.

At noon, he decides to grab a quick sandwich at a food truck emblazoned with a message that highlights how likely he is to reach for a smoke after he finishes the meal he's about to eat.

Hi, I'm lunch. First I'll make you full. Then I'll make you want to smoke.

re-learn **eating meals** without cigarettes. re-learn **anything** without cigarettes.

ex

BecomeAnEX.org

A food truck emblazoned with this message serves as a reminder for smokers to be aware of their triggers.

It's 3:30 P.M. It's time for the afternoon smoke break. He heads for the elevator to take him down to the main floor where he'll head outside to the sidewalk for his smoke. But on his ride down, he'll notice the elevator TV screen and find a message that reads: "Hi, I'm either taking you up to work or back down to freedom. Either way, I make you want to smoke. Learn more at BecomeAnEX.org." He chuckles to himself, knowing he is just about to light up with his "afternoon break" cigarette. EX has him pegged.

It's 3:35 P.M. When he gets to the street, he notices an interesting billboard that asks him to vote with his cigarette butt for the most compelling trigger in his life: drinking, big meals, coffee, driving, or sex. Looks like driving has the most "votes," which brings us to our next trigger.

It's 5:30 P.M. and he's driving home. He's listening to the radio, window rolled down to let the smoke out of the car, when he hears the following radio commercial that plays sound effects from everyday life moments accompanied by short bursts of a pop music chorus singing about the triggers that each moment represents:

SFX: Subway train going down tracks.
SINGER: Train is packed and stinky!
BACK UP: Makin' you want to smoke!
SFX: A lady on her cell phone talking loudly about herself.
SINGER: Annoying lady!
BACK UP: Makin' you want to smoke!
SFX: Sports on TV.
SINGER: Your team lost to a bad team!
SFX: Doorbell.
SINGER: Eight kinds of meat on a pizza!
SFX: A bed squeak.
SINGER: Afternoon deligh-hight!
BACK UP: Makin' you want to smoke!
ANNOUNCER: Learn what makes you smoke, and you can re-learn life without cigarettes. You can do it at BecomeAnEX .org.

It's 8:00 P.M. and he's back home. He turns on ESPN's *Sports Center* to get caught up on the latest highlights as the analysts discuss the EX "Play of the Day." They show a basketball play and explain how practice and preparation always help the team succeed. They go on to explain that it's the same when you're trying to quit smoking. That's something he hadn't thought of before and it's really starting to sink in. He's had plenty of failed attempts in the past—but hadn't thought about preparing to quit. He decides to log on to BecomeAnEX.org to learn more.

RETHINKING PLUS RELEARNING

Getting people to rethink the process of quitting is no small task. To help achieve that goal, we created a brochure that expanded upon the ideas we tested throughout our mass marketing. The brochure provided more substantive information on the quit process and all the triggers the smoker needed to consider in order to quit successfully.

While the advertising and the brochure help smokers rethink what quitting entails, our Web site provides the tools and know-how to relearn life without cigarettes. BecomeAnEX.org is more than a Web site. It is an online personal quit plan. It's a base where users find resources, information, and tools to relearn life without cigarettes. It's based on the idea of "learning and doing"—it presents facts and information so that users can learn how to quit smoking, and then it provides them with exercises where they can utilize their new knowledge in real-life situations.

The site gets smokers thinking about quitting in a holistic way by addressing the behavioral, physical, and social factors related to addiction. There is a cigarette tracker tool that helps smokers identify when and why they smoke each cigarette throughout the day along with tips for separating each activity from the act of smoking. There is a section on the physical nature of addiction that provides the most up-to-date information on the use of medication and nicotine replacement therapies, which when used correctly can double the chances of success. There is a section on social support that connects smokers with other smokers struggling to quit as well as to ex-smokers who can provide compassionate support and advice.

This site has the power to transform the seemingly impossible process of quitting—of relearning life without cigarettes—into something possible and fulfill the purpose of the organization in the process.

WINNING ON PURPOSE

The American Legacy Foundation only has one true measure of success when it comes to cessation: increasing the number of successful quit attempts. We want to see more people entering the quit process with a game plan—prepared to face all the triggers and challenges that stand ready to sabotage even the best intentions.

Excerpt from EX brochure that smokers receive to help them relearn life without cigarettes.

HIGHER EDUCATION

SOLUTIONSFOROURFUTURE.org

HOW PURPOSE
CAN CREATE
A GRASSROOTS MOVEMENT

*To transform lives for the betterment of society.
One student, one discovery at a time.*

I can't tell you how many purpose projects we've engaged in that began with the warning: *"You'll never be able to find a purpose that all of our various players will be able to agree to."* The good news: There's a lot of common ground on higher ground. The further you go to understand the difference that you make, the more likely you are to find agreement on the ultimate purpose of the organization—a purpose where all can find a role to play.

The American Council on Education (ACE) is essentially the trade association for all of higher education. They have over eighteen hundred college and university members—from Ivy Leagues to community colleges, small liberal arts colleges to massive research universities. ACE was interested in figuring out a way to develop broad-based public support for government funding of higher education. Why?

Support for higher education in America hasn't kept pace with the rest of the world. While we've maintained the status quo, the rest of the world has been significantly increasing their level of investment in higher education. As a result, among OECD[1] countries, the U.S. has slipped to sixteenth in high school graduation rates, ninth in postsecondary enrollments, and twelfth in college completions. We've seen college tuitions rise by more than 65 percent over the past decade (largely in response to cuts in state appropriations) while median family income has risen by only 5 percent, making college affordability for the next generation of Americans a growing problem.

Bob Utley, chairman of the board for Inland American Communities Group and an advocate for higher education, is on a personal crusade to strengthen America's educational system. He introduced our firm to ACE and asked us to tackle the following question: How can we increase public support for higher education?

The only way to develop a broad base of public support for higher education was to speak to the market with one powerful voice explaining the difference that higher education made to society at large. To have eighteen hundred institutions promoting their unique benefits to the world might help with individual enrollment goals, but it wouldn't help create a clear and compelling case with enough firepower to make higher education a top priority on the nation's agenda.

When we first proposed the idea of developing a unifying purpose for higher education, we were met with a great deal of skepticism and in some cases downright reluctance at the thought of developing a purpose that hundreds of colleges and universities would have to share. How in the world could an Ivy League university and a local community college possibly share a similar purpose? When you stop focusing on the differences that exist between institutions (and there are many) and start focusing on the difference that they make, finding common ground moves from the realm of the impossible to the possible.

FROM ME TO WE:
THE PATH FROM PERSONAL BENEFIT TO COLLECTIVE GOOD

Our research among the mainstream public quickly revealed that no one in America is not "for" higher education. Why would you possibly be against it? The question is: Who should pay for it? For decades, the idea that higher education leads to higher income and a higher quality of life for the individual has led millions of parents to struggle and do whatever it takes to send their kids to college and live the American dream. And four-year college graduates do, in fact, earn an average of about 60 percent more than high school graduates in similar demographic groups. If that individual benefits, then—the thinking goes—that individual should have to pay for it.

The public is very well aware of the high rate of return for the individual who receives the education. What they don't understand is the high rate of return for society—a rate of return that would suggest everyone has a personal stake in higher education.

When we asked Americans what they cared about most—specifically in terms of what issues they wanted to see their tax dollars address—they cited a host of issues including a strong economy, job security, health care, crime, terrorism, energy solutions, poverty, and homelessness, among others. What they didn't realize was that higher education was inextricably linked to solutions for almost every one of the issues they cared about.

When it comes to the economy, colleges and universities are an engine for economic growth in the United States. It has been estimated that increasing the country's average level of schooling by one year could increase economic growth by 6 to 15 percent, adding between 600 billion to 1.5 trillion to U.S. economic output.

Colleges and universities are also home to the laboratories and research centers that generate the scientific and technological advances that have fueled the U.S. economy and been the source for innovations in medicine, business, national security, environmental quality, and many other fields.

University-based research has led to breakthroughs that the general public benefits from on a daily basis—things like Internet search engines, overnight delivery, long-term kidney dialysis, birth control devices, laser eye surgery, child-proof safety caps, and the digital signal processing that's used in everything from cell phones to medical diagnosis equipment.

Our colleges and universities teach students how to learn and think critically, and they prepare citizens to solve the problems that our country faces. Whether it's a community college training a first responder, a research university cracking the code on cancer, a small liberal arts school cultivating critical thinking skills, or a public university teaching the founder of the next high-tech company that might change the way we work, higher education is responsible for producing solutions that benefit everyone.

Every student passing through the halls of higher education has the potential to undergo some form of transformation for the betterment of society. Be it self-sufficiency, critical thinking, or civic engagement, the outcome does in some way, shape, or form affect everyone.

To that end, we articulated the core purpose of higher education as:

Transforming lives for the betterment of society.
One student. One discovery at a time.

Contrary to all initial concerns, all the constituents on the ACE council were able to see how their institution fulfilled the promise of this purpose in some meaningful way. With the internal constituents aligned, we translated that purpose into a positioning platform that would be most relevant to the general public—who needed to be transformed from passive supporters to active advocates of higher education.

Solutions for Our Future

Higher education is a source of solutions to our most pressing problems. We all benefit from what colleges and universities do to prepare the people who solve the problems and teach the people who change the world.

BRINGING IT TO LIFE

Think about advertising that you've seen for higher education. I'm guessing that a montage of students holding beakers in a laboratory, carrying books across a pristine campus, and smiling from ear to ear donning a cap and gown comes to mind. To build a brand for higher education that was relevant to the general public, we needed to get off campus and into the lives of everyday Americans who don't realize how those beakers and books and caps and gowns translate into solutions that they benefit from everyday.

People say they're worried about crime. We open on a 911 dispatcher taking an emergency call.

HOMEOWNER: Someone's trying to break into my house!

911 OPERATOR: Sorry ma'am, our local community college had its budget cut, so we're a little short on police at the moment . . . do you happen to have a rolling pin or a golf club?

HOMEOWNER: No! (We see her husband sheepishly holding a flimsy squash racket.)

911 OPERATOR: Know any kicks or pressure holds? How about jujitsu?

HOMEOWNER: Jujitsu?!

VOICE-OVER: Less support for higher education means fewer trained police. Eighty-three percent of first responders are trained in community colleges.

911 OPERATOR: Are you limber? Can you run?

VOICE-OVER: America's colleges and universities. We teach the people who solve the problems and change the world. For ways to help, visit solutionsforourfuture.org.

People say they're worried about health care and finding cures for the diseases that affect themselves and their family members. We open in a modern emergency room. An EMT wheels in a man on a gurney whose hand is stuck in a pickle jar.

NURSE: We got a 63-year-old male, hand stuck in a pickle jar.

DOCTOR: This man needs bloodletting, stat.

NURSE: Right away!

We see a room somewhere else in the hospital where a doctor is examining a patient with a group of residents.

DOCTOR: Cough. Lightheaded. What would you prescribe?

RESIDENT: Bloodletting?

DOCTOR: Bloodletting. Very good.

We see a ward full of incredibly pale patients as a resident
   wheels out a cart with countless pints of blood. A doctor ex-
   amines a patient's broken leg:

DOCTOR: Still broken. Take six more pints.

VOICE-OVER: Less support for higher education means fewer
   medical breakthroughs. Open-heart surgery and other ad-
   vancements came from colleges and universities. America's
   colleges and universities. We teach the people who solve the
   problems and change the world.

People say they're worried about America remaining a leader in innovation. We created another ad that shows a woman walking into a
neighborhood mail center to have a package shipped and then see the
employee take the package to a loading dock, remove a pigeon from a
cage, and try to shoo it toward Sacramento. It ends with the reminder: Less support for higher education means fewer innovations
like FedEx and the Google search engine.

CREATING A GRASSROOTS MOVEMENT

Every single college and university in America develops communications to build its brand in some way, shape, or form. We realized that
if we could seed the idea of *Solutions for our Future* into thousands of
communications plans across America, we could radically expand the
power of the idea and extend the life of the campaign indefinitely.

To that end, www.solutionsforourfuture.org was developed to
provide college and university communicators with a plan for incor-
porating the *Solutions for Our Future* message into their existing
communications channels—admissions, orientation, and student life
materials; Web sites and e-letters; faculty/staff publications, alumni
magazines, and newsletters; parent and alumni association communications and events; business advisory council meetings; and outreach
activities.

The more seamlessly they could incorporate the idea of solutions into their existing materials, the better. When you're trying to develop a grassroots effort with over three thousand plus colleges and universities throughout the country, you really want to keep the "to do's" to a minimum or it's unlikely people will bother to adopt the program.

To that end, the Web site provides a very simple toolkit filled with key talking points and communication strategies designed for easy implementation. We encouraged communication strategists to tell the stories of the solutions coming out of their campus, to weave it into the speeches and presentations of presidents and chancellors who routinely address large groups, to create a solutions page on their institutional Web site, and to invite students, faculty, and alumni to contribute solution stories to their site.

The solutionsforourfuture.org site also serves as a repository of solution stories from hundreds of colleges and universities across the country—stories that are shared through a weekly e-newsletter that highlights the newest and most notable solutions coming out of higher education.

WINNING ON PURPOSE

We knew the campaign had taken root when we began to see headlines like: *Northeastern Solving Real-Life Problems, University of Minnesota Scientist Makes Key Cancer Gene Discovery, College Offers Opportunity for Former Criminals to Turn Their Lives Around.*

College and university administrators and communicators have begun looking at the work of their institutions through the lens of solutions. As a result, the public is beginning to understand how supporting higher education will ultimately benefit everyone—not just the individual student.

Prior to this campaign there was no national, unified voice building support for higher education. Today, hundreds of colleges and universities have adopted the language of *Solutions*. The general public is beginning to recognize the value of higher education beyond personal opportunity and we see higher education becoming a greater priority on the national agenda.

18

HOW PURPOSE
CAN EXPLAIN
THE UNEXPLAINABLE

*To develop leaders of character
dedicated to serving the greater good.*

There is a saying at Texas A&M: *From the outside looking in, you can't understand it. From the inside looking out, you can't explain it.* This saying has been uttered for decades with a certain amount of pride—inspired by the unique culture that you encounter when you step foot in "Aggieland" that is like nothing you'll experience on any other college campus.

Dr. Robert Gates, previously the president of Texas A&M and now secretary of defense, was involved with the *Solutions for Our Future* effort and believed that if we could explain higher education in a way that would rally America, we could certainly explain Texas A&M to the constituents it needed to reach: prospective/current/former students, parents, and corporate recruiters.

Having established that higher education was really in the solutions business, we approached Texas A&M with the central question: *What solution is Texas A&M delivering to the world? How do traditions*

*like Silver Taps, Muster, the 12th Man, Midnight Yell, Fish Camp, Big
Event, and the famous Aggie Ring (to name but a few) transform students for the betterment of society?* When we spoke with the com-
mandant of the Corps of Cadets, LTG John Van Alstyne, he told us:
*"The great enduring traditions of Texas A&M teach the values of loy-
alty, service, and helping one another through direct experience."*
Other leaders explained the traditions this way: *"I view our Aggie
traditions as one of the ways Aggies pass on our core values from
class to class and generation to generation. Aggie Bonfire taught
the value of teamwork. 12th man taught the value of commitment.
Fish Camp taught the value reaching out and serving others."* The
commitment to Aggie traditions, Aggie spirit, and participation in
student-led organization has led many students to value what's
known as "the other education" (e.g., the values-driven education
that's received outside the classroom) as much as they do the academic training they receive at Texas A&M. This other education is actively cultivated, celebrated, and sets Texas A&M in stark contrast
with many other "values-neutral" institutions.

> *It's very unique for a university to espouse a set of values. You
> won't find many University Presidents saying they're here to build
> character, loyalty or integrity. . . . [So, why do we it?] Our society is
> increasingly 'what's in it for me?' . . . Texas A&M stands for the
> opposite. We can band together and do good things for society.*
> —Dr. Gates, former president of Texas A&M

It became very clear to us that the people of Texas A&M were incredibly passionate about cultivating people of character and values
with an orientation toward serving the greater good.

Is this a solution that America needs? Millennials (the generation
A&M needs to recruit), the general public, and the corporate recruiters seem to think so. In contrast to the "me generations" that
have come before them, the millennials have a service orientation and
a desire to restore values, character, and civic-mindedness in America.
While they certainly want to go on to do well and make money,
they're equally interested in exploring ways to make a difference.

When we talked with corporate recruiters from Fortune 100 companies, they too expressed a desire for colleges and universities to produce not only competent, educated individuals but also individuals with leadership skills, a sense of responsibility, a team orientation, and a code of ethics. One recruiter told us that he routinely recruited from Texas A&M for the character of the applicants: *"If everyone wore an Aggie Ring, we'd never have to do background checks."* That insight actually became a headline in one of our print ads.

And then we asked the general public, *What are the most important roles that a university can play in contributing to the overall health and vitality of our nation?* Not surprisingly, "academic excellence" and a "global view" topped the list but so did roles like "instilling character," "teaching leadership," and "cultivating selflessness." People were clearly hungry for a solution to the crisis of character, integrity, and leadership in the workforce and in the country. And because so few other colleges and universities are willing to talk about cultivating values in the students that traverse their halls, we saw a great opportunity for Texas A&M to explain—once and for all—the purpose of all their quirky, seemingly inexplicable traits:

Developing leaders of character dedicated to serving the greater good.

All the various assets of the institution could play a role in fulfilling this purpose.

Academic excellence gives students the know-how and the desire to solve today's most challenging problems. *Cutting-edge research* makes headway on pressing problems facing society. *Student-led organizations* give students firsthand leadership opportunities serving causes they care about. The *Corps of Cadets* is designed to cultivate values-based leaders. And *Aggie traditions* enable values to be put into action. So no matter what area of university life we are talking about, we can frame it in the context of the overall purpose and create a highly relevant and highly unique brand identity for Texas A&M in the process.

BRINGING IT TO LIFE

The first thing we did was create what we called the Aggieland Anthem. Because the culture, traditions, and rituals found at Texas A&M are so unique, we chose to develop work that was more akin to tourism advertising than to conventional college and university outreach efforts. It gave the impression that Aggieland was an entirely different world—a world where *"tradition is a way of life, character is stitched into the local fabric, and leaders are a natural resource."* That's how we began the anthem that now hangs in dormitories all over campus. It was also brought to life in a video that plays on the Web to attract like-minded students, inspire current students, reinforce those values among former students, and let the world know what they can expect from Texas A&M students. It goes like this:

WELCOME TO AGGIELAND

There is a place where tradition is a way of life,
character is stitched into the local fabric
and leaders are a natural resource.
It's a place where the future is knocking at the door,
but the past always has a seat at the table.

Here everyone's glass is half full,
and cynicism is on a permanent leave of absence.
It's where fish learn to swim, elephants never forget,
and a horse could carry someone
all the way to a Nobel Prize.

Every man or woman can make a
difference here—especially the twelfth one.
And you're as likely to get a statue for
a selfless act as you are for a heroic one.
The greater good is a required course,
and a helping hand is a required gesture.

This is Aggieland, where optimism
is an alternative energy source and acts

of integrity are on everyone's to-do list.
History is made every day and
remembered every year.
It's a place where pushing ideas forward
doesn't mean pushing values aside.

Welcome to Aggieland.   Enjoy your stay.

The print campaign focused on individual traditions and academic accomplishments and how they fulfilled the purpose of the university:

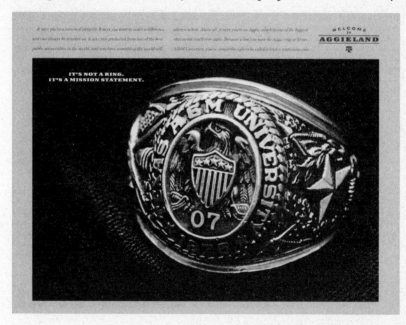

WINNING ON PURPOSE

Your purpose will determine which rankings ultimately matter to you.
While Texas A&M doesn't register in the top fifty universities in the
U.S. News & World Report's college rankings, it ranked number one
the year after we launched the campaign on the *Washington Monthly*
college rankings.

While *U.S. News & World Report* looks at values-neutral factors like class size, student/faculty ratio, and SAT scores, the relatively new *Washington Monthly* college ranking system wanted to go beyond basics stats. Its ranking is based on three factors: social mobility, research, and service. To be first on this list—above such prestigious institutions as UC Berkeley, Stanford, Harvard, Georgetown, and Duke—sends a message about Texas A&M's commitment to serving the greater good.

The most meaningful measure of success—the way that A&M really knows that it has *developed a leader of character dedicated to serving the greater good*—can be felt when you sit down and talk with seniors about their experience at Texas A&M. When we talked with one Hispanic student from the Texas valley who had come to Texas A&M on a Pell Grant, he described his own personal transformation this way:

> *I came to Texas A&M because of their amazing reputation in engineering. I come from a poor family and the only thought that I had in mind when I came here was getting the best education that I could, working the Aggie Network, and landing the highest paying job that I could. But I can honestly tell you that my time here has taught me the importance of giving back. I have some very high-paying offers from highly reputable firms in Houston but I'm not going to pursue that right now. I want to go back to the Valley and figure out how I can apply what I've learned to help that community. It's in bad shape. I can always make money—and I plan to—but I feel really drawn to give back. This place will do that to you.*

That's what Aggieland is all about.

SPORTS ORGANIZATIONS

19

HOW PURPOSE

CAN TEE YOU UP

TO BE EXCEPTIONAL

To be the exception in sports.

If you turn on ESPN these days, you're as likely to see a story about dog fighting, betting scandals, and steroid abuse as you are a great sporting event. In a world where some athletes and sports leagues have traded sportsmanship for selfishness, respect for spectacle and integrity for glory, there is an exception: the PGA Tour.

If you find yourself operating in an environment that is plagued with problems, leveraging what you stand for can invigorate existing fans and create new fans in the process. The PGA Tour lives by a set of values that enables it to do just that.

GOLF: IT'S MORE THAN A GAME

Golf has a nonnegotiable code of conduct that is sacred to every professional golfer. The PGA Tour is designed to uphold and demonstrate those core values, beliefs, and guiding principles in everything it does. The PGA Tour represents the *values* of honesty, integrity, respect for rules as well as other golfers, and winning the "the right way" rather than at all costs.

It is a *tradition-rich* tour characterized by timeless ritual and a gentlemanly attitude. The tour holds *sportsmanship* sacred—playing fairly, honestly, and respectfully, and treating opponents and the game with dignity. And it believes—more than any other existing sports organization—in giving back. In fact, it's approaching the $2 billion mark in contributions made to charity since the inception of the PGA Tour.

Tim Finchem, the PGA Tour commissioner, is fanatical about preserving the core values of golf. To him, golf is more than just a game. Golf embodies the best of sportsmanship. It always has and, in the current environment, that's more relevant than ever. In a world of sports gone wild, the PGA Tour profits by holding itself to a higher standard.

Every professional golfer pays the price to be exceptional. There are no guaranteed contracts—if a player doesn't make the cut, he doesn't get paid. Golfers honor the rules of the game, calling penalties on themselves in the heat of the battle—no wiggle room, no exceptions.

DISCOVERING AN EXCEPTIONAL PURPOSE

The purpose and values embedded in all that the PGA Tour does and stands for is a beacon for others to follow. In all that they do, the players, and the people of the PGA Tour pay the price to be exceptional. And therein lies the foundation of its purpose:

To be the exception in sports.

POSITIONING: THESE GUYS ARE GOOD

When your purpose is *to be the exception in sports,* everything you do must be able to live up to that claim. Players must play with dignity and integrity and the PGA Tour must demonstrate exceptional practices that clearly set itself apart from the field.

For the PGA Tour to thrive and do the good work that it does, it needs to create excitement and interest in the game of golf—a game that, on the surface, might not seem as highly interesting as other sports. But selling what the game of golf and its players stand for is of very high interest. People are hungry for athletes who represent integrity and true sportsmanship.

We created a manifesto to tell the world exactly what the PGA Tour and its players stand for. It goes like this, and it has driven one of the longest-running campaigns in the world of sports.

> *Behind every shot there is a story. Around every turn there is a challenge. On every tee box, fairway, bunker, or green there is an opportunity for greatness, grandeur, or gaffs. There is no screaming, no pads, no place to hide. To survive and thrive on the PGA Tour, you've got to be good. Real good.*
>
> *The wind changes without warning. The pin placements seem to get more diabolical daily. And a pulled drive, or a 7-iron caught thin can be the difference between glory and emptiness. Every shot is fourth and one. Every lie is a moment of truth.*
>
> *To survive and thrive on the PGA Tour you've got to be good. Real good.*
>
> *So what is this game called the PGA Tour? A game where only the best of the best get a shot. A game where you don't get paid unless you suit up and play. A mind game. In fact, it's a game within a game. It's between me, myself, and I. And if you are careless or sloppy or timid or tired, you need not apply.*
>
> *Indeed, in order to survive and thrive on the PGA Tour you've got to be good. Real good.*
>
> *These guys are good.*

BRINGING IT TO LIFE

One of the most remarkable areas in which the PGA Tour is true to its purpose is its commitment to charity. The PGA TOUR and its tournaments give back to each of the communities in which it plays— to over two thousand charities in total. We celebrate the PGA Tours' charitable orientation in a spot that features PGA Tour player Ernie Els volunteering at a Boys & Girls Club. He is teaching the young children a very unique mathematical formula. We hear Els ask, "What does 4+4+3+5+2+4+3 equal?" He calls on one of the students who answers, "3 under par." Els responds, "Very good." *These guys are good.*

A NEW ERA OF GOLF

These guys are good embraces the pride and heritage of golf embodied in Hogan, Snead, Palmer, Player, Rodriguez, and Nicklaus. But the future for the Tour had to embrace . . . well, the future.

There's a new set of stars rising up in the sport of golf—the brightest, of course, being Tiger Woods. These new players are bringing a new level of interest and energy to the game of golf. Commissioner Finchem wanted to develop something innovative that would capitalize on that newfound interest—and do so in a way that respected the heritage and integrity of the game.

Together, in the summer of 2006, we created and launched a concept called *A New Era in Golf*. It was anchored in the idea that professional golf needed a playoff season—something they had never had before. The playoff format enabled us to really maximize the growing interest in golf that players like Tiger Woods have generated in recent years. It enabled us to preserve the core values of the game and stimulate progress in a sport that has remained largely unchanged for hundreds of years. The PGA Tour launched the FedExCup and a new era of golf began.

In one advertising spot, we celebrate the history and heritage of golf by showing the evolution of the game and its players through eras past and present. There is sentimental music playing as footage of players from different eras is featured in chronological order, culminating with players from the new era of golf.

We took the same approach with our print ads by celebrating great accomplishments from past eras while setting up intrigue for the new era.

Finally, we created anticipation and excitement in an ad featuring Tiger Woods. In this spot, Woods is tying his shoes just before he heads out to the course. While tying, he is also whistling the song "Eye of the Tiger." When he is finished, he gets up and walks out as "The playoffs are coming" appears on the screen.

WINNING ON PURPOSE

Since the inception of *These guys are good,* all the key indicators of the strength of the PGA Tour are positive. Tournament purses have skyrocketed, sponsorships have been strong, charitable contributions continue to increase, and the fans' perception of the PGA Tour and its players is overwhelmingly favorable—more so than for any other sport.

PART IV

Are You Bringing Your Purpose to Life in the Marketplace?

Are you bringing your purpose to life in the marketplace?

The following survey is intended to gauge whether or not you are bringing the purpose of your organization to life in a way that is relevant and relatable to employees, customers, and other key stakeholders.

Question	Yes	No
1. Have you articulated your purpose in a simple, clear, and compelling way that everyone can understand?	___	___
2. Do you have a keen understanding of how you need to be positioned in the marketplace in order to win? Do you know the answer to the question: *What do we have that people want that the competition isn't giving them?*	___	___
3. Do your employees know what you stand for? Have you created experiences or programs that bring the purpose to life for them?	___	___
4. Do your customers know what you stand for?	___	___
5. Do your vendors, suppliers, and partners know what you stand for?	___	___
6. Do the communities you operate in know what you stand for?	___	___
7. Have you prioritized brand-building experiences that will be most influential in enhancing perceptions of the brand?	___	___
8. Do you think about how you can use various marketing tools (promotions, sponsorships, events, etc.) to fulfill the purpose of your organization?	___	___

Question	Yes	No

9. Do you think of *integration* as an exercise in bringing your purpose and values to life in meaningful ways throughout the organization and throughout the customer experience?

10. Are you creating advertising that is an *invited guest* in people's lives—intriguing them, entertaining them, and persuading them with the right messages, at the right times, and in the right places?

If you answered yes to the majority of the questions, congratulations, your purpose is alive and well in the marketplace. You know what you stand for and you're telling the world about it. Your employees buy in and help you fulfill it day in and day out. Customers and community members have a sense of who you are as well as what you sell. You're on the lookout for new ways to bring it to life, and you approach marketing assignments as opportunities to serve the purpose.

If you answered yes to roughly half of the questions, you're on the right path to building a brand of great purpose. Try to identify the weak links in your communication strategy. Is the articulation of your purpose too complicated for people to understand? Are you overlooking your employees? Are you treating promotions or special events as something "separate from" a brand-building exercise? Identify the areas where your purpose and values are absent and begin doing the work that needs to be done to express who you are, what you stand for, and what difference you make everywhere you can.

If you answered yes to only a handful of questions, it may be that you: (a) don't know your purpose—and therefore need to revisit the purpose discovery section of this book until you identify one; (b) aren't properly positioned—so no one will listen to what you have to say; or (c) don't subscribe to purpose-based branding principles—and have never bothered telling anyone what you stand for. Identify the breakdown and get to work.

SUMMARY

20

KEY PRINCIPLES FROM THE BOOK

There are three fundamental building blocks of high-performing, high-purpose organizations.

1. They are built to make a meaningful difference.
2. They are led by leaders of great purpose who act as stewards of the purpose.
3. They bring the purpose to life in meaningful and relevant ways in the marketplace.

An organization must be firing on all three cylinders to achieve the levels of performance experienced by truly great purpose-driven organizations. Let's take one last look at each area.

BUILDING AN ORGANIZATION THAT MAKES A DIFFERENCE

Although all the organizations that we've profiled throughout this book are different—different industries, different business models, different market situations—they share some amazingly similar characteristics. To follow in their footsteps and create an organization that is capable of making a difference, making money, and—with a little luck—making history, we recommend three steps.

Find the Thrill

Companies with a purpose are motivated by the idea of making a difference. They look at unmet needs, underserved populations, and areas for improvement in the marketplace and find opportunities to create something remarkable in that environment.

The thrill for you may come from anywhere. You may want to revolutionize your industry or just delight your customers in a way no one else is doing. You may find a noble cause to serve or just see an opportunity that no one else has been able to see. Take stock of your unique strengths and your genuine passions, and listen to what the world is calling you to do.

Have the Will

It's not enough to have a desire to make a difference in the marketplace. You must create a business model that is in alignment with the purpose that enables a difference to be made.

True purpose-driven organizations find new ways to think about their business and provide something different or innovative in their space. They love questioning the status quo and testing things that people say can't be done. In the process, they develop products, services, or experiences that are innovative in the marketplace—but not just for innovation's sake. Innovations are developed and deployed in direct relation to their ability to help fulfill the overarching purpose of the organization.

There is no "right way" to go about building purpose-based organizations. Every organization will need to look at how they do business and identify which aspects of the business are working in the service of the purpose and which aren't. From there, you can begin to prune away the products or practices that undermine the purpose and build up those that help facilitate the purpose.

This may mean taking a look at your economic model, your cost structure, and other processes to see what can be brought into closer alignment with your purpose. You may need to walk for a while in your customers' shoes to identify the real problems and opportunities. Each situation is unique and the strategies employed to align the operational model with the purpose will vary accordingly.

The point is to remember that you must behave in ways that fulfill the promise of your purpose. Purpose is not a marketing gimmick. It takes hard work, operational alignment, and 100 percent commitment.

Ignite the Passion

When the thrill has been found and the will has taken root, passion can be ignited throughout the organization with little trouble. In fact, passion tends to emerge naturally as a result of giving people something they can believe in.

Create some simple feedback mechanisms that enable your employees to have a firsthand appreciation for the role of the organization in the lives of the people it touches. Share customer stories. Track the difference that you are making and share those results with your employees. And don't be afraid to aim high and dream big because passionate employees who believe in the purpose of the company can pull off extraordinary things.

Use the passion of the workforce to continually push forward. For purpose-based companies there is no finish line, no having "made it." Your people should constantly be on the lookout for new and better ways to fulfill the purpose of the organization.

BECOMING A LEADER OF GREAT PURPOSE

If you are the leader of an organization with a purpose, your primary function is to build, nurture, and fulfill the purpose of the organization. You are the chief steward of the purpose of the organization. The following principles should help you to fulfill that role.

Make It Job Number One to Be the Torch Bearer of Purpose

Great leaders recognize that without their support and commitment, the core values and core purpose of the organization will not flourish. Evangelizing the purpose is always on their to-do list.

Believe In Purpose Before Profit

Great leaders do not adopt a purpose to increase their profitability. They believe deeply in the purpose and the profitability follows.

Use Purpose to Create Alignment and Drive Performance

Great leaders use purpose to channel the collective talent and energy of the organization toward an inspiring and meaningful goal.

Keep In Mind What You're Fighting For

Great leaders know what they're fighting for and inspire employees to fight for the same. They understand that asking employees to fight for something they believe in will create a much more competitive organization (versus an organization that asks employees to fight for increased earnings or profitability).

Use Purpose, Not Just Personality, to Lead

Great leaders know that the real secret to inspiring the troops is appealing to their core human values and need for fulfilling work.

Do Right by Your Purpose

Great leaders look at every decision, big or small, and ask whether or not it will support or subvert the core purpose of the organization.

BRINGING YOUR PURPOSE TO LIFE IN THE MARKETPLACE

If you've built an organization that makes a difference and are leading the organization with the purpose as your guide, you should be ready to bring your purpose to life in the marketplace and build a great brand in the process.

The simple fact of the matter is this: Great brands are born out of great leaders who have created great organizations that create something that actually matters to people.

When you have done the hard work to create something remarkable, bringing it to life in the marketplace becomes a matter of telling your story in the most relevant and compelling way possible.

Articulating Your Purpose

If it hasn't already been done, the first step is to take a good hard look at the difference that your organization makes and articulate the core purpose in a clear and compelling manner. Ultimately, you can't fulfill your purpose if you haven't articulated it in a way that everyone can understand.

Positioning Strategy: What Do We Have that People Want that the Competition Can't Deliver?

Once everyone has agreed to the core purpose of the organization, study the marketplace and identify the barriers to the fulfillment of your purpose. Then use the power of marketing to begin to change the attitudes and behaviors that stand in the way. Unlike your purpose—which never changes—your positioning strategy is responsive to current marketplace dynamics. You want to be able to answer the question: What does your organization have that people want that the competition can't deliver? The answer to that question will help you to fulfill your purpose, build your brand, and grow your business.

Bringing It to Life

With purpose in place and brilliant positioning insights in hand, it's time to create visionary ideas that will move the business forward.

Get Your Employees on Board

You have to bring the purpose to life inside the organization before you do anything else. Ultimately, your employees will be responsible for making the difference you are trying to make.

Prioritize Brand-Building Experiences

Before you jump into the creation of a traditional advertising campaign, stop and look at the way your customer experiences the brand. In doing so, you might find a host of highly influential areas (store environment, product design, customer service experiences, environmental practices, etc.) that affect how your brand is perceived. Focus on these high-impact areas first.

Fulfill Your Purpose Everywhere You Can

Think about all the initiatives on your to-do list. How many of them are helping to contribute to the overall purpose of the organization? How many of them are contributing to the story of your brand in the marketplace? How much more powerful would your brand be if everything you were putting out in the world was attempting to fulfill the promise of your purpose in some new and exciting way? Stop investing your precious time, energy, and money on initiatives that don't support the overall purpose of the company; start thinking about how to bring the purpose to life in all the projects that come across your desk.

Don't Be an Uninvited Guest

When it's time to tell your story, don't do it in a way that interrupts and irritates the people you are trying to reach. We recommend that all advertisers think about how they can transform their messaging from being an uninvited guest to becoming a welcome and invited guest in people's lives. Think about how you can intrigue, entertain, and persuade people with your story.

Acknowledgments

ROY SPENCE

I have been blessed with so many wonderful mentors, extraordinary clients, and purpose-based leaders, business colleagues, and friends. Most important, I'm blessed by a loving, supportive, and highly engaging family interested in all things of great passion and purpose—my wife, Mary Couri Spence, and our three children, Courtney Couri Spence, Ashley Elizabeth Spence, and Shay Milam Spence. My family is the true treasure of my life.

To my partner in purpose, Haley Rushing, our "chief purposeologist" and coauthor of *It's Not What You Sell, It's What You Stand For*, who is the best in the world at discovering and bringing to life purpose in any organization that seeks it. You are the reason this labor of love happened. To my business partner, Judy Trabulsi, and my dear colleague and best-selling author, Jim Collins, who inspired this idea, my deepest thanks for keeping the faith and keeping us focused as we went on this journey. A very special thanks to MaryEllen Rasnick for countless hours and never counting us out. She dogged this mission with tenacity, discipline, and humor. And I could not have done this without my trusted executive assistant of thirty years, Karen Greer Bearden. And that's for sure.

To my other business partners of some thirty-seven years, Steve Gurasich and Tim McClure and all the purpose-based leaders and employees of GSD&M Idea City, what a road of discovery and friendship and partnership this has been so far.

I also give deep thanks to my mom, Ruth Griffin Spence, my dad, Roy Milam Spence, and my sister, Mary Gordon Spence. It was a treat growing up in a family of great passion and creativity.

Most important, I want to dedicate this book to my oldest sister, Susan Spence. Susan had such a profound influence on my life. She was born with spina bifida and lived to be forty-nine years old. She never walked, but every day she taught me that you do not have to have legs to fly. In fact, it is a hindrance. And boy, did she ever fly. Her purpose was all about grit and determination and love and inspiring others. She believed that no matter what, everyone can live and practice a life of purpose by simply practicing the Golden Rule, reaching out to others when a helping hand is needed, and never giving up when things look too tough to handle.

And although she was never able to stand physically, she stood above all others I have known in my life. Godspeed, Sister Susan.

HALEY RUSHING

This journey started back in 2001, with a simple question from Roy: *"What's at the heart of the most successful brands on our roster?"* By exploring that question, we stumbled upon purpose. His unwavering enthusiasm and support of the work that I've done in this area have meant the world to me. He's been a mentor, a supporter, and a friend.

Much gratitude is owed to *all* the founders of GSD&M for creating a firm with enough spirit to attract the type of clients that care as much about making a difference as they do about making money. Roy, Judy, Steve, and Tim are all living role models of the purpose-driven leaders that we describe in this book.

And then there is the team of people who believed in the book—

Adrian Zackheim and Jeffrey Krames at Portfolio, our literary agent
Jim Hornfischer, and the small team of dedicated people who made
this book happen: Carol Keesee, MaryEllen Rasnick, and Amie
Raftus. A special thanks to colleagues and clients who have champi-
oned purpose and evolved my thinking along the way: Gia Medeiros,
Tony Rogers, Greg Chandler, John Davies, Bob Gates, Steve Moore,
Dave Jeffers, Judy Trabulsi, Maryam Banikarim, Richard Leider, Raj
Sisodia, Jeff Klein, Chip Conley, Simon Sinek, and John Mackey. And
a very heartfelt thank you to Mr. Robert Utley—probably the biggest
advocate of purpose I know (outside of Roy). You are a true Renaissance man.

My parents, Hal and Gene Martin, embody the purpose of all
great parents—to be the biggest cheerleaders for their children. They
have always cheered me on, and I hope that through the writing of
this book, they may come to have some faint understanding of what I
do for a living.

And to my sweet little twin angels, India Vida and Ziggy, you
make me want to make a difference.

Notes

Chapter 1: What Is a Purpose and Why Should You Want One?

1. John Kotter and James Heskett, *Corporate Culture and Performance*, Simon & Schuster, 1992.

2. Rajendra Sisodia, David Wolfe, and Jagdish Sheth, *Firms of Endearment*, Wharton, 2007.

3. Larry Dorman, "A General in the Army of Volunteers," *New York Times*, February 17, 2008.

4. Perry Pascarella and Mark Frohman, *The Purpose Driven Organization*, John Wiley, 1989.

5. Rodd Wagner and James K. Harter, *12: The Elements of Great Managing*, Gallup Press, 2006.

6. Mihaly Czikszentmihalyi, *Flow*, HarperCollins, 1990.

7. Richard Leider, *The Power of Purpose*, Berrett-Koehler, 1997.

Chapter 2: Discovering Your Purpose

1. Jim Collins, *Good to Great*, Collins, 2001.

Chapter 3: Articulating Your Purpose

1. "How to Write a Mission Statement," *Drucker Foundation Self-Assessment Tool*, 1999, Leader to Leader Institute, November 27, 2005.

2. Nikos Mourkogiannis, *Purpose: The Starting Point of Great Companies*. Palgrave Macmillan, 2006.

Chapter 4: Find the Thrill!

1. Don Soderquist, *The Wal-Mart Way: The Inside Story of the Success of the World's Largest Company*, Thomas Nelson, 2005.
2. *About SWA, History*, www.southwest.com.
3. Charles Schwab, *Charles Schwab's Guide to Financial Independence*, Three Rivers Press, 1998.
4. Bill Novelli, opening statement by AARP CEO Bill Novelli at a press briefing in January 2005.
5. Bill Novelli, "How America Can Afford to Grow Older: A Vision for the Future," speech given at The National Press Club, Newsmaker Luncheon, February 2005.
6. John Mackey, quoted from *Interview Show: Marketplace*, SYND, November 27, 2003.
7. John Mackey, quoted in an article by Charles Fishman, "The Anarchist's Cookbook," Fast Company, Issue 84, July 2004.

Chapter 5: Have the Will!

1. Sam Walton, *Made in America*, Bantam Books, 1993.
2. Ibid.
3. Kevin Freibergand Jackie Freiberg, *Nuts! Southwest Airline's Crazy Recipe for Business and Personal Success*, Bard Press, 1996.
4. Ibid.
5. Ibid.
6. *The Priorities Book, AARP Public Policy Priorities*, AARP.
7. John Mackey, quoted in an article by Charles Fishman, "The Anarchist's Cookbook," Fast Company, Issue 84, July 2004.
8. Ibid.

Chapter 6: Ignite the Passion!

1. Don Soderquist, *The Wal-Mart Way: The Inside Story of the Success of the World's Largest Company*, Thomas Nelson, 2005.
2. Declaration of Interdependence: Final Thoughts, www.wholefoods.com.

Chapter 7: Stewards of Purpose

1. www.hotelterrajacksonhole.com.
2. Ashley Morgan, quoted in an interview entitled "Green Hotel Guru" available on www.sprig.com, January 30, 2008.
3. Nikos Mourkogiannis, *Purpose: The Starting Point of Great Companies*, Palgrave Macmillan, 2006.
4. Ibid.
5. Kevin Freiberg and Jackie Freiberg, *Nuts! Southwest Airline's Crazy Recipe for Business and Personal Success*, Bard Press, 1996.
6. Ibid.

7. Lamar Muse, as quoted in "Inspiring Muse," *Time* magazine, November 17, 1980.

8. "Muse Air Founder Competes Against His Own Creation with an Aura of Class," *Air Transport World*, October 1981.

Chapter 8: Purpose-Based Leadership Principles

1. Kevin Freiberg and Jackie Freiberg, *Nuts! Southwest Airline's Crazy Recipe for Business and Personal Success*, Bard Press, 1996.

2. David Magee, *The John Deere Way*, John Wiley, 2005.

3. Thomas Cleary translation of Sun-tzu, *The Art of War*, Shambhala, 1991.

4. Marc Gunther, "Wal-Mart's Mixed Green Bag," *Fortune*, November 16, 2007.

Chapter 10: How Purpose Can Take You Higher

1. "Consumers will benefit from 'free love,' " Texas Public Policy Institute, November 2, 2005, cited on www.setlovefree.com.

2. http://www.setlovefree.com/pdf/DOT_SouthwestEffect.pdf; "The Southwest Effect," US DOT, May 1993.

3. http://www.setlovefree.com/southwesteffect.html.

Chapter 11: How Purpose Can Make You Better

1. Douglas Smith, *On Value and Values: Think Differently About We . . . in an Age of Me*, FT Prentice Hall Books, 2004.

2. Television spots created by the Martin Agency.

3. Sustainability Progress Report: Progress to Date 2007–2008, message from Lee Scott.

Chapter 12: How Purpose Can Accelerate Your Momentum

1. *Strategic Vision*, JD Power, 2005.

2. The Onion postcampaign reporting, June 25–July 1, 2007.

3. BMW's call center partner who tracks and reports on Performance Driving School incoming-call volume; 2007 data are reported through October 24.

4. *AdViews, AdRelevance, Automotive News*; October year to date, 2007 (Note: Does not include CPO spending.)

Chapter 17: How Purpose Can Create a Grassroots Movement

1. Organization for Economic Cooperation and Development consists of thirty member countries committed to democracy and the market economy.

Bibliography

Arena, Christine. *The High-Purpose Company: The Truly Responsible (and Highly Profitable) Firms That Are Changing Business Now*. New York: HarperCollins, 2007.

Bergdahl, Michael. *The 10 Rules of Sam Walton: Success Secrets for Remarkable Results*. New York: John Wiley & Sons, Inc., 2006.

Collins, Jim. *Good to Great: Why Some Companies Make the Leap and Others Don't*. New York: HarperCollins Business, 2001.

Collins, Jim, and Jerry Porras. *Built to Last: Successful Habits of Visionary Companies*. New York: Harper Collins, 1994.

Czikszentmihalyi, Mihaly. *Flow*. New York: HarperCollins, 1990.

Freiberg, Kevin, and Jackie Freiberg. *Nuts! Southwest Airlines' Crazy Recipe for Business and Personal Success*. Austin, TX: Bard Press, 1996.

Godin, Seth. *Purple Cow: Transform Your Business by Being Remarkable*. New York: Portfolio, 2003.

Kador, John. *Charles Schwab: How One Company Beat Wall Street and Reinvented the Brokerage Industry*. New York: John Wiley & Sons, Inc., 2002.

Kotter, John, and James Heskett. *Corporate Culture and Performance*. New York: Simon & Schuster, 1992.

Loehr, Jim, and Tony Schwartz. *The Power of Full Engagement: Managing Energy, Not Time, Is the Key to High Performance and Personal Renewal*. New York: Free Press, 2003.

Leider, Richard. *The Power of Purpose*. San Francisco: Berrett-Koehler, 1997.

Magee, David. *The John Deere Way: Performance That Endures*. New York: John Wiley & Sons, Inc., 2005.

Mourkogiannis, Nikos, and Roger Fisher. *Purpose: The Starting Point of Great Companies*. Basingstoke, England: Palgrave Macmillan, 2006.

Novelli, Bill, and Boe Workman. *50+: Igniting a Revolution to Reinvent America.* New York: St. Martin's, 2006.

Pascarella, Perry, and Mark Frohman. *The Purpose-Driven Organization.* New York: John Wiley & Sons, Inc., 1989.

Schwab, Charles. *Charles Schwab's Guide to Financial Independence: Simple Solutions for Busy People.* New York: Three Rivers Press, 1998.

Sisodia, Rajendra, et al. *Firms of Endearment: How World-Class Companies Profit from Passion and Purpose.* Philadelphia: Wharton School Publishing, 2007.

Smith, Douglas K. *On Value and Values: Thinking Differently About We in an Age of Me.* New York: FT Prentice Hall, 2004.

Soderquist, Don. *The Wal-Mart Way: The Inside Story of the Success of the World's Largest Company.* Lawrenceville, GA: Nelson Business, 2005.

Sun-tzu. *The Art of War.* New York: Shambhala, 2005.

Wagner, Rodd, and James K. Harter. *12: The Elements of Great Managing.* Washington, D.C.: Gallup Press, 2006.

Walton, Sam. *Made in America.* New York: Bantam Books, 1993.

Index